"Because I Live Here"

Other Books by S. R. SLAVSON

Science and the New Education, 1934
  (with Robert K. Speer)
Creative Group Education, 1937
  translated into Japanese
Character Education in a Democracy, 1939
  also in Braille
An Introduction to Group Therapy, 1942
  translated into German and Japanese
Recreation and the Total Personality, 1946
The Practice of Group Therapy, 1947
  (with collaborators)
Analytic Group Psychotherapy, 1950
  translated into French and Japanese
Child Psychotherapy, 1952
Re-Educating the Delinquent, 1954
  translated into Italian and Serbo-Croatian
The Fields of Group Psychotherapy, 1956
Child-Centered Group Guidance of Parents, 1958
  (with collaborators)
A Textbook of Analytic Group Psychotherapy, 1964
*Reclaiming the Delinquent by Para-Analytic Group
Psychotherapy and the Inversion Technique*, 1965

"Because I Live Here"

THE THEORY AND PRACTICE
OF VITA-ERG WARD THERAPY
WITH
DETERIORATED PSYCHOTIC WOMEN

by
S. R. SLAVSON

INTERNATIONAL UNIVERSITIES PRESS, INC.
New York

New York

Copyright 1970, International Universities Press, Inc.

Library of Congress Catalog Card Number: 70-125477

Manufactured in the United States of America

To the memory of

NATHAN BECKENSTEIN, M.D., 1904-1968

It has been said that "he who forgets the past is doomed to eternal error," but on the other hand—he who adheres to the past is doomed to barrenness.

Contents

Foreword

Every living organism carries within itself the germ of its decline and death. Even in inanimate objects the potentials for decay and demise are ever-present, and survival rests upon efforts at preventing or delaying these declining processes. Unless their conditions are buttressed by care, maintenance and restoration, things fall into progressive disrepair. If not repaired or restored, everything deteriorates and, depending on its nature, ultimately ceases to function adequately or is relegated to the scrap heap. Whether it be a tree, a fence, a building, furniture, vestments or living organisms, the common denominator in their survival is renewal, effort, and attention, for life itself is the dynamic process of renewal.

All of this holds true for human individuals and their institutions as well. Aggregates, such as families, communities, institutions and nations—all impose on their members efforts at keeping them alive and maintaining their health and integrity by readjustments, accommodations, and expansion. Without such continuous efforts, the inherent deteriorative forces automatically take over: disruption, tensions, conflicts, decimation, inertia, inevitable gradual decomposition, and finally demise become inevitable.

A mental hospital is a special type of organism, quite unlike

1

any other: it is a compact community in which pathology is king. To be effective, it has to invoke rational and health-inducing human relations and administrative procedures, unlike the situation in general hospitals where patients are predominantly isolated individuals, having minimal or no relations with one another or staff. Their usually brief stay terminates with some kind of recovery and permanent separation. This is not the case with the mental hospital. The mental hospital is in a real sense a true community where recovery or improvement is conditioned by survival as a social atom. Here interaction and cooperation must be made part and parcel of the therapy itself; it is the *living situation* in which patients can find comfort and from which they can draw strength for their return to comparative normality.

The dichotomy of the two oppositional forces—the isolative life pattern the patient adopts and the social needs for inner change—impose heavy burdens on the hospital and its staff. This dichotomy between the nature of the illness or condition with its intense self-centeredness and encapsulation as well as the remedy for it, human relatedness, place a Herculean task of extremes in emotional resources, flexibility and inventiveness on the shoulders of those who are responsible for the conduct of the hospital and especially of the ward staffs. Their task exceeds in complexity any other in the realm of human relations, except, perhaps, that of dealing with conflicting international affairs, the irrationality of which unfortunately finds resolution in mutual mass slaughter. In fact, so complex are the problems that in self-defense, inflexible bureaucratic procedures have been evolved and so rigidly traditionalized that to a distressing degree they negate the basic intents of a mental hospital.

The present volume is the saga of an extensive effort at breaking down entrenched rigidities and traditionalism in dealing with mental patients as rejected members of the human family. To demonstrate the potentials of the innovative VITA-ERG procedures, completely inaccessible and intransigent long-term segregated female patients on two disturbed wards had been chosen.

This volume details many of the numerous trial and error approaches, the vast number of alterations and modifications that became necessary as our project progressed, the steps toward creating a humanistic community through integration of the variegated contributions of many individuals and facilities, and altering attitudes in staff toward patients as members of the human family and in both toward themselves.

The inevitable, though unexpected, resistances that stemmed from deeply ingrained traditionalism, habituated conduct bordering on sadism and antiquated role-concepts which were brought into relief and threatened by the project, have been only scantily narrated. But anyone knowledgeable in universal institutional rigidities and others who know of them by heresay will require little effort to conjure up the difficulties and frustrations that have been encountered by the departures from tradition in our approach.

The term VITA-ERG is derived from Latin roots (vita = life; erg = work) to designate the essential nature of this technique. Its essence, however, does not lie in occupations alone as the name might suggest. While realistic occupations flowing from spontaneous interests and group participation reawaken the smoldering life-force in the psychotic and aid his return to and his ability to deal with attenuated reality, VITA-ERG treatment strongly relies on benign human relations in rehabilitating patients.

Despite many impediments, its effects have immeasurably exceeded initial expectations. The findings by various observers, official and unofficial, recorded in this volume, attest to this fact. The title of this book itself— "*Because I Live Here*"—is derived from a remark by a patient in response to a visitor's inquiry as to why she was working so hard at a domestic chore. However, the reader is cautioned against seeking in the present volume abstruse disquisitions on the complex and contending theories of the nature of psychosis, psychiatry, or psychotherapy. VITA-ERG therapy, as its name implies, consists mainly of a life-setting in which the patient is viewed as a person who, partially because of insurmountable pressures and intolerable stresses in the complex of family and social setting, withdrew from reality and created a world for himself which in his enfeebled psychic state, he can no longer manage. The task is, therefore, to find means to facilitate his return to the world of men through an unthreatening life-setting and warm human relations which are the ingredients of VITA-ERG therapy.

When the psychotic is treated with the regard given a normal individual, particularly by staff and others with whom he comes in contact, he responds more normally and more rationally. These were the primary assumptions of VITA-ERG therapy derived from our understanding of the internal psychic process in the psychotic state. For the most part, our results served to validate these assumptions. However, in the concluding chapter the reader will find a frank statement of the limitations of our method as a total treatment modality.

The project was carried on through a grant from the National Institute of Mental Health (No. 2M-61-64) to the New York State Department of Mental Hygiene.

New York, N. Y.
November, 1969

S.R.S.

4

1. *Introduction*

Einstein held the view that for an idea or theory to be valid it must have "inner coherence"; that one cannot rely on results alone. In unravelling the implications of this significant statement, one can speculate that results can be the favorable or unfavorable outcomes of a set of circumstances accidentally combined, and that, given some other condition or circumstance, the same theory or idea would yield results of a quite different nature. The principle of "inner coherence" applies especially to biochemical and pharmacological research where seemingly valid hypotheses are reversed by the presence of unrecognized or unidentified elements in a given chemical combination. On the other hand, a great many, and some of the most significant advances in knowledge and science have been the result of serendipity (i.e., accident).

What is true of the physical sciences holds true, and occurs frequently in the behavioral sciences and in sociology generally. It is not unusual for workers in these fields to propound explanations for phenomena and suggest managerial and remedial steps for their continuance or elimination that fall far short of validity. The vast number of dynamic factors that underlie human conduct—its effects and results—and the innumerable and obscure forces in social phenomena, have often led to the formulation of invalid principles and guidelines. A more thorough scrutiny reveals that it is the presence of unrecognized factors that result in the lack of an inner coherence in formulations.

A major task of the thoroughgoing researcher is to uncover, identify, and describe hidden elements and thus complete the picture of an operational complex. The more involved a phenomenon, the more caution is needed in formulating judgments and making deductions. This is particularly true in the realm of human affairs.

In line with these considerations, the reader will have to keep firmly in mind several basic factors in understanding and evaluating outcomes of our project. Foremost is the fact that ours were not the usual mental hospital wards, and that our patients were not typically encountered in a comparatively modernized "open-door" mental hospital. Ours were the "dregs," as it were. They were the rejects. And because of their assumed inaccessibility by the comparative freedom of action and movement on the other wards, and because they could not be involved in the many structured recreational, educational and social activities that the hospital provided, they had been sequestered. The patients presented extremes of agitation or depression. Our wards housed also all the idiots, imbeciles, mental defectives, as well as all the organic cases. (The latter exerted a destructive effect upon the others and imposed excessive strain on staff.)

The second element by which the project can be best understood is that changes, alterations and expansions could be made only within rigidly defined limits of the state laws and regulations and the limiting factors of budget, which did not include provisions for expenditures an activity program necessitated. Funds for this purpose were raised by the director of the hospital from sources other than the state allowances. Another limiting policy was that monies within the budget could not be transferred from one item to another. Even when such a step would have produced better results, a particular fund could not be applied to any other but the originally specified items, no matter how beneficial such a step may have proven to the patients.

INTRODUCTION

We were also required to strictly adhere to the existing departmental delineations and to accept the staff assigned to us by the supervisors of the various departments, as woefully inadequate as some of them were for our particular purpose. Our problem was therefore to maintain cordial relations with the departmental heads, for only on that basis was it possible to obtain the services we needed from them. We were also required to retain the staff we found on the wards, whether or not they proved suitable for the new program we envisaged.

In this connection it may be said that in addition to describing the objectives of the project, the details in setting it up and in conducting it, the evidence of its effectiveness, its successes and failures, the reader will find also an abridged account of some of the tribulations endured by some of us who were involved, as well as the frustrations in store for anyone who embarks on a path of innovation and change in these special circumstances.

THE PSYCHOSOCIAL CLIMATE AND PHYSICAL SETTING

Brooklyn State Hospital was, until recent decades, situated on the outskirts of the borough of Brooklyn in New York City, but as the population expanded and the construction of homes kept apace, it became surrounded by a multitude of small private homes and a sprinkling of apartment houses. Small business establishments and such amusement facilities as moving picture houses now are within walking distance and are accessible to patients.

The grounds of the hospital can be described as an oasis of greenery in an otherwise fairly drab setting of pavement and a motley assortment of buildings and garages. Some distance away, and not within sight of the hospital campus, the wide streets, lined with comfortable private homes and spacious lawns, recall a former suburban affluence. The hospital campus is a large parklike extent of land with well-kept lawns and neat paved walks. Opportunity for quiet relaxation is provided by numerous comfortable benches, some along the wide walks; others in tree-shaded areas that abound on the grounds.

Shaded recreational areas, several of which are enclosed by high wire fences, contain seats and benches conducive to quiet reading. These areas are also suitable for shuffle-board or for tossing a medicine ball. A large baseball diamond and a tennis court are available to the recreation department and are at the disposal of patients and staff members. In addition, there are several nooks and corners in this pastoral setting which offer relative privacy.

The spacious, well-kept lawns, innumerable trees, and many shrubs and flowerbeds give the grounds the aspect of a luxurious park, especially when bathed in golden sunshine. The solarium in the care of a horticulturist provides shelter for the potted flowers during the winter months, and is a popular place with patients. The transplanting of these plants in springtime makes for excellent occupational therapy. Our women patients grew enthusiastic about this plant sanctuary and displayed great interest in learning the names of the flowers and the trees on the grounds, but unfortunately none of our staff could satisfy their curiosity.

Among the many indoor recreational facilities, there is a rather dimly lit basement lounge with settings for billiards, cards, checkers and chess, reading, or lounging. A brighter and better-equipped smaller lounge located in another building is used for small parties and patients' meetings. We utilized this lounge for music and various creative activities with smaller groups. A well-stocked library, supervised by a librarian, is open during the daytime hours for patients who are free to come and go at will, since the hospital is conducted on an open-door plan. A large bus is available for transporting patients to places of educational and strictly pleasurable interests, although it is inappropriately marked "Ambulance," because it is also used to transport patients to and from other mental hospitals.[1]

Patients can take part in the score or more conveniently located centers where various forms of planned occupational, artistic, and some educational and vocational training, as well as

[1] Our suggestion that this sign be made removable was not followed up.

opportunities for creative expression, are available to them. They are free to move about the buildings and grounds, and many who can manage themselves with safety can leave the campus and roam the neighborhood, do window-shopping, or purchase various articles and food which they may need or desire. "Walking" groups with one or two attendants can always be seen on the hospital grounds and adjoining streets. There is a capacious assembly hall designed for large community meetings which has a well-equipped stage in addition to a variety of musical instruments and other equipment for theatrical presentations and the preparation of refreshments.

However, there were four patient wards—two for women and two for men—for whom this liberalized climate and enriched life had to be restricted or altogether denied. The residents of these wards were patients who could not navigate with the freedom and comparative responsibility of the majority. They were the long-term, chronic, severely disturbed and assaultive members of the community, who had to be segregated for their own and others' safety. To these wards were also relegated the constitutionally deficient, the mental defectives, imbeciles, and idiots. These wards were kept locked, the movements of their "inmates" were rigidly restricted and their every move strictly supervised. Many of them had not left their wards for years, even decades. The patients here were subjected to various types of punishment, deprivations, and restrictions for purposes of control.

Two of these wards—those in which the women resided—were chosen for our demonstration. The attendants on these wards seemed to have been specially selected in the past for the arduous physical tasks that they were called upon to perform, i.e., custodial and disciplinary treatment of the highly disturbed and violent patients.

The hospital admits patients 16 years of age and over who suffer from a variety of psychiatric disorders. It is divided into the following services: Reception, Continued Treatment, Infirmary, Medical and Surgical, Clinical and Pathological Laboratory, and a Biochemical Research center. A school of psychiatric nursing is attached to the hospital. At the time our project was introduced, the average daily population was about 2900. In addition, there are usually about 45 patients on day care (sleep home at night); about 100 are on leave status (trial home visit for 30 days), and about 580 on convalescent care. The hospital is affiliated with a constellation of community psychiatric clinics which treat both children and adults.

A hospital community is in many respects a microculture reflecting the macroculture in which it operates. The humaneness of a community and its culture can best be judged by the way it treats its weakest members—children, the ill, the aged, the criminal and, in some instances, the women. Liberalized schooling, rehabilitation of prisoners and delinquents, care of the ill and the aged and humanization of mental hospitals in the progressive countries of the world are direct outgrowths of the democratic and egalitarian values in which the dignity and the sanctity of the individual is the primary principle of life. Gone are the ball and chain that fettered the insane. Patients now move about with comparative freedom. They now sleep in beds between clean sheets instead of on dirty earthen or concrete floors; they no longer wallow in their filth, but frequent showering is imposed. Their diet is no longer bread and water; it is now planned by scientifically trained dieticians who draw on the best available knowledge of nutrition for health.

Similarly, some opportunities for diversion and recreation are part of the equipment in most hospitals of most Western countries. Considerable freedom of visitation has been extended and "leave status" allowed patients to spend time with families and friends. The aim, though not the methods, currently employed in the treatment of patients, is to return them to their homes and the community. Despite this objective, the culture within mental hospitals is still repressive, isolative and almost entirely custodial. Patients have little autonomy and they expect to be taken care of with little, and predominantly, no effort at participation on their part. Their lives are parasitical and in all respects akin to small children whose every need is supplied because of their supposed helplessness. And indeed many are helpless and require "baby care" for a time at least. The tragedy is that dependence and helplessness become permanent, even irrevocable, conditions through hospital confinement. Improvement, and in some cases recovery, when they do occur, are almost always spontaneous as a result of reduced pressures and demands of everyday living in a complex world outside. Remissions are inevitable, since no structural change occurs in the patient. As the anxieties and overloading of ego in family and communal living again set in, the defensive escape into regression re-occurs, and return to the sheltered life in the hospital follows.

Perhaps we should let a former patient in another hospital speak for herself as she did in a letter to a newspaper:

I have experienced mental illness myself, and feel very angry, and sorry about existing facilities in mental hospitals. Possibly the worst aspect, and the most humiliating, is the negative attitude of nurses and doctors toward their patients, almost verging on the brink of callousness. Incentive to live a vital, active and normal life is withdrawn in slow subtle stages, beginning with suspicion, supervision and inhibition of personal freedom. Ridiculous and unnecessary measures are taken in this respect—one even begins to doubt one's rights to ownership of even modest belongings, and excursions beyond the walls of the institute are regulated with fearful care.

Once the patient has been categorized, however wrongly, there is nothing he or she can do to impede the prescribed cure or even approach the doctors on a sane and equal basis. It is of course possible for the more energetic to refuse drugs and fight against electro-convulsive therapy, but certification of short duration (e.g., one month or three months) can make the treatment compulsory. Indeed, plunged into such an incredibly unreal situation, it is all too easy to be completely overcome with the hopelessness of it all.

It was our intention to create a "therapeutic climate" which would include both appropriate stimulations for activities as well as benign attitudes and, hopefully, relationships *among* the attendants—among themselves and other staff on and off the wards—and, above all, between attendants and patients and among patients. The plan, as it was conceived, would have first involved the training of the staffs of the two wards by a continuous weekly practicum seminar, later to be extended to the eight wards in the women's service (building). It was intended that in succeeding years the training program would spread to other buildings. We envisioned that as patients were prepared through milieu and relationship therapy, other forms of more intensive treatment would be introduced. Some of this work would probably have involved individual and group psychotherapy of an order suitable for psychotic patients, and conducted by properly qualified psychiatrists and members of allied professions under their supervision. In view of the numbers of patients in need of psychiatric treatment, for which there is limited or no personnel, we considered it important to develop methods by which larger numbers might have access to direct psychotherapy. In the opinion of the hospital director, the group method was a step in that direction, a position which we had fully supported at the time. Experience, however, caused us to abandon this position, the reason for which will become clear later on.

As a first step in putting these plans into operation, a planning meeting was held among the Director of the hospital, Dr. Nathan Beckenstein, Dr. Abbott Lippman, the consulting psychiatrist for the project, and the present author, on June 4th, 1964. The following is a summary of the transactions of that meeting:

(June 4, 1964) The purpose of this conference was to discuss and formulate procedures of introducing to the personnel of the hospital the plan we had originally outlined. The following steps were decided upon:

1. That Dr. Beckenstein as director of the hospital would take an active part initially in introducing the project to the hospital.

2. A copy of the description of the project should be distributed to the department heads.

3. The initial step would be a meeting with the department heads, especially those who may in any way become involved in the project.

4. In view of the fact that the basic personnel for putting the project into operation would be the attendants on the wards (none of whom have had the training and experience in working on this level with patients), the occupational therapists would be responsible for implementing the activity plans which will evolve during the staff group discussions (seminars). However, the responsibility for seeing that plans are carried

out would rest with the supervising psychiatrist of the building (service.)[2]

5. In the initial stages an experienced and personality-wise qualified occupational therapist would spend all of her time in introducing arts and crafts on each ward and training the ward personnel (attendants) to ultimately take over this function. When the ward personnel become ready to do so, the occupational therapist would act as a consultant or a resource person.

6. Indoctrination meetings of the active staff, namely the ward personnel and occupational therapists, will be held on a weekly basis.[3] The supervisory staff, psychiatrists, and department heads who will be "auditors" in the morning sessions, will meet at lunch to discuss the preceding sessions, react to what had transpired and make whatever suggestions they may have and thus involve themselves and their staffs in the project.

7. Consideration must be given at all times to the feedback from the personnel who will have encountered specific problems and difficulties as well as successes in the application of the techniques as formulated during discussions. The major emphasis should be on the participation of the staff in the discussions rather than making them didactic.

8. The aims of all the sessions with the attendants and supervisory staff will be:

a) to help personnel to understand *sensitively*, and appreciate feelings and attitudes patients reveal through behavior;

b) evolve through participatory discussion individual and group techniques for dealing constructively and therapeutically with patients' and staff reactions, and

c) above all, evolve techniques that would yield satisfaction through creative activity in staff and patients through the use of arts and crafts materials, various other occupations and through human relations. Particular emphasis will be directed toward helping patients to interact, relate to, and cooperate with each other and staff.

As a first step, a brief outline of the project was circulated among the department heads to orient them for a meeting which was held on the morning of June 11th, 1964.

The first steps in our work with the regressed, highly dis-

[2] For reasons too extensive to detail here this responsibility has never been assumed by supervising psychiatrists or the nurses.

[3] At our suggestion, it was decided that no disagreement or controversy be introduced by the professional staff during the seminars with the attendants, so as to prevent confusion in their minds. Any difference of opinion would be discussed at the "follow up" sessions with the supervisory personnel.

turbed psychotic patients with which this book deals were inaugurated without any rigid assumptions beyond the common sense recognition that patients are human beings in specially distressing physical and mental states, and that like all human beings, they require "affectional ties" (Bowlby) and are entitled to dignity, respect, and the opportunity for each to pursue her own interests in life. But as our work took root and yielded favorable results, we felt it necessary to identify factors beyond these simple assumptions before expanding our project further.

Upon extensive reflection and painstaking study of the content of our seminar session protocols, conversations with and feedback from various staff members, the entries in our diary of the numerous events, spontaneous comments, and reactions from staff, visitors and observers, as well as from the conduct of patients themselves, some definite patterns began to take shape. That is, it became apparent that an *inner coherence* had emerged which influenced our approaches and determined our plans and lines of action at different stages.

Among the major elements in the holistic nature of our work were: the characters of our patients—their assets, defects, potentials and limitations; the nature of the members at the various staff levels and their interrelationships; the quality of their functions and the degree of their involvement; the physical conditions and the emotional and social climates on the wards and in the hospital as a whole and, particularly, its social structure and its indigenous culture.

All of these elements, and more, are fully discussed in considerable detail in subsequent chapters. At this juncture we shall only briefly delineate initial impressions of the total situation as we found it, and as it came more clearly into focus in relation to the crystallization of our thinking. We shall also point out briefly the steps taken in dealing with and altering it as far as rigid traditionalism would allow.

The outstanding characteristic that impressed us most was the pervasive air of hopelessness on the part of all who were involved. The patients appeared to have resigned themselves to the emptiness of their lives, to their inactivity, to the inescapable fate

14

which was theirs, and as one former mental hospital patient described it in her communication to a newspaper—"to rot." The attitude of the staff was similarly devoid of hope. Theirs was the task of *caring* for persons interminably doomed to helplessness and utter dependence, intermixed with directing, disciplining, and punishing intransigence and disobedience. They were permeated with the conviction that their charges had reached the end of the line; that there was no hope or escape for them; in essence, that their patients would end their days in their current pathological states. As a result, the staff concentrated attention and effort on custodial care and management, rather than on attempting to rescue their charges from the morass into which they had sunk.

These roles of the patients and of the staff appeared to be clearly defined and rigidly adhered to within an intra- as well as an interpersonal context. The patients' roles, as well as their fate, had been fixed in the traditions of the past and bore the stamp of the antiquated practices that prevailed when mental hospitals were terminal dumping grounds for social rejects. Though health regimens and physical cleanliness were scrupulously enforced and medication regularly provided, the attitude that patients be treated *as persons* received no attention.

It should however be noted that this situation did not prevail in the hospital as a whole. Considerable efforts were being made by staff elsewhere in the hospital to "activate" (not motivate) patients to take part in occupational and recreational therapies, as well as to participate in various other activities. The patients' lounges and the "community store," where a variety of merchandise was available, were furnished with tables, chairs and other equipment which patients were allowed to utilize.

None of these were freely accessible to the 130 residents of the two "disturbed womens' wards" with which this volume deals. Forced to live under lock and key, only a small number, holders of "honor cards," were allowed off the wards, provided that they were in the company of another patient or in the company of an attendant. Others who did not rate such a privilege—and they were in the preponderant majority—would be taken down for brief periods in small groups under the supervision of *two* attendants. Thus it must be borne in mind that while the regimen in the hospital generally was to a degree an enlightened one and to a very limited extent in conformity with modern trends in mental hospital living, the two wards with which we are concerned lagged far behind these.

Obviously, to strengthen our patients' egos and prepare them to bear up under pressures and deal with the demands of the ordinary community life within the limits of each one's potentials required revolutionary steps. While ultimate results will be achieved mainly through appropriate biochemical means as yet to be evolved, until then the instrumentality of the *living process of graded reality* was essential.[4] To develop such a reality was the pivot of our work.

An erroneous belief is prevalent among lay persons that the medication now available is a "cure" for psychosis (or schizophrenia). Though very effective in giving temporary relief from tensions or depressions, their effect is short-lived. The value of these medications lies in regulating behavior; they do not reconstitute personality. Encouraging reports of significant steps in this direction through biochemical means appear from time to time, however.[5]

While the Brooklyn State Hospital is, as already stated, conducted on progressive lines, with open wards and free movement on and off the campus, and opportunities for recreational and occupational therapy activities, a patients' library, frequent movies, and a variety of gatherings, the important point is that all these are arranged and programmed *for* them and not *by* them. They were not employed to activate inner responses and aim-directed interests which to the general run of patients are essential for lasting improvement. Activity opportunities are *handed to* them and participation is in most instances urged or

[4] There is a definite similarity between the growth and treatment of psychotic persons and those of children. In the case of the latter as well, the "living situation" is the chief operational medium.

[5] Slavson, S. R. (1961). Group Psychotherapy and the Nature of Schizophrenia. *Internat. J. Group Psychother.*, 11:3-32.

imposed. The instinctive drive "to be the cause"[6] is not utilized. Patients in hospitals are, as are children in traditional homes and schools, recipients, not self-motivated activists.

Full-blown psychotics who are still subjected to sequestration under prevailing social conditions need to be viewed from two complementary points of view. One is that their state is an illness in need of medical intervention, on the one hand, while on the other, they are persons uniquely constituted organically. The nature and degree of their particular organicity, defective as it is in terms of biochemical homeostasis, compels them to act detrimentally to the *particular* prevailing social patterns. But if we consider the population generally, we find among it, as well, numerous individuals who, by their somatic and other idiosyncrasies are deviant of the so-called norms. Falling outside those norms they create social and interpersonal tensions. Some of the idiosyncrasies are psychogenic, conditioned by the circumstances of their early lives, but many of these social deviations from the hypothetical norms are somatically determined.

Irritability, irascibility, neurasthenia, egotism, self-centeredness, autonomic imbalance, depression, fatigue, and numerous other para-pathologic states may result also from nueronic sensitivity and imbalance and/or from glandular peculiarities. These are understood or endured in the ordinary person, even when not fully approved, as the individual's *state of being* or his *condition*. Schizophrenia and the psychotic state are in some instances also psychogenic as in induced schizophrenia (see footnote 5, p. 16), but in the vast majority of cases, more frequently organic—that is, *conditions* which are outcomes of organic equipment and defensive measures against them that take the form of specific flights from reality.

We consider this thesis as crucial if we are to be effective in the treatment of hospitalized patients, for if we expect the full-blown psychotic (with his deficient organic resources) to live up

6 Slavson, S. R. (1934), *Science in the New Education*. New York: Prentice-Hall, pp. 137, 140, 292.

to the pressures of the world and duplicate them in the hospital, even the most intensive psychological care will prove ineffective. As long as his ego is overloaded and his weak defenses assailed by the conditions under which he is compelled to live in the hospital, he will continue to retreat from reality as a form of defense.

What he rather requires is a comfortable and unthreatening human and physical milieu, simple and undemanding, on the one hand; on the other the opportunity to engage in meaningful interests and to use his powers in freely chosen pursuits and in active voluntary participation in the life around him—all within the limits of his capacities. Such a milieu requires a carefully planned physical setting, but what is even more important are the attitudes of, and relationships with, understanding and empathetic people who, in the case of a hospital, are the staff, and especially the attendants.

Our project was, therefore, set up with the view of creating a suitable physical and human living condition. All agreed that the state in which we first found our patients and the climate in which they lived were such as to make them inaccessible to any form of direct psychotherapy, individual or group, even if it had been available, which it was not. What they rather needed was an *appropriate life-setting in consonance with their condition*. That most of the heretofore "hopeless" patients had greatly improved and many were discharged (without direct psychotherapy) was a byproduct which we did not anticipate.

2. The Patients and Basic Approaches

Each of the two wards, A and B, selected for our project, was populated by 65 of the most intractable as well as the most withdrawn women in the hospital. With very few exceptions the women looked decrepit, disheveled, dirty, unkept and wore expressions of typical hospitalized, deteriorated mental patients. In the state we had found them, most wore inward-directed, lethargic expressions on their faces, while a small number presented a distinctly wild-eyed appearance. All but a few were uncommunicative; some were to various degrees manic, following the attendants around wherever they went, especially the supervising psychiatrist on his daily rounds, imploring him to be allowed to go home, demanding in chorus sundry privileges. For all the world they acted like baby sheep trailing their mother.

The physical appearances of the two wards were as decrepit as were the patients. The worn walls, in spots with peeling paint, presented a depressing sight. The paint on the doors displayed the effects of violent kicking and scratching. The plaster on the walls, too, seemed to have sustained a similar fate.

Most of the women sat about inert with vacuous expressions on their faces, in a manner suggesting total resignation from life. Ten or twelve lay on the floors, some asleep; others were milling around aimlessly. Screeching and screaming arose from time to time. These sounds were for the most part ignored by the attendants. There were always several patients in restraint (camisoles). On my first visit to one of the wards, I observed a woman under medical care confined to bed (in one of the small rooms used as overflow dormitories), as a result of a severe beating administered by a fellow patient. Several endlessly paced back and forth the full length of the ward, some barefoot, others shoeless, still others with unmatching shoes. Screams were emanating from one of the "isolation" rooms in which a patient was locked and in a camisole. On another ward, a small, frightened looking, bearded woman (Shirley, see p. 202) with sunken cheeks and deep-set sad eyes was tied to a bench, mumbling incoherent meaningless sounds, and waving one hand before her face pendulumlike.

On another ward, two girls, one Negro and the other white, had their arms tightly around each other so that their plump bodies were pressed into one another. One of them was bright-eyed, attractive, immaculately dressed, clean looking, and highly rouged and powdered. The other, was extremely fat and flabby, garbed in a dirty, ill-fitting dark dress, with oily face and staring, insane eyes. The two kept marching back and forth but stopped long enough to exchange a few words with the director, who accompanied me, and to inquire as to who I was and what I "wanted." This Siameselike relation between the girls was of long duration, I was told. It continued on the same basis for five or six months into our program until it automatically dissolved when the doors were unlocked and the patients calmed down. The white patient ventured out into the hospital community where she established friendships and joined her own social group.

Of the two wards, ward A was the more disturbed and the more violent. In ward B there was some semblance of order, but here, too, great mobility, evidences of destructibility and a climate of tension reigned. Here, too, patients sat around aimlessly while others were lying on the floor and on two or three chairs strung into benches. A number were asleep where they lay since the dormitory was kept locked during the day. There was much purposeless milling about and sitting around on the long rows of chairs arranged back to back. A few patients were watching television, though the vast majority did not take advantage even of this solitary opportunity for interest and stimulation.

Some patients on both wards were in a state of stupor and in various degrees of frozen catatonia. One girl, Julia (see p. 297) in particular, attracted attention by her foetal position. She sat from morning till night with her back against a wall, always at a particular spot with legs trussed up and encircled by her arms, her face buried in her knees, dressed in her not too clean nightgown. When her head was lifted by a staff member, it proved to be limp and her eyes unseeing and unfocussed. She did not respond to her name or to any other communication. As with her neck, her body, was similarly limp, and her mind blurred. She had remained in this state for years, we were told, though when she first came to the hospital she acted "normally" and responded well. Now, when she was forced to rise and walk she would do so as if asleep. Often, as she sat so immobile and incapsulated, a stream of urine would be seen flowing from under her into the room, an occurrence which seemingly went unnoticed. Neither patients nor staff appeared to be in the least concerned.

As the hospital director and I were entering the dormitory that led off from the day room, on one of our early brief visits to observe the ward, a woman was standing statuelike at the door jamb. Her eyes seemed to focus on us, but as we came abreast, her expression grew clouded and she sank into a catatonic state. To test her condition, the director lifted one of her arms, which remained in that position. [This experience made us suspect that assuming a catatonic posture may be one means of attracting attention (i.e., love) from staff (as parent substitutes).]

Our attention was drawn by an attractive, rather healthier and more intelligent-looking woman, who sat immobile, with a stony countenance and a hardly perceptible, permanent Mona Lisa smile. The smile and the fixed outward look of her clear and intelligent eyes never left her as she sat rigidly on a chair, always placed tightly against the wall. When addressed or asked a direct question, the immobility of her head, face and eyes remained totally undisturbed. Having assumed a pattern of complete detachment, she would not respond by gesture, word, or movement, but one somehow felt, after seeing her for a long time afterward, that this was almost a studied posture, arising from underlying intense hatred and bitter spite. During the more than two years that I knew her on the ward, I never heard her utter a word, participate with, or in any way make contact with or address staff or a fellow patient. The only relation in which she engaged was with an elderly woman who existed in a permanent state of torpor and who had to be taken care of like a baby—bathing, toileting and feeding. However, the relationship between the two was a completely nonverbal one in which they would sit close together in total silence, seemingly oblivious of one another's presence.[1]

One of the strikingly atypical persons was Justina. Justina was under five feet in height, squat, with a permanently dirty, sallow face and soiled hands. Her appearance bore a remarkable resemblance to that of the classical Neanderthal woman—low forehead, stubby nose, heavy jaws, large teeth, and small chin. With the rigidity of a statue, she would stand against the same wall, most often in precisely the same spot, perpetually shifting her weight from one foot to the other, with an impassive expression and an unseeing stare. While in this inert posture, her fingers would be busily preoccupied with her genitals or anus, and periodically she would smell her fingers. Justina could not speak or make any sound, and seemed to be completely deaf, for she did not respond when called, and had to be touched to attract her attention. Her self-manipulative practices particularly annoyed the ward staff and understandably precipitated attack on herself from other patients when, during her menstrual periods, she would displace the sanitary napkins, covering her dress and

---

[1] Like her companion, this woman was a "problem eater" and had to be helped with her food. Interestingly she relinquished this pattern of spite as our project got under way.

THE PATIENTS AND BASIC APPROACHES

hand with blood. Justina was one of the "recliners," i.e., she was not infrequently seen lying on the floor in a far, dark corner at the end of the passageway, removed from the central part of the ward, and thus from the other patients.

Try as I might, I was unable to elicit any response from her for eight months, despite my smiles and regular greetings which were always accompanied by a friendly remark each time I visited the ward. Throughout, she remained immobile and unresponsive, failing even to change the direction of her unseeing stare. In time, she did, on occasion, when so addressed, purse her lips and turn her face away, seemingly annoyed by the intrusion. On rare occasions she could be seen sitting, probably because someone had left a chair on the spot where she usually stood. Once, about four feet away from her, another vacant chair was at hand, and in my efforts to try to evoke some response from her, I sat down in that chair. For a lengthy period she appeared to be totally unaware of my presence, but when it did in fact register, she abruptly rose from her chair and walked away with an air that was unmistakably resentful.

As our story unfolds, we shall be able to describe how this patient gradually developed a strong attachment to me, her strange smile, her attempts at monopolization of me, and her jealousy of my attention to other patients. In a manner markedly unlike her former state of immobility, she would, upon seeing me entering the ward, approach me with an outstretched arm, and then walk along with me, hand-in-hand, until another patient would peremptorily claim my attention. She would then peremptorily leave me as if in anger, but without any change in her bland, impassive facial expression. As her attachment grew, she would, on occasion, purse her lips, and turn her face upward, indicating her desire to kiss me, which she would do as I stooped down. However, her kisses consisted of touching the cheek with her lips, her kissing reflex seemed to have remained dormant.

Then there was Hannah whose face in structure and expression was that of a classic psychotic. Of all the 130 patients, she was the most typical of this particular classification. Tall,

23

stooped, with heavy features, large yellow teeth, a dark-sallow face distorted by rage and always looking dirty even after a thorough scrubbing. Her unkept, scraggly hair was always in disorder and she wore her misfitted shoes on bare feet. Hannah was perpetually trotting back and forth the length of the ward, emitting periodically ear-splitting screeches followed by a screaming scramble of syllables and incomprehensible babble. At these short-lived but exhaustingly frequent periods, her watery blue-gray eyes would flash beams of hatred from a face distorted by rage. Just as suddenly she would fall into a withdrawn silence, only to burst forth again in a few minutes with her typical agitation.

Sometimes she would lie inert on the floor, apparently exhausted and withdrawn, at the extreme dark end of the passageway, seemingly wishing to be completely alone. At these periods she would respond to our approaches with a vacuous, uncomprehending gaze. Like Justina, Hannah, too, was isolated from the ward population and had never participated in any of the activities or made any contact whatsoever with anyone on the ward. For years she had never left its premises, even for a short walk, nor taken part in any of the trips to other precincts of the hospital.

For almost a year she ignored me and would, on occasion, explode with violent rage at the sight of me, emitting an incomprehensible jumble of words and loud sounds with facial contortions while maintaining her rapid pace at walking. Once in a while she would push me slightly or strike me with an open hand on my back almost automatically as she passed by. Most of her time was spent lying on the floor at the very end of the corridor quietly as though in contemplation, or fast asleep.

However, it would appear that my consistently greeting her by name in a friendly fashion and patting her (when she would let me) bore fruit after nine or 10 months. After the program got under way and the physical and interpersonal relations on the ward vastly improved—also perhaps because she grew accustomed to seeing me or because she may have perceived that I was responsible for the improvements in the life of the ward—

she became increasingly friendly toward me, which she demonstrated in a variety of ways. At first she would thrust a piece of paper—perhaps a wrapper of a stick of chewing gum or part of a newspaper—into my hand as she passed by me without a word or interruption in her forward movement. Later she would kiss me on the shoulder, again in the act of passing by. Still later she would stop, lift one of my hands and kiss it, then without a word resume her walking. Subsequently she took to announcing, upon seeing me, in a childish shrill voice, "I like you," and kiss either my cheek or my hand; I would then tell her that I liked her too.

In time the loudness and recurrence of her explosive screeching was greatly reduced and sometimes an entire morning would go by without a sound from Hannah. The frequency of her outbursts and the intensity of her rage seemed to correspond to the degree of disturbance on the ward. When the ward was quiet and serene, her outbursts would occur less frequently, and in diminished volume, only to reappear again in full force when even subsurface tensions set in on the ward. It would seem that her rages and screams proceeded from anxiety intensified by her environment. In one of our staff seminars, we called attention to this fact and suggested that Hannah could be viewed as the "barometer of emotional tensions" on the ward. It was many months before she was able to venture from the ward to a lounge with a "mixed" group (consisting of patients from both wards) where, though not taking part in the activities, she sat quietly in seemingly better contact, with an expression of serenity and even pleasure.

At first we did not believe she would be capable of such progress. Once stepping out of the elevator, during this period of Hannah's emergence, I was confronted by a group of patients going for a walk, who were waiting for the lift. Hannah, attractively dressed in contrast to her habitual disheveled attire and appearance, was among them. On seeing me, she exclaimed with a broad smile, "I am in heaven! I am going out for a walk!" This was the first time that she utilized clearly enunciated words— usually her raucous speech, although discernible, was jumbled.

Cornelia, a slight, dark-eyed, brown-haired, middle-aged woman would usually sit on the floor with her back against a wall, repeatedly crossing herself as she moved her lips in an inaudible whisper, obviously praying. When I would pass her, even without looking directly at her, she would cover her face with her hands, a towel, or any object of clothing, as though it were a sin to look at a man. When surprised standing in an open space, she would rush over to the nearest corner and turn her face away, as though seeking security by obliterating me from her vision. Insofar as I never had the opportunity to observe her in the presence of another male, I had no way of determining whether her need to hide her face from me was a specific fear of maleness or a general fear of human contact. This mannerism somewhat abated with time. That is, she no longer rushed for the "safety" of a corner, nor did she duck through the nearest open doorway with the same impetuosity as before. At times it appeared that the simple act of turning her head had become a sufficient avoidance tactic, but Cornelia never gave up her reserve and withdrawal at the sight of me. Nor did she stop crossing herself and moving her lips as if in prayer.

She was one of the self-incapsulated patients having no relations with anyone. She never spoke to anyone. The staff, as did the patients, scrupulously ignored her since she in no way obtruded herself, nor did she present any problem. Cornelia kept herself scrupulously clean, showering and washing her hair frequently. She was seen more often than was any other patient on the ward, with a towel tied around her head subsequent to showering. Years later I was told that Cornelia was of Greek origin, but would become enraged if addressed in her native tongue by a staff member hailing from that country.

Natalia presented us with quite a different problem. She was a youthful, short, squat girl with a round, clean face, dark hair and eyes, and a charming little-girl-like lisp and smile. Being mentally retarded in addition to being psychotic, her vocabulary was seriously limited and when addressed she would repeat what was said to her with her charming lisp. There was

26

always a question as to whether she understood the meaning of what was said beyond the simplest routines involving personal habits. It was certain that she was unable to grasp any abstractions. She had a very infectious smile and engaging babylike manner. However, her quiet exterior and baby-face masked a violent temper and an explosiveness that surprised one by its suddenness and physical violence. In fact, assaultiveness in Natalia did not require special provocation. She would suddenly attack the nearest person, screaming unfounded accusations against her victim, who would emerge from the melee with scratched face, minus a handful of hair, or with bruised shins.

Her special target was Shirley, an elderly woman, of whom a more detailed study appears elsewhere in this volume (see Chapter X). When questioned why she attacked Shirley (who could not defend herself as she was completely out of contact) Natalia would scream that Shirley "messed up" the ward (by her incontinence as she shuffled along the ward). There was some ground for anger since Natalia was the one who was ordered by the healthier patients to clean up the mess. It is interesting that while she meekly submitted to these orders, as an obedient small child would, this would mobilize her rage against poor, completely detached Shirley, who would receive without any resistance pummellings and severe hair-pullings.

However, Shirley was not the only victim of Natalia's explosive rage. Almost any patient who may have looked at her askance (or so Natalia thought) or whose cigarette Natalia demanded and was not readily given would become the target of her assaults. Like a little child, Natalia would want a chair already occupied by someone and on being refused, the occupant would suffer at her hands before she was forcefully stopped by an attendant.

Natalia was the source of much disturbance on the "better" of the two wards, Ward B. Ward A, where the assaultive and the more deeply psychotic patients seemed to have been concentrated, was plagued by almost constant violence. Though there were others on Ward B who occasionally created turmoil by their unprovoked physical assaults, the assaults, as were the

27

screams, screeching, and wailing, were outlets for intrapsychic pressures, mounting anxiety, as well as the accumulated hostility and anger characteristic of the psychotic process. All of this was further intensified by boredom, inactivity, the perpetual invasion of privacy, and the confinement and congregate living peculiar to an institutional setting.

Natalia was the only patient on both wards whose regression led her to eat feces from the toilet bowls, and unless she was watched, she would emerge with feces covering her face. She also drank water from toilet bowls. On occasion I observed her drinking steaming, almost boiling hot tap water from cans used for slops. When I suggested that she "put some cold water in because this water is too hot," she flashed her childlike infectious smile and, looking up at me, repeated, "Put in cold water, this is too hot," which led me to believe she did not grasp meanings of words, for she proceeded to drink the contents of the can. In time, these propensities greatly diminished, as did her combativeness, and ultimately almost disappeared. Among Natalia's idiosyncrasies was a penchant for marching around in bare feet. The staff found it impossible to keep her shod, for she would discard shoes almost as quickly as they were put on her. She was also one of the few patients who would suddenly appear stark naked on the ward, to the consternation of the others.

Natalia made hardly any contact with fellow patients, but responded to staff with deference and submission. She was particularly attached to the charge nurse and spent much time sitting in the office looking at people in a detached but smiling way. At times she seemed to understand a conversation, as for example, when the nurse related a story (later proved to be untrue) about the death of one of the attendants' husbands, as a reason for her absence that day. Natalia grew visibly pale and her eyes anxious as the nurse progressed in her narrative. While I signalled to the nurse to change the subject, Natalia was saying to herself, though looking at me, "Christina died, too." (Christina was a patient who, some weeks earlier, during a midday meal in the dining room, suddenly dropped to the floor dead.)

28

Natalia would be visited infrequently by an older sister, a woman in her middle thirties, who dressed well and appeared to be cultured. She seemed quite fond of her younger sister. Our patient harbored murderous hatred for this older sibling and treated her with contempt, refusing to speak to, or remain in the same room with her. She would scream abuses and vulgar expletives, shouting that the sister "get out." Entreaties by the latter bore no fruit. Natalie would only become more enraged—practically foaming at the mouth—and finally tear out of the room, leaving her sister to dejectedly turn and depart from the hospital. Natalia would not even accept the presents and food her sister would bring her, although otherwise a voracious eater.

For a long time, her behavior was predominantly morose and tense. She was very much withdrawn and usually spent much time either in one of the smaller rooms or in the foyer of the toilet. Pugnacious outbursts were frequent and her loud, angry, quarrelsome shouting resounded on the ward. Her tantrums were typically violent and a source of tension and disorder. Once she threw a tantrum it was not easy to quiet her down. Though usually meek and obedient with staff members, she would, at such times, even challenge them, an action leading to her forcible removal from the ward and placement in isolation.

Her attitude toward me when I first came on the ward consisted of ignoring me most of the time, though her face would pale somewhat and her manner grow diffident. As I kept greeting her on each of my visits with a friendly manner and smile, and as she became aware of my role, she showed some signs of relenting and would smilingly respond to my greeting by saying perfunctorily, "Hello, Mr. Slavson." It was interesting that despite her limited intellect, she learned to pronounce my name correctly and clearly. After some months, Natalia took the initiative in greeting me when I appeared. This she always did to the accompaniment of her fetching smile, narrowed eyes, and a display of well-formed white teeth. She seemed genuinely happy to see me, once she broke through her initial wariness and perhaps her fear.

29

With time, as the atmosphere on the ward grew calmer (i.e., fewer episodes of panicky screaming, less frequent fights, patient participation in manual work, table games, or quiet relaxation), Natalia's outbursts greatly diminished. She became more tolerant of Shirley, no longer attacking her even on the now much more infrequent occasions when the latter soiled the floor. On the whole, Natalia had become more amenable and if a request was made of her by an attendant, especially the ward nurse to whom she continued to be attached, she would undertake and carry out various chores.

Our luck did not hold as well with Geraldine. She was considered to have the most violent temper of the approximately 1,600 women patients in the hospital. Her perpetual rage was manifested by compressed lips, eyes which flashed anger, and easily provoked hatred directed at all comers. A short, heavily built woman with a clean, attractive face and somewhat heavy features, Geraldine was always cleanly and well dressed, and could be seen nearly all the time sitting apart at one side of the ward, radiating anger. She looked for all the world like a tigress in her lair, set to spring on any prey that would come her way. The intense hatred in her eyes made it difficult to look at her directly for more than a flash, partly because it was difficult to sustain such hostility and partly because one felt intuitively that a direct gaze would inflame her anger to a point where it would set off screams, threats and vituperations.

Her violent temper is well illustrated by an episode during my early inexperience with hospitalized psychotic patients. While I was walking on the ward in Geraldine's proximity, not noticing her presence, she suddenly jumped up screaming, "Get out of here! Get out of here!" and ran to a table nearby and with a violent sweep of her arm sent a set of assembled chessmen crashing to the floor, scattering them far and wide. She then proceeded without a stop to another chair and sat down looking daggers at me. I stooped down to help a few nearby patients pick up the chessmen. Without anyone uttering a word, we replaced the scattered objects on the table (although not setting them up for a game).

I did not perceive the significance of the patient's act at once, but later, in reflecting upon the event, its meaning became clear. Her anger was really directed toward me and her scream to get out was meant for me, as was also the attack on the chess game as a substitute for myself. The chief administrator, who happened to be on one of his occasional visits to the ward at the time, later called to my attention that there had been a sharp knife lying on the table near the chess game and its possible danger to me. The knife, part of the O.T. equipment when our project began operation, was apparently left there by a careless staff member. However, it served to expose the absurdity of universally practiced overcaution and rigid preventive measures against anticipated dangers in mental hospitals that lead to restrictions, thus preventing improvement in patients. We had encountered numerous similar demonstrations of this fact, some of which will be noted at various junctures later.

But returning to Geraldine, I should like to cite another occasion in which her outbursts of rage share certain parallelisms with that of a tigress.

Once Geraldine was stretched out with eyes open at her accustomed location on three chairs which she fashioned into a couch. I came within her sight though at least 30 feet away and quite unaware of her. Suddenly my attention was arrested by her screaming, "Get away from here! I am sleeping." Of course there was no alternative but to ignore her shouts and disappear from her range of vision! It was very much later when I had the opportunity to observe her in various and many conflicts on the ward that I became convinced that Geraldine was really a very frightened woman who reacted to her fears through rage. She limited herself to verbal attacks only and was very much afraid of physical conflict which she successfully managed to avoid. She limited herself to screaming, threatening, and calling names, always stopping short of physically attacking anyone, though for all the world the aspect of her rages bid fair to culminate in a vicious onslaught.

She arrogated to herself the management of the phonograph, which we had introduced on the ward, and laid sole claim to it. She would stand near the table on which the instrument was resting, thus detaching herself from other patients and staff (which was characteristic of her) and turn on the instrument to its highest pitch, thereby filling the room with ear-splitting raucous sound, then looking around to see the effect it had upon the others on the ward. When asked to turn down the volume, she would flatly and insultingly refuse at first, but some minutes later, comply. It was obvious that she used the phonograph as a means of aggression and a tool for attracting attention to herself.

Geraldine's behavior toward me was consistently hostile. It was later that I ascertained through her case history that this unreasonable antagonism had its roots in a traumatic relation with a man that resulted in out-of-wedlock motherhood and which precipitated her breakdown. Once when I was standing at the doorway to the dining room with the new (male) psychiatrist, she stopped in passing into the room and, before I was able to prevent it, kissed me intensively on the lips five or six times, holding my head between her hands so that I could not turn away my face. At the time she murmured, addressing the psychiatrist, some name that was unclear to me. Apparently in her fantasy, I had become someone else. This kissing episode was repeated once more on the ward as I was standing talking to another patient, but this time she was not as intense, nor were her kisses as numerous. Just what she was specifically living over in her fantasy during these episodes never became clear to us.

Delia, 35, on the other hand, was a psychotic mental defective who neglected herself physically and was completely unaware of and indifferent to her appearance. She was permanently in a state of limited contact, though not in a psychotic way, because of her native dullness in perceiving and her extremely infantile personality. Her pinched face, shaped like an inverted cone, terminated in a weak, pointed chin. Her mouth was completely toothless, resulting in pursed lips, and with her watery, expressionless small blue eyes and extremely spare, grotesquely clad body, she presented an appearance of permanent discontent, as she slowly ambled along with protruding abdomen and slight shuffle. She had the classic appearance of a mental hospital inmate.

Delia's characteristic response to the slightest frustration or unavoidable denial was an instantaneous copious flow of tears, which seemed to come to her with the greatest of ease and was accompanied by an even greater contraction of her already pinched face, all of which served to create a grotesque and laughter-provoking appearance. The tears streaming down her face in considerable rivulets were accompanied by a hardly audible, slight tragic wail, and at such times Delia was at once a comical and appealing figure.

Her speech impediment, which was exaggerated by the absence of teeth and a flapping tongue, rendered her requests clipped. Her vocabulary was limited and almost incomprehensible. When she became accustomed to my presence on the ward and learned what my functions were, she would be the first to accost me on my arrival with a demand like, "party, party, party" (meaning that she wanted to know whether there would be a ward party with coffee and cake) or "cigarettes, cigarettes, cigarettes." She was unable to fashion a sentence and would convey her wish by one word, the central noun. Many months later when she had partially given up her extreme infantile mechanism and would help with some chores, such as sweeping the floor and emptying the wastepaper basket, her face would be enlivened and her eyes lose their blank expression. She would announce, with a happy smile on her face, to no one in particular: "I'm working, I'm working." These moments were rare however, and would be followed by a demand for cigarettes as compensation.

When she came to know me, which took some months, her typical reaction to my appearance on the ward was to rush over, lock arms with me, and walk along wherever I went. She would stop and look with her bland bovine eyes as I talked to a patient or a staff member, not comprehending what was being said, but frequently interrupting the conversation by repeating, "party, party, party." We discovered, however, that when such matters as cigarettes, food, parties, and walks were under discussion, she appeared to understand parts of the conversation.

At first I met Delia's demands, conveyed as they were by accompanying tears, but when our relationship was established on a sounder footing, I decided to take measures which were to affect some degree of maturity. This was accomplished by directly admonishing her to stop crying, telling her sternly that she was no longer a little child. "Only little children cry when they want something," we would say sternly. At first this strategy was not very effective and the ward nurse would intercede in an attempt to stem the flood of tears. Delia responded to this nurse well and would be comparatively easily consoled by her. However, I continued to admonish her when she repeated her lacrimonious performance next time and in addition would guide her to the O.T. worker showing her that she could make her own cigarettes with the equipment and supplies which we had provided for this purpose.

Delia resisted assuming any responsibility for many weeks, but with the help from the ward nurse, she accepted the new plan to meet her wish for smokes by making her own cigarettes. In time, and this took many months, she gave up her demands and weeping spells but, still holding my arm, would drag herself along on my ward peregrinations. With the passing of time, Delia relinquished her clinging behavior and would greet me in a considerably more mature, less monopolistic manner. Along with this change, there was evidence of generally more mature conduct and visible improvement in physical appearance. Her face filled out; she looked less emaciated; her eyes grew more alive; she dressed better; and occasionally she even bore herself with comparative dignity and self-assurance.

On occasion, when her desires were not met, Delia would still regress to weeping spells. One incident both significant and amusing, occurred during her slow ascent from arrested infancy, yet before the full improvements described above. She had reached a stage where she would sit with the other women at the O.T. table busying herself with some very simple occupation, most often rolling cigarettes. It was on one such occasion that I saw her from a distance in tears as she was sitting there. I

34

walked up to her and sternly said, "Delia, stop crying! You know, only little children cry. Grown women don't cry. How old are you?" She looked up at me as I was stooping over her and said through her sobs, "Five years." I said, "No, you are 35." She repeated, sobbing as streams of tears rolled down her face, "Five years." As I continued chiding her, she raised her right arm and placed it around my neck from her sitting position and blurted out imploringly through her tears, "You like me. You like me. I'll stop. I'll stop."

Delia is a good example of what may be described as progressive ego integration and improved identity. She now seldom looked bedraggled, her mendicancy almost completely disappeared, and her infantile dependency and hang-dog countenance were no longer in evidence. She still remained an unusually limited person with many handicaps and slight vocabulary, but was now able to formulate phrases and at times even a sentence. However, it was her improved appearance and air of self-confidence that were so impressive. When seen almost three years later she seemed to have retained her improvement and no longer resorted to tears to get her way.

Dorothy was among the more enigmatic, least predictable of all our patients, and consequently a source of great annoyance to the staff. She was tall, gaunt, with a prominently curved back, flat chest, and deeply stooped posture. Her hair was reddish and always clean-looking; her eyes small and clear blue; her face normally rosy, but when she was upset, which occurred very often, she looked deathly pale, with lifeless eyes. Although totally toothless, she had a rather attractive, long, aquiline face which terminated in a sharp pointed chin. The curvature of her spine and her permanently stiff neck caused her eyes to be directed downward. When she wanted to look up she would straighten her entire body as far as she could, and when it was necessary that she look sideways, she would partially turn her torso. Due to her towering height, however, it was seldom necessary for her to stretch, as she found herself looking down at people of ordinary size.

35

One of her striking features was her hands, which were unusually large, with long, stiff, misshapen arthritic fingers. Although she could partially flex a few of them, she could not make a fist and therefore was unable to hold objects. Dorothy was one of the two patients on our wards whom we could not train to hold a tray of food due to the condition of her hands, and had to be fed. Dorothy had a way of stretching out her hands to anyone nearby which, appearing as they did like the talons of a predatory bird, had a threatening aspect and aroused fear in the uninitiated. Her hands were often covered with bandages which she would constantly be tearing off in order to scratch the underlying sores. This necessitated placing one of her arms in a camisole until the sores had disappeared. As the project advanced and the ward climate grew calm, the frequency of her skin outbreaks greatly diminished. During the second year of our project, she never required such restraint.

Dorothy's arms were inordinately strong, a fact of which I was made aware when, in her animal-like affection, she would embrace me with a "bear-hug" that would almost take my breath away. At times I found her stranglehold so overwhelming that it required the help of a staff member to disengage me.

She could not articulate even one word clearly and was thus incapable of directly communicating her needs or wishes. When she wanted something or was eager to convey a thought or feeling, she would emit a loud, repetitious grunt. When one did not understand the meaning of these grunts, her small cat-like eyes would slowly fill with a rising anger, often culminating in a high-pitched rage. She would then either attack the uncomprehending culprit or begin to bellow, emitting piercing animal-like sounds, not unlike a sow being slaughtered. Both her rages and her voice were deafening. These and her vicious facial expression instilled fear into the uninitiated beholder.

Dorothy was given to tearing up books and magazines and breaking objects during her fits of rage. Once she reached this level, there was no question of bringing her under control short of forceful restraint and isolation, of which she had been a frequent victim. As a result, she had in the past spent much time in restraint. Only one of the attendants could sometimes, with luck, succeed in cajoling her into comparative quiet. This remarkable attendant was the gentlest, most maternal, and most dedicated woman, whose genuine kindness and interest could occasionally penetrate even this somatopsychic defective.

One of the problems was Dorothy's unpredictable mood swings. While this was true of most of our women, and is more or less characteristic of psychotic patients, it is generally possible upon protracted observation, to discern a behavioral pattern which foretells an outbreak. Thus a perceptive and interested staff member could ordinarily take steps, if she so wished, to prevent or reduce the intensity of the onsetting disturbance. This however was not the case with Dorothy. Her mood swings and agitation would spring up without warning, often from seeming calm, and with no transition. We have observed, however, that Dorothy, like Hannah, responded sensitively to the climate of the ward. When tension prevailed, her face would grow pale, drawn, and strained; her eyes would take on a lusterless quality as she sat by herself, stalked back and forth, or lay on the floor with an expression of deep dejection.

During periods of aggressive stalking about the ward, which were generally accompanied by threatening emanations, she would finally pounce on something that she could destroy, such as a newspaper, magazine, book, or a picture on the wall. If Dorothy's favorite attendant happened to be on the ward during one of these outbursts, she would attempt to quiet the former, who responded with inflexible, blind stubbornness. At times she would abruptly break out into heart-rending weeping in the midst of such rages, putting her head, childlike, on the shoulder of whatever staff member happened to be administering to her at the moment. Weeping usually would calm her down. At other times, should a staff member attempt to invade her privacy when she was looking upset and angry, she would stop and prohibitively glare at the intruder, which always frightened the latter away.

One incident will serve to illustrate Dorothy's explosive violence. During the early period when the so-called "problem eaters" were fed separately by attendants in advance of the bulk of the patients (a practice that was eliminated as our project got under way), one of our two youthful (19-year-old) attendants was attempting to spoonfeed Dorothy mashed potatoes. Refusing to eat them, she mumbled something that neither the young attendant, another attendant nearby, nor I could understand. Dorothy kept refusing the potatoes, while the attendant just as persistently tried to force the food upon her, while soothingly urging her to eat. (A more perceptive and sympathetic person, less given to carrying out routines come what may, would have suspected some reason for the patient's adamant refusal and would have desisted from force-feeding.) Suddenly Dorothy, emitting a loud roar, violently swept the tray to the floor splashing a variety of foods over a wide area and on everyone nearby. Having done this, Dorothy, enraged, abruptly got up and with a mixture of suppressed weeping and rage, stalked out of the dining room and into the ward where she continued pacing back and forth, weeping.

(I later tasted the mashed potatoes as they were served to the patients and found them to be very hot. Apparently it was this that Dorothy vainly attempted to convey to the attendant.)

I had a somewhat similar experience with Dorothy on another occasion, but with a less disturbing outcome. Finding her, on one of my visits to the ward, in an excessively distraught condition, I decided, contrary to my general practice, to give her a piece of candy (which I obtained from the coin machine in the hallway near the door of the ward). I unwrapped it and gave it to her. Because of her condition, she was unable to grasp the small candy bar in order to feed herself and I, therefore, attempted to place it in her mouth. As I was doing so, she emitted sounds which I could not understand. However, noting that she was using the back of her hand to push the chocolate in, her unintelligible sounds became clear to me: she was trying to tell me that the piece of chocolate was "too big" to fit into her mouth.

On the ward, Dorothy presented a picture of utter loneliness, but she somehow emanated an air of longing for association. Ward staff at their best are unable to give of themselves to individual patients, but pressed as they were by the innumerable chores, occupations and activities, dealing with outbursts, crises and routines, they had little time to deal intensively with individuals and had been, anyway, not disposed to do so. I therefore made it a point to greet Dorothy effusively whenever I visited her ward, and attempted to speak with her. At the beginning she remained completely unresponsive, fixing her steely cold gaze on me, but with no trace of anger or resentment. When I persisted in my attentions, she would smile wanly and walk away, but in time her smiles became warm and friendly in response to my courting of her friendship. Later she took the initiative in greeting me upon my arrival and attempted to talk to me in sounds that I was unable to understand.

She seemed particularly pleased when I would tell her that she was a "good girl" and would flash a broad, toothless smile uttering sounds that seemed to say, "You like me?" I would assure her that I did. Dorothy frequently formulated sounds which one of the attendants, who was well acquainted with her through the years, would understand as being "kill" and "die" (apparently verbalizing the central fears that occupied her mind). Later, she would make sounds that, though not too clearly, seemed to spell the phrase, "I like you." On occasion in an outburst of affection, she would throw her long arms around my neck and give one of her prolonged bear-hugs.

Dorothy never became what one might call a model patient, but in time her outbursts grew less frequent and she became somewhat more tractable. In the latter part of the first year of our project, she was seen only once in a camisole, and in the second year she had no need of it at all. She had never participated in any of the activities or games, which she could not understand, but once when I happened to enter the "recreation lounge" (in another building), where a group of about 25 patients from our two wards were concentratedly engaged in various quiet activities while a patient played the piano and sang for the group, Dorothy, who had never left the ward before, was sitting in their midst, unoccupied, with a serenity on her smiling face that gladdened one's heart. From that time on, she joined walking groups, and would lumber along either by herself, or accompanied by an attendant.

Jeanne, our only permanent catatonic, spent her days sitting on the floor in a foetal position, and was incontinent. About a year after our project was started and Miss Eipiniki Kralides (see Ch. 6) was assigned to us on a full-time basis, she turned her attention in her spare moments to Jeanne. Once when Jeanne had her face exposed but her eyes were still blanketed by her characteristic nonseeing permanent withdrawal, Miss K. asked her to toss a medicine ball with her. When Jeanne did not respond, Miss K. physically helped her up and led her to a free space on the ward room. Once Jeanne was placed in a position facing Miss K. and the ball was lightly thrown to her, Jeanne actually caught it and made a feeble effort to return it. The ball was then tossed back and forth for several minutes, but Jeanne never succeeded in throwing it far enough for Miss K. to catch it. Soon Jeanne gave up and sat down on a nearby chair.

This maneuver to activate her was repeated on several occasions, as a result of which she began to respond as though she were in more contact with her environment. The music therapist, who had worked with her for some years past, reported to us that in some of her wakeful periods, he too had been able to interest her in coming to the "music room" with a group. In those instances, Jeanne would partially awaken and evince an interest in the music played on a hi-fi. Insofar as she was unable to navigate on her own, the music therapist would lead her down the flight of stairs to the music room, as well as help her get into the elevator and into the ward on the group's return. Jeanne would then sink back into oblivion.

Miss K.'s efforts with Jeanne bore a glimmer of hope for her. While she still often retreated into her incapsulating catatonic withdrawal, she would at times sit on a chair instead of on the floor and look straight ahead of her with her misty, unfocused eyes. On rare occasions, she would even take a few steps away from her usual perch. Whenever it was possible for

Miss K., she gave Jeanne some attention, either by speaking to her or attempting to engage her in a game. Much to my surprise, I once saw Jeanne actually going through the motions of playing checkers with Miss K. On another occasion, several months after Miss K. had made Jeanne a subject of her attention, an event occurred that remained permanently impressed in my memory.

Miss K., a female attendant, several patients, and I were talking one day at a table near the spot where Jeanne always sat on the floor. She voluntarily rose, made the few steps toward us, sat down on a vacant chair at the table, and attentively listened to our conversation. I turned to Jeanne and asked her what thoughts she had on the subject, which concerned some event on the ward. Jeanne mumbled a few words in a low whisper. Unfortunately the attendant who was with us, rather happy at the developments, pounced on Jeanne, plying her encouragingly with questions. Faced with this verbal barrage, Jeanne abruptly ended her participation in the conversation. [The attendant was an elderly woman from the "old school" who talked to patients in a condescending, cajoling voice used by baby-nurses, and who treated patients as though they were little children. She was new to the ward, having been transferred for a period of training in the new procedures of our project.]

Another significant episode with Jeanne deserves recording, as it reveals the basic incestuous content of the psychotic's psyche. When the new resident psychiatrist, a young man of about 30 years of age, was in the second year of our project assigned full time to our wards, I escorted him around to acquaint him with our practices. As we were standing and quietly talking, with no one nearby, Jeanne, who now walked by herself, came up to us and whispered so low that whatever she was saying remained inaudible. I, therefore, placed my ear near her face to better hear, and to my amazement heard her repeat in a continuous stream the following words: "I want a fuck. Fuck me. I want a fuck. Fuck me." Without replying I turned to my companion while Jeanne remained standing nearby whispering the same words, which remained inaudible to him, but decipherable to me since I now knew the sounds. In order to curtail this be-

41

havior, I guided the resident toward the door leading out of the ward. Jeanne followed a step behind us repeating her whispered entreaty during our walk and then proceeded to follow us into the foyer, but was restrained by an attendant. [It was on this occasion when the resident and I were standing inside, near the door of the dining room, that Geraldine kissed me repeatedly on the lips, mistaking me in her delusional state for someone else.]

Anna had a face resembling that of a ground hog. It was sallow and always dirty, a skeletonized face with sunken cheeks partly due to absence of all her side teeth (as well as most of those at the front of her mouth). The several front teeth that she still possessed were interspersed and inordinately long. The length of her teeth necessitated that her cavernous mouth remain permanently open. Her black, small eyes glittered with fear and examined one quizzically and suspiciously. Her eyes had a permanent haunted look that registered at once a mixture of suspicion and fear, which automatically precluded any entry into the abyss of her life. She repelled every effort at friendliness by staff and fellow patients. The first time I saw her she sat, her arms in a camisole, emotionally though not physically isolated, her calves almost completely covered with lacerations. When I greeted her, she did not respond. Instead she threw a hostile look at me and angrily muttered, "Who are you? I don't know you!"

Anna always sat on one of a long row of chairs which, before we rearranged them, were strung out across the width of the "day room" (ward) in two rows back to back. She always sat in the row that faced the larger part of the ward so that she had at all times a full view of what went on. She was inordinately curious and suspicious, while possessing a vicious and explosive temper which she freely discharged at everyone she perceived as annoying or threatening to her. An uninhibited torrent of expletives, curses, and obscenities flowed from her lips with remarkable rapidity. Her rages and flashing hostile glares caused most of her fellow patients to shy away, though not infrequently some aroused patient would administer a thrashing that sent Anna to her sickbed. She was given to paranoid complaints and accusations against fellow patients which she enunciated in a loud voice with free-flowing, well-constructed sentences, always believably coherent, even though the content was delusional. Anna had an excellent command of language and a good vocabulary, although she spoke typical Brooklynese. Her manner was essentially that of a shrew.

She had an irritating personality and a sadomasochistic quality that seemed to compulsively provoke rejection, physical attack, and a feeling of revulsion. These feelings were enhanced by the open deep sores with which her calves were nearly always covered. One of her most repellent postures involved her sitting with her skirt drawn up to her knees, exposing legs bandaged and soaked in a yellowish, filthy salve. Anna's clothes were always loose and ill-fitting; her blouse, open at the front, partially displayed her dried-up flabby breasts, which she furtively but unsuccessfully tried to cover at the sight of a male staff member.

Altogether she was a pitiful individual, though looking at her hawklike expression one could not escape the recognition that she was cruel, selfish, and predatory. When free of the leg sores, which occurred very seldom, her suffering mien would be replaced by a shrewd and aggressive expression. She was indeed inordinately shrewd, practical, and money conscious, and was known to have single-handedly transacted a number of "business enterprises" among her fellow patients on her own, as well as on other wards.

The dermatitis was undoubtedly related to her emotional state, for she was always extremely disturbed, but reluctant to act out her aggressions. A full-blown paranoid, she held under control much of her potential for murderous hostility, though enough broke through her controls (derived from fear) to create difficulties on the ward. The great quantum of repressed hostility, ready anger, and acidity lay at the root of her dermatitis. When her abrasions itched she would remove the bandages and scratch them, thereby spreading and deepening the sores. Consequently her calves and parts of her feet would become one large continuous wound. Staff admonishment against this behavior was to no avail and camisoles were frequently employed as a restraint against her further self-mutilation.

My early months on the ward saw Anna in a perpetual state of leprouslike debility. Her legs had been covered by the festering sores which the attendants sought to treat by salves and powders while she remained in restraint for weeks on end. She would sit dejectedly, with hopelessness and suffering imprinted on her face, incommunicado, except for an occasional outburst of her screaming accusations against fellow patients, shouting expletives at them and against fancied injustices. I assumed that this mode of existence was to be her lot in life. Within the general context of the ward atmosphere, the resemblance of this and other patients to drawings of medieval asylums and the English "bedlam" was indeed striking. Anna, like Hannah, Dorothy, Jeanne, Delia and others, could, for all the world, have stepped out from those pages.

Entering the ward one morning some months later, I was pleasantly surprised to find Anna fully dressed with shoes on, her face devoid of its usual pallor. Her complexion was much healthier and the fear and suspicion that always spread over her countenance seemed greatly diminished, though still wary and reserved. This time when I greeted her, she responded in a half-hearted and noncommittal manner. After a few days, she became a busybody and general factotum, running errands for other patients, at a price, counting change, bartering and selling sundry objects such as powdered coffee, candy, and shoe laces, which she seemed to have gathered no one knew where. Having been approved as essentially responsible, she was granted an "honor card" through which she enjoyed the privilege of free movement in the hospital.

After some weeks, however, Anna was again struck down by her affliction and with it her manner, appearance and reactions become overtly pathological. This time the period of her disability was much shorter and recovery much quicker. In time, although the dermatitis kept recurring, it did so much less frequently and its duration was considerably briefer. Sometimes months would pass before it made a reappearance.

Now that she was up and about, her real character asserted itself. She was acquisitive and predatory, sometimes taking possession of other patients' personal articles of clothing, and her voracity for accumulating and consuming food reached great proportions, which brought her into conflict and fights with her co-residents. Anna always emerged the loser from these battles, as she was basically frightened and a physical coward. For the most part, her strength was in her tongue.

My relationship with Anna remained till the end a distant one. I would greet her whenever I came on the ward and she would respond, but in an offhand way. She was incapable of friendship and warmth, giving the impression of being solely preoccupied with herself and her survival. In this respect, she was almost "normal."

When she addressed me, and this she did more frequently now, it was to complain of some injustice from the hospital or staff, against treatment received at the hands of another patient, or a failure in some business transaction. Once she complained that "they don't give a woman a chance to earn a living here," referring to her commercial enterprises on the ward. Given her pathology, Anna was bright and very shrewd. Thus as the ward life began to run more smoothly (fewer conflicts, less tensions) and when relations between staff and patients became friendlier and mellower, Anna's ego integration was more in evidence and the periods of comparative balance grew more extensive. She now dressed with greater care, presented a cleaner appearance, and less bizarre reactions. Nonetheless, from time to time, she would revert to her periods of depression and outbreaks of dermatitis, but these were now milder and of shorter duration.

One of the patients was a well-dressed, immaculately clean-looking, middle-aged woman with sandy hair, a pretty, well-rouged face, piercing black eyes, a small attractive mouth, and sensuous lips, who spoke in cultured Oxfordian tones. She insisted that she had come from a superior family, that her husband was a wealthy man, and that she was wealthy in her own right. Upon each one of my visits to the ward, I would be fur-

45

ther regaled with the story of her forcible abduction from a New York hotel suite, as a result of which she had had to leave behind costly jewelry, expensive dresses, and high-priced fur coats. She continually insisted that she be returned to her quarters.

Although she repeated her story numerous times, it was told with an air of newness and confidentiality on each occasion. Not being aware of the veracity or falsity of her claims, I always listened attentively to what sounded like a broken record, although occasionally she would add a detail or two.

A remarkable obsessional maneuver (in addition to her paranoid structure) were her hypnotically self-induced orgasms in which she indulged quite frequently. She accomplished these by sitting up rigidly ramrod-like in an armchair, her back tight against the back of the chair, elbows resting on its arms, while grasping and pulling on the latter with her hands. Her eyes were tightly shut with lids occasionally flickering, tensing her entire body which quivered occasionally, until orgasm was achieved. She would then relax.

At first her posture and general aspect attracted my attention as being unusual, but their meaning escaped me and I passed them off as one type of irrational psychotic behavior. However, the persistence of the phenomenon was sufficient to arouse my curiosity to the point where I took a seat at a distance to observe her. Though her eyes were shut, she would become aware of being observed (in the mysterious way that people do become aware through other than the recognized senses) and would half open them, taking a furtive and what seemed like an unseeing momentary look in my direction. This done, she would immediately close them again and continue with her contortions. During the fleeting gaze, her eyes revealed a dreamlike ecstasy characteristic of the passion evoked during coitus. It was this ecstatic look, together with the strange, glazed, dreamy appearance of her eyes and subsequent relaxation of her body that revealed the meaning of her behavior.

As bizarre as the aspect of individual patients was, their

effect upon the observer in aggregate was even more startling and not a little frightening, especially to the neophyte. The contorted faces, the many distorted and bloated bodies, the variety of bizarre positions, the sudden screeches and screaming, unexpected outbursts of hair-pulling and fist-fights, the strange and variegated expressions of eyes that ran from inverted withdrawal to murderous hostility—were bound to frighten those unaccustomed to such sights, and could be similarly disturbing even to those who had lived with them for long periods. Actually, it became evident to us in time, and it was further confirmed by other observers, that as much as they attempted to conceal it, the majority of the staff were genuinely afraid of the patients in the states they were in at the time we began our project.[2] In fact, the rules prohibited an attendant from entering a room with a patient except when accompanied by at least one other staff member, lest she be attacked.

We also discovered that the cause of many fights among patients took place over the possession of articles of seasonal clothing, usually coats required for outdoor walks. The staff had failed to appreciate the importance of clothing as an element in self-identity, especially for children and for childish adults. Articles of clothing were generally regarded as common property. An additional factor that aggravated this situation was the absence of individual lockers (which we later supplied). Underwear and dresses were kept in heaps on the floor and coats hung on racks in a locked "clothing room," outside one of the passageways leading to the ward. There were a few patients who had their clothes supplied by families, and these were sacrosanct. But even these garments would be delusionally claimed by others as theirs, to the consternation of their rightful owners, who often responded with savage combativeness to protect their private property.

Having no safe place for personal belongings, many of the women carried with them paper shopping bags which they

---

[2] A few years later, some attendants had grown sufficiently secure to openly admit this in a seminar session. Many unmistakably *acted* frightened.

clutched for dear life, never allowing them out of their sight. In deference to the rule against toting the bags to the dining room, they were left for safekeeping in the ward office, which was usually locked during mealtimes, to be retrieved immediately after the meal. An interesting and psychologically significant phenomenon was the fact that some of the women continued carrying bags even after we had made available to them individual lockers. It seemed that these belongings, which consisted mostly of odds and ends, paper, magazines, and sundry other generally useless items, had psychologic significance: they seemed to be extensions of the patients' bodies, feelings that flowed from defective body images and perhaps also from the cuddling instinct.

To assume that fights sprang only from conflict over possessions would be erroneous. Face scratching, blackening of eyes, hair pulling, and infrequently more serious injuries resulted without such "legitimate" grounds, as delusional as they may have been. Belligerency would erupt spontaneously from the seething homicidal hostility that is part of the schizophrenic syndrome. Those patients who sat for days, months and years without adequately externalizing energies, and who had no outer interests, would flee into a world of private dreams, introspectively reliving painful and frightening situations of their past and delusionally attacking anyone who became, in their fantasies, the threatening person or thing of their backgrounds. Serious fisticuffs would flare up with great frequency for the possession of a chair, while a dozen or more stood vacant in the immediate vicinity.

A patient would come up to another and order her to give up her seat. The frightened and meek would immediately arise and walk away. More often, however, a struggle would ensue requiring intercession of a staff member to prevent injuries. More importantly, such explosions, unless quickly extinguished, generated anxiety in nearby patients, setting off a chain reaction of emotional contagion which terminated in chaos. Another common source of embroilment was the differential preferences for radio and television programs on which the combatants could not agree. This, too, required the attention of the attendants. The staff were unaware that possession of objects and personal preferences were not the primary cause of these flare-ups. Rather the acting out was a channel by which the psychotics' diffuse hostility could be discharged.

As we shall see later, the frequency of physical encounters and other forms of conflict and aggression had enormously diminished and for many days on end occurred not at all. As the attendants grew more benevolent, the activities more involving, the total ward climate grew tranquil, patient relationships comparatively sanguine, the physical encounters completely disappeared for long periods.

The physical appearance of many of the women reflected the fact that they had spent years in sequestration, under lock and key, harboring hatred in a climate of fear; that they had abandoned all hope and had withdrawn from life with crushed egos, devoid of all motivation. For the most part their manner of dress was hopeless in terms of style and fit, except in those rare cases where families supplied the clothing. As previously mentioned, many wore unmatched shoes, or walked about in bare feet or in stockings, while a few were shod in only one shoe. Others on the ward wore heavy winter coats, some of which were men's overcoats, and still others a conglomerate of odd articles of clothing. A small number, especially those in the younger group, wore bizarre kinds of make-up. Several were inappropriately and highly rouged; one had her face painted white giving her a truly ghostly appearance; another—a heavy-set young white woman constantly peregrinating on the ward—splashed wide black stripes on her forehead and cheeks in the manner of African tribesmen. She employed this adornment for many months, sometimes altering the color to brick-red and, later, pure white. Later she took to painting her calves instead of her face.

However, as our project got under way, and comparative calm settled over the ward, these patients relinquished their various disguises and changes in identities. At the same time they grew more communicative; that is, relatively speaking, and exhibited a greater willingness and ability to relate to fellow-patients and staff. More than a year had passed before the patient who painted stripes on her face openly took notice of me and as she passed would say in a semiwhisper, "Hello," accompanied by a rather charming smile. She never actually stopped to talk to me during the long period of my visits to the ward. She was one of our "strollers," spending most of her time walking back and forth with a tentative, almost furtive expression on her face.

A number of the patients were nearly always to be seen in restraint. This was taken for granted. Others sat or lay on chairs and floors, snuggled awake or asleep against walls, some with despairing expressions on their faces, but most with singular blandness and detachment. The rather large foyer of the lavatory seemed to be the preferred location for self-isolation. A considerable number of women on the few chairs and on the floor could always be seen there. Screams of fear and anguish would periodically assail one's ears but were unheeded. For a long time after the initiation of our project, this form of retreat continued, but was eventually given up by all but a few. When the weather turned cold, many patients chose to be near the heat radiators on the ward, usually with their backs against the coils, even though the temperature on the wards was always adequate and often excessive. Here and there one could hear the even, calm voice or the whisper of hallucinating patients, some of whom sat apart, while others continued their self-addressed communications as they sat adjoining those who remained quite oblivious to these murmurings.

While we considered most disconcerting the noise, turmoil, tension and the frequent irrational outbursts of unprovoked violence and screaming among the patients, their total indifference toward their environment, toward themselves, and life itself, was even more distressing. Also discouraging was their seeming unconcern about anything around them, their lack of striving or interest in anything (beyond obtaining cigarettes and candy or a professed desire to "go home"). In short, the general air of hopelessness and resignation which constituted the climate on the wards did not, on the face of it, promise great success.

In addition, the staff, from the psychiatric residents down, seemed to be as devoid of hope for ameliorating the lives of their charges or improving their life-setting as were the patients themselves. Nor was there any apparent desire to effect any kind of a change in what to us seemed intolerable conditions.

Having had no previous experience with patients in a mental hospital, the fear which I definitely felt at the sights that confronted me would have caused me to retreat were it not for the ease and good humor displayed by Dr. Beckenstein, who accompanied me on my first two or three visits. His hearty greeting of each patient by name, ease of manner and semihumorous banter lifted the spirits of the patients, diminished my fear and increased my confidence, which was recognized by the patients and served to put them at ease with me. However, one incident in this area may be worth recording. Once while I was standing on the ward, the "Siamese twins" stopped in front of me and the white patient said challengingly: "Mr. Slavson, you're afraid of your shadow," immediately raising her fingers toward my eyes. I, too, raised my hand to block her, whereupon she abruptly dropped her hand, as if frightened of my gesture. This encounter was never brought up between us when we later became good friends. When I narrated this incident to some of the attendants, they told me that it was characteristic of this patient to scratch at the eyes during fights. Months later this same patient began confiding in me her thoughts and preoccupations, as well as the problems she had with her family.

Once, when she returned from a home visit where she had attacked her mother, she accosted me to tell me that she "really did not want to go home." Her mother "bothered" her. She would interfere with her movements and question where she had been whenever she went out of the house. This annoyed our patient and made her angry. "My mother never leaves me alone," she complained. "She's always after me. I can't do anything. She always interferes." On two other occasions, the

51

theme of her complaints was her brother's sexual advances toward her. In a complaining voice she would say, "My brother asks me to undress down to my waist, Mr. Slavson. Now, this is not right. I am not his wife. This is incest, don't you think?"

These confidences were part of the warm friendliness she apparently acquired toward me. Whenever she caught sight of me entering the ward, she would exclaim in a friendly voice and smile, "Hello, Mr. Slavson! How are you?" As her attachment to her companion dissolved, when she found her social metier off the ward, I saw her very infrequently. We would come upon each other only when I was on the ward at lunch or dinner time, which occurred infrequently. On such occasions, her face would beam with pleasure as she greeted me in a friendly, loud voice. She continued to be the very well-dressed girl and radiated health and happiness.

It is interesting to note that perhaps because of this patient's attitude, her Negro companion, too, grew friendly toward me. While they were still walking around clasping each other, the other girl, who, by the way, was a heavy drinker, said nothing, but looked at me with her staring wild eyes while the white girl would engage me in a brief conversation. When the separation of the two occurred, the Negro girl attached herself to me and invariably during my visits to the ward, engaged me in conversation. But unlike her former friend, she would make requests for various privileges, such as freedom to go off the ward (which at that time was still prohibited), to go on home visits, to have special clothing, etc. The most frequent topic of conversation was a missing front tooth, which she wanted to have corrected. When I suggested that she arrange for the dental work through the ward-charge, she had me explain how the dentist would make the correction, whether the clasps would be seen, whether the process would give her pain, etc. These matters were the concern of her inquiries for many months, though I repeatedly explained the process of capping adjoining teeth and attaching the artificial tooth to them and that it involved no pain. After some four or five months of this reassurance, she finally decided not to have it done.

52

It gradually became clear to us that our patients' need to relate on a dependency basis only was stronger than we all had assumed. Their welcoming smiles when I came in to the wards, their warm responses to greetings, their inquiries as to the state of my health, and other nonverbal approach responses, bore witness to this fact. One of the younger patients, for example, adopted me as her grandfather and would regularly address me by that name. Another said to me once with feeling, "It's too bad you have to work so hard. You should be retired by now." On some occasions when I seemed tired, she would say, "You look tired. Why don't you go home and rest?" On one such occasion before a weekend, as I was bidding goodbye to the patients, she said with genuine concern and kindness spreading over her smiling face, "Goodbye. I don't want to see you till next week." It must be noted that as a rigid policy, I gave nothing of a material nature to the patients, and they accepted the fact after a period of my consistent explanation, that I could not give them things.

The reaction of the patients to both Dr. Beckenstein's and my early calls to the wards was both interesting and enlightening. As soon as he stepped into the ward, he was instantaneously surrounded by a score of more women asking him for a vast variety of things: visits home, "honor cards," freedom to go to the community store, new dresses, candy, cigarettes, etc. They appeared for all the world as a group of mendicants in an Eastern bazaar besieging a Western traveller. The behavior of these chronologically mature women suggested that they were actually psychologically small children in the habit of being catered to by a parent.

I have observed the same phenomenon re-enacted less frequently when the supervising psychiatrist would appear on the ward for his very brief rounds. Similarly, in the first year of our project, when the psychiatrist who was assigned to us on a part-time basis and only occasionally visited the wards, did not appear on a given day, the patients constantly and anxiously asked for her. They seemed like children abandoned. However, this was not true when there was a full-time psychiatrist, in the sec-

53

ond year, who visited the wards daily and spent some time with the patients—that is, his absence did not provoke anxiety. From this it might be surmised that once the patients were assured of constancy and attention, the feeling of dependency abated.

The observation of the patients' reactions to Dr. Becken-stein helped me to formulate a program of activities within the context of an anxiety-reducing climate. Changing the relations between attendants and patients, as well as the pattern of their functions, became our aim, thereby reducing the prevalent anxiety. Basically, it was essential that the patients acquire a sense of dignity and self-worth and that the staff concentrate on this aspect of the rehabilitation of the patients, in addition to the behavior-regulating medication.

A feature that militated against the development of such attitudes was the appearance of the patients, both in manner and dress. Having been treated as helpless wards, requiring constant care and supervision, and needing to be reminded of such simple and ordinary functions as combing hair, bathing, changing underwear and dresses, the patients seemed to have surrendered every vestige of autonomy in all matters, which included grooming and personal care. There were, of course, the exceptional few patients who had maintained standards of personal appearance, usually to the point of compulsiveness.

As the records of the seminar discussions revealed, the matter of improving the appearance of patients as a therapeutic step, i.e., to raise their self-concepts and self-respect, frequently occurred. This question was first broached in the luncheon seminar of the administrative personnel where a division of opinion appeared. Following the traditional procedures that had been deeply ingrained through training and practice, some of the participants held out for the behavioristic approach of stricter supervision and control by attendants. We held out for the genetic approach; namely that personal care and cleanliness must proceed from improved personal dignity, self-awareness, and self-regard, and this would require (a) *opportunities* for improving appearance and (b) *engendering* desire for it by raising values and attitudes through an enriched life on the wards and through respect for the personality of each patient according to her particular needs and capacities.

These attributes, we held, would require a complete reversal of the philosophy that determined the perceptions, and above all, the treatment of patients by personnel, especially the attendants. However, we later discovered that the professional staff, as well, needed re-education in this regard. After many discussions of the subject in the seminars, the attendants, for example, considered it a great step in liberalism when they reported that they "let" a patient "choose" her clothes from the pile. This is only one instance of the extent to which the attendants infantilized their charges and thus rendered them completely incapable of the slightest degree of autonomy.

As a first practical step in this direction, the seminar members concluded that better choice of clothes in terms of size and color be made by the laundry staff, who washed and supplied them to the wards. We also requested that the outer garments be pressed, instead of being returned in a crumpled state. This had taken many months before it was achieved and would lapse periodically. None of the staff—attendants, nurses, psychiatrists —ever commented on the re-appearance of the deteriorated aspect of the patients. Invariably it was necessary for us to bring it to the attention of the staff always at a seminar session. These events recurred until, more than a year later, it was finally discovered that to have dresses pressed, they had to be delivered to the laundry in special baskets as "private" clothes, which received special treatment. Heretofore they had been dropped down the chute and treated with the mass of garments in the laundry.

Another practice that entrenched infantile characteristics and countered emergence of self-respect in patients was the commonly accepted practice of what we termed "the mendicancy syndrome," i.e., begging from visitors and staff. Upon being sighted coming into the ward, the newcomer, whoever he might be, would be surrounded by a number of the residents begging for cigarettes or money "to buy candy" (from the coin box situated in the foyer between the two wards). The attendants exploited the patients' propensities for "being given" by bribing them to help with chores that were part and parcel of their own personal lives and comfort, such as bed-making, sweeping the floors, helping in the dining room, emptying wastebaskets, or gathering articles for the laundry—chores that should have been performed as a matter of course and which they later did carry out as our program got under way.

Some attendants were so patronizing as to offer cigarettes to patients for being "good girls." A few brought cooked food and articles of clothing for their favorite patients and one night nurse in charge of one of the wards regularly appropriated excess food from the evening meals to compensate "deserving patients," as she referred to them. One attendant used to bring food regularly from home which was indigenous to her nationality and which she distributed every morning to some of her co-nationals among the patients. She was greatly puzzled by our disapproval of this practice. What *could* she do with such good food that the patients liked and enjoyed so much? It took some months of the operation of the program before she perceived, in her simple way, what we were aiming at by our program, and grudgingly capitulated. There was actually no valid reason for supplementing food, for the diet at the hospital was ample in quantity, excellent in taste and quality, and of a good variety.

The attendants were honestly convinced, and understandably so, that they were acting in kindness and devotion to their charges. The discussion of the effect of these acts occupied many of our seminar sessions. This proved to be a knotty topic for, in the light of our social mores, such "charitable" acts could be understood only as indications of interest. It took many repetitions and elaborations of their effect upon patients as such, and on the interpersonal relations. We pointed out that bestowing attention on selected individuals inevitably generated resentment against the attendants in those who were not so favored and also set off rivalrous feelings among the patients themselves which led to physical encounters, even though the cause of these remained unrecognized by the staff. Such *cumulative* resentments and built-up anger were instrumental in precipitating negative treatment by attendants as well as frustrations born of unkept promises by relatives, staff, and administration. During our seminar discussions, we were able, in many instances, to make these facts palpable by tracing patient outbursts to specific anger-evoking antecedent events which we had observed, or by helping the attendants by dogged questioning to recall such events.

The ingrained habit of attributing blame impulsively and automatically upon patients without making any effort at understanding the meaning of their disturbing acts often seemed inaccessible to "educational" ministration. To counteract this tendency, we introduced full two-hour case-studies in our seminars of the most troublesome patients in the hope that these would fix in the minds of staff the law of cause and effect in human behavior, be it that of the psychotic or the nonpsychotic. However, while the attendants and other staff came to intellectually understand the dynamic causes of deviant and troublesome behavior, their defensive armor prevented them from applying them under the stress of ward life. It is a sad commentary that even the members of the highest echelon did not react epistemologically to their patients' behavior.

Obtaining cigarettes is a major preoccupation of residents in all institutions: "reform" schools, jails, prisons, and mental hospitals. "Smokes" serve a realistic need in terms of habituation and physiologic conditioning, while at the same time having a variety of symbolic meanings. The socializing effect of tobacco on the life of the wards was indicated by the readiness with which patients shared them, allowing others to take puffs at their stogies, giving lights to fellow-patients from their cigarettes and, on numerous occasions, actually offering a partially-smoked cigarette to a fellow-patient. The patients on our wards had been accustomed to "being given" these highly valued objects by attendants who would use this "beneficence" partially out of custom and partially out of a need to allay their fear of patients' anger. "Smokes" also were used as bribes for doing simple housework chores and as a means of getting patients "off their backs."

However, because of our aim to help patients grow toward self-reliance and to give up mendicancy, we introduced cigarette making as one of the occupational therapy projects by supplying loose tobacco, cigarette paper, and a simple rolling device which patients could easily use after being shown how by the worker. The patients, however, did not readily take to this activity. There was considerable resistance on their part to giving up the wonted benevolence and attention from the attendants. To justify their resistance, they complained about the quality of the tobacco which was by far of a higher grade than the best of the store-bought kind. Neither did the attendants take kindly to our plan, for it deprived them of a potent tool for pacifying patients and buying their obedience.

At first, patients approached me, as they did everyone who came to the wards, with a variety of demands, begging cigarettes, matches, money, candy, home visits, trips to the community store, etc. As part of the demonstration for the attendants, we steadfastly refused these with an appropriate explanation. As far as cigarettes were concerned, we would take the patient to the table and point out the makings for cigarettes. [I never carried cigarettes or matches as I am a nonsmoker, a fact that I invariably made known, but which patients promptly "forgot."] As to money, I would explain that I was *not allowed* by the hospital rules to give away money. However, in the course of two years I did give a small sum of money to a patient, and on two occasions I got a piece of chocolate from the coin machine outside the ward for two mentally defective patients for therapeutic and relationship reasons. On one occasion I *lent* a small sum of money to a patient, who promptly returned it the following week. Jealousy was prevented by the fact that these transactions took place out of the earshot of others.

The following tables offer a picture of the ward population in terms of age, schooling, duration of hospitalization, occupation, and clinical diagnoses upon admission.

58

THE PATIENTS AND BASIC APPROACHES

TABLE ONE

Age Distribution of Patients at Time of Project Initiation

Age range: Years	Number
21 - 25	4
26 - 30	20
31 - 35	15
36 - 40	19
41 - 45	20
46 - 50	17
51 - 55	17
56 - 60	10
61 - 65	5
66 and over	3
Total	130

TABLE TWO

Schooling of Population on the Wards[3]

Type of School	Number
Grammar	38
High School	62
Business School (after H.S.)	6
Business School (No H.S.)	2
College	15
School for the Deaf	2
No schooling	3
Special school	2
Total	130

[3] In all instances patients did not complete academic schools.

TABLE THREE
Length of Stay in Hospital[4]

Years	Number
Under 2 years	4
2 to 5	14
5 to 10	38
11 to 15	25
16 to 20	39
21 to 25	6
Over 25	4
Total	130

[4] Previous hospitalizations are not included.

TABLE FOUR
Occupations of Patients Preceding Hospitalization

Type of Occupation	Number
Homemaking	21[5]
Domestic Service	7
Factory Work	22
Office Work	33
Bookkeeping	6
Dress Designing	1
Teaching	2
Student	5
Salesgirl	3
Usherette	1
Farming	1
Variety of Jobs	1
No occupation	27
Total	130

[5] Three women in this category had held a variety of jobs.

TABLE FIVE

Clinical Diagnoses at Time of Admission[6]

Category	Number
Schizophrenia	
Catatonic	64
Paranoid	24
Hebephrenia	11
Simple	1
Mixed	14
Manic Depressive	1
Affective Reactions	1
Psychosis	
With Mental Deficiency	10
(episodes of excitement and depression)	
With Alcoholism	1
With Brain Damage	1
With Senility	1
With Cerebral Atherosclerosis	2
With Convulsive Disorders	
(epileptic, excitement)	4
Involutionary (Melancholia)	2
Involutionary with Paranoia	1
Primary Behavior Disorder	1
Total	139

[6] As they appeared in patients' charts.

The records showed that seven of the patients had had head injuries and six had undergone lobotomies in the hospital or had come to the hospital after such operations elsewhere. Six cases, listed above under various categories were, in addition, mental defectives, making the number of patients with this deficiency 16. On one of the wards seven patients had been classified as having "organic deficiencies," some with deterioration. Four patients were deaf-mutes. Another qualifying term that often appeared was "excitement" (perhaps implying "agitation") and "violent outbursts." After we became acquainted with the ward residents, we realized that a number were idiots

[Dorothy and Shirley], imbeciles and feeble-minded [Natalia and Delia], simple psychotics [Cornelia and Hannah], a variety of types of schizophrenics, alcoholics [with and without psychoses] and other character disorders. In our opinion, a goodly number of our patients should not have been committed to a mental hospital altogether, since they were not accessible to therapeutic and quasitherapeutic efforts.

Whatever the clinical and/or functional categories recorded, they do not truly convey the actual picture of the ward population *en masse*. In the first place, the number of agitated patients was much higher than the statistics have shown.[7] Nor do figures accurately convey the intensity and the frequency of incidents of agitation, group contagion, or the great variety of stresses and the instances of panic that large numbers of such patient conglomerates inevitably generate.

To make matters worse, the population of the two "disturbed" wards was fluid during the first three months of our project. The practice of transferring unmanageable female patients—those in temporary states of agitation—from the entire hospital to these two wards and returning them after they calmed down was continued. Many, however, were added to our permanent list.

The transients who remained for several days or weeks were known as "lodgers," and appeared under that classification on the daily roster kept by the nurses or attendants in charge. About 12 beds, in addition to some of the 65 in the large dormitory, on each ward had been available for this purpose in three smaller dormitory rooms giving out of the passageways at each end of the "day room." [These rooms had also been used for punitive isolation. As part of our project, most of these rooms were transformed into kitchens, laundries, beauty parlors, and conference rooms.]

Thus, one would find new patients almost every day on each of the wards. As indicated, some of them remained permanently on these "locked, disturbed" wards. One young girl, for

[7] It is certainly within the realm of possibilities that many of these had become agitated as a result of the conditions on the wards.

example, was required to remain under restriction by court order, even during our liberal and freedom oriented regime because she was sexually promiscuous (carrying out the mores of both her parents who openly indulged in extramarital relations). The judge had committed her specifying that she remain under constant surveillance.

While there had been a calming effect on the "lodgers" as a result of the growing quiet on the wards, following on the heels of the changes in the physical setting and equipment, the creative and pacifying activities, the degree of social participation and, above all, the new attitudes of compassion and respect for the patients on the part of the staff, nevertheless, before they had brought themselves under control they succeeded in infecting the others with their tensions and aggressions through group contagion. We have, therefore, decided to no longer accommodate "lodgers." By thus stabilizing our population we could better judge the effectiveness of our program. This decision was supported by the hospital director who has always held that temporary intransigence of patients should be dealt with *in situ* on their own wards by "therapeutic isolation," by special attention from staff and, when necessary, by increased medication.

The four tables that appear in the preceding pages should, therefore, be considered as psychologic contours, rather than as reflections of the actual clinical situation as we found it. However, the tables are as fair a representation of the cross-section of our patient population, as it is, we daresay, of the *disturbed* wards in any state hospital. In delineating our ward population, added factors in changes that inevitably occur in a hospital need to be considered: transfers of patients to other wards as they improved, absences of patients on probationary release to the community, patients on home visits of various durations [as our project progressed some of them were able to remain from six weeks to three months without untoward incidents, while some had been discharged and replaced by others], as well as patients requiring prolonged medical attention off the wards and some who had to be confined for medical reasons in one of the smaller rooms reserved for this purpose.

3. *The Wards*

Despite the age of the W. Building, on the fourth (top) floor on which wards A and B were situated, the latter were spacious and sunny. They were furnished plainly but adequately for custodial care of patients and because they had been planned originally for 85 to 90 occupants, the current population of 65 made them seem uncrowded. Nonetheless this number as well far exceeded the requirements for effective therapeutic work.

Upon entering a ward from the wide foyer between the two wards through a wide, glass-panelled door, one encountered the ''office.'' From this one-windowed comparatively small room the ward was administered by a trained nurse when one was available. In addition to a desk, two chairs, and a small bulletin board on the wall, there was a locked cupboard which held the medication. Unlike all the other wards on the service (building) for which medication was prepared in the ''treatment room'' on the fourth floor, in the case of wards A and B the medication was prepared and dispensed by an attendant under the perfunctory supervision of the ward nurse.

While the wards were intended to be left in charge of a nurse, because of absences and other assignments, this responsibility actually devolved almost entirely upon an attendant of the longest period of service in the hospital. Even when a nurse was

64

theoretically "on assignment," the two days off a week, sick-leave, other assignments, and time allowances resulted in a situation whereby the nurses on our two wards were physically present on what could only be described as an occasional basis.[1]

Next to the office was the "clothes" room. This room was kept under lock and key and could be entered by patients only accompanied by an attendant. Beyond this was a third door leading to a room that had been used as an "overflow" dormitory accommodating four patients. Opposite these three rooms were three other chambers that served as storage room for the cleaning equipment, dressing room for the staff, and another overflow small dormitory. The "overflow" small dormitories were also used for medical as well as punitive isolation. Next to these rooms and a distance away was a door leading to the general dormitory with 65 cots.

As one moved on beyond the small rooms, one encountered a rather long narrow glass-enclosed room with a row of windows giving out to the outdoors. The walls of this room were lined with chairs. This room was known as the "sun room" where patients could be seen at all times sitting around the walls staring quietly into space, some mumbling to themselves, some crying, or occasionally screaming. Opposite the "sun room" was the door leading to the showers. Beyond this "sun room" was the large, bright "day hall" with its rows of chairs placed back to back across its width, and a number of large oblong tables in the middle of the room, surrounded by a few arm chairs. The narrower spaces between the small rooms on each end of the ward we designated as the "passageways."

The scenes we described in the preceding chapter took place mostly in the day room and to a lesser extent in the passageways. A wide-screened porch, the full length of the day room, looked out onto the grounds and could be reached by three wide French double doors. When all the doors were open the porch became part of the day room and added to its spa-

[1] Ward A operated without a nurse during the major part of the duration of our project.

ciousness and brightness. Beyond the day room, two small rooms, one on each side of the short passageway, had been used as overflow dormitories and for temporary isolation of individual patients. This passageway ended in a solid, fireproofed door, which was always kept locked and led to an emergency stairway. A door from the common foyer (outside the wards) led to another stairway connecting all the floors of the building.

The general dormitories were large, bright rooms, having a series of round columns running through their middle, and two walls consisting almost entirely of windows, thereby assuring excellent ventilation and sunshine. At all times, but especially on sunny days, this room presented a cheerful aspect that lifted one's spirits. Because of its simplicity and utilitarian design, it was easy to keep clean and was always kept neat. The dormitories, as well as all the other rooms, except the utilities storage room, had always been locked.

At one end of the outer foyer and between the two wards, a door led to the "treatment room." This room was left in the charge of a special nurse and it was here that patients from the entire building who did not require hospital attention were examined and treated by physicians. It was also in this room that the nurse prepared medication for the six additional wards on the service. An inside door connected the treatment room with an examining room equipped with an examining table and appropriate tools of the trade. A door, always kept locked, at the left of the foyer behind the front passenger elevator shaft, led to the attendants' toilet.

Directly opposite the treatment room at the other end of the foyer, a wide double door led into the adequately large and cheerful dining room. This room was identical in size and construction with the dormitory. Both were so situated that they formed two distinct wings projecting from the main body of the building far enough apart so that each was bathed on two sides in the sunshine and spaciousness of the outdoors. Tables seating eight arranged in four long rows gave the room, at all times spotless, a neat and pleasant appearance.

At its far end, partially walled off with two wide proscenia, was the "kitchen alcove" where the food was dispensed, cafeteria style, by the staff of one or two, aided by attendants from each ward on a rotating basis. The food was prepared in a central kitchen and brought to the wards on wagons by a rear elevator. Patients formed a line the full length of the dining hall on the right, and entered the alcove where, unaided, they picked up trays and utensils. The meals were dispensed as they passed a long counter behind which the staff prepared the "plates" for them. They then exited by the other proscenium at the left and found tables for themselves. Seats were not assigned but each ward had alotted to it two rows of tables and patients were required to confine their choices to these. The rows were supervised by two or three attendants attached to the respective wards who kept walking back and forth watching the diners.

When the meal was over an attendant signaled that the diners line up again at the left of the room to return the used plates and utensils. This operation was presided over by an attendant, but the actual work of scraping, washing, and sterilizing the utensils and pots was carried out by a few of the more intact patients who had been receiving a small compensation for this work. After delivering their burdens, the patients would turn about face and leave the dining room to return to their respective wards under the watchful eyes of the attendants in charge.

The patients' anger and violence took their toll in the physical appearance of the wards. In addition to the fact that because of staff maintenance limitations the walls and ceilings in the various rooms had remained unpainted for years, there were everywhere areas of peeled, scratched off or kicked off paint and plaster. Understandably, the locked doors leading out of the wards had been the special targets of aggression. The raw wood and plaster being exposed at many points gave the wards a shabby appearance. The well-used floor covering being of plain dark linoleum added to the uninspiring appearance of the "home-away-from-home" for the 65 residents.

The smaller rooms giving out on the passageways which

were used for showers, utilities and a clothes store room, appeared to be in a state of disorder and were far from being up to the standard of hospital regulations. The two huge floor-washing mops on each ward were, for example, strung over the partition in the showering room. Since these mops were used to clean up the fecal matter and urine of incontinent patients, they emitted a revolting odor. The showering rooms were dark, dingy, and damp from the vapor that eternally hung in the air. No ventilation was provided and the one window with opaque glass panes could not be kept open. The buildings had been designed and built many decades ago and reflected the lack of imagination and utility characteristic of the building industry of that period. As a result, the showering rooms remained uninviting and depressing even after matters had improved through the implementation of our program.

Not wishing to appear in an authoritarian role, we have repeatedly brought up the question with the staff of storing the mops with their nefarious odor elsewhere than in the showering rooms. The matter was fully discussed at many seminar sessions and decisions made accordingly, but still for many months, none of the plans had been carried out by the staff in charge of the wards. Whether it was inconvenience, forgetfulness, resistance or a strategy of sabotaging, we were unable to ascertain. The latter explanation, however, seemed the most likely one in the light of the conduct of "officials" in other situations. Relocation of the perpetually wet, ill-smelling, and unclean mops to the open air landings of the staircases was effected only after the *director* had voiced his disapproval of the existing arrangement.

The physical layout of the damp, dark showering rooms was such that patients had to dress and undress, shower, and dry themselves in the presence of several others who were waiting their turn. Showering took place in pairs under two separate sprinklers having no partition between them. Only one long metal bench was provided for dressing and undressing in full view of the other patients.

Since they received daylight through a window with clear glass, the utilities store rooms where brooms, pails, and other cleaning utensils and supplies were stored seemed more bearable. These small rooms were equipped with "slop sinks" and other appurtenances required for house cleaning. Because the equipment was not kept adequately clean and the lone window seldom open, the odors in these rooms, as well, were offensive. The director was aware of these conditions and decried them, but, as he explained, because of the unsuitable structural features in the antiquated buildings, little could be done to make some parts of the wards pleasant in appearance and efficient in use. Nonetheless, subsequent months saw considerable improvement in them as the patients assumed more responsibility for the wards. The staff, freed from dealing with the interminable crises with patients, could now turn more of their attention to these details.

In the room that was strictly kept locked where a mass of dresses and other items of feminine apparel were kept, there was always a high pile of dresses on the floor due to insufficiency of space and racks. When needed, dresses would be pulled out of the pile and *given* to patients. Sometimes a patient was "allowed" to select one for herself under the watchful eye of an attendant. Although the dresses were washed regularly in the central laundry, they were not ironed, and no provisions were made on the wards to this end before our project was introduced. No special attention was directed to appropriateness of size or color. There was, therefore, little wonder that the patients presented so decrepit an appearance individually and *en masse.*

More shocking were the otherwise large, bright, exceptionally clean toilets on the wards. They were long, narrow rooms, facing the bright outdoors with the sun streaming in nearly all day through a long row of translucent windows. An adequate, full-length glass mirror hung on a wall of the foyer of this room in each ward. At least one, and not unusually a few patients could be seen before these mirrors doing their hair, putting on rouge, or just looking at their reflections. The shock about this otherwise adequate setup lay in the fact that in a turn around the corner, from the foyer, obscured from view from the "day room," 10 toilet bowls were strung out, six in one row and four opposite them, with no partitions or curtains between them. As in the showering rooms here, too, no privacy was provided. For one with no previous experience in a state hospital, this spectacle was indeed appalling. One could not easily conceive or accept the fact of such indignity against fellow creatures; it was difficult to contain one's ire at the sight of such an affront to human dignity. To provide enclosures for individual toilet bowls, therefore, received our first priority, second only to fresh paint for the wards. [We were to discover much later through bitter experience the rigid controls and inflexible rules in state institutions that prevented needed improvements because funds could not be converted from one budgetary item to another.]

We took immediate steps to remedy most of the deficiencies in the physical setting and appearance of the wards. Due to lack of budgetary funds, the director raised money from sources other than the state treasury for some of the improvements. Where work was to be done by the maintenance staff of the hospital it was done by them, though the limited personnel necessitated great delay. We recommended new paint for both wards, but of the utmost importance, we felt, was the construction of cubicles around the toilet bowls as soon as possible. On this point we were most insistent. The following entry in the minutes of a planning conference with the director on this subject is typical of our efforts: "The basic aim of the project is to elevate the patients' self-images and arouse in them a sense of self-dignity. How can this be done when we expose them to such extremely demeaning indignity?" We also recommended minor structural changes in the showering rooms by providing curtains between patients during their showering activities and separate enclosed benches for privacy in dressing and undressing.

The director of the hospital whole-heartedly supported the suggestions and despite numerous other demands on the maintenance and constructional staffs in his large plant, the partitions in the toilets were the first changes made, to the great joy of the patients (which will be described later).

70

Heretofore, there had been no lockers in which to keep shoes, clothing, or other personal belongings, so that these would be either strewn about or toted around by patients in shopping and smaller paper bags. We therefore set in motion a project for supplying individual lockers. This required some doing, however, for whereas wood for partitions in the toilets, and cloth and rods for curtains in the shower rooms could be drawn from the general supplies, while installation was accomplished by available hospital staff on the grounds, the lockers had to be made in one of the out-of-town state prisons. Since there was no budgetary provision to meet the cost (as well as other materials and equipment which we later needed), the money had to come from another source. This source was an auxiliary community organization, The Ivy League, whose members dedicated themselves to aiding the patients and with which the director maintained a close liaison. His influence upon the organization was considerable. This group supported us financially, and made possible many activities during the life of the project, without which our work would have of necessity been seriously curtailed.

Delivery of the lockers was delayed almost eight months, as a result of which, the patients' patience was strained to the utmost. They had looked forward to having a suitable place to house their belongings and had made repeated inquiries as to when the lockers would arrive. When they all but lost hope of ever having them, the lockers came and were received with great joy.

The lockers, properly tagged with each patient's name, were placed in the dormitory near the bed of each. The problem of managing keys by patients such as ours were at the time, who had little or no contact, proved a difficult one to solve.

After the wards had been painted, the partitions in the toilets installed, the lockers provided, the ward climate more tranquil as many patients displayed an interest in work with their hands and took on limited responsibilities, we turned our attention to further improving the physical aspects of the wards. Accordingly, the attention of the staff to possibilities for doing so was drawn at our seminars on a number of occasions. Various suggestions came from them and a number of projects was decided upon. Among these were the making of curtains for the numerous windows on the wards, in the dining room, and in the dormitories, as well as the hanging of pictures on the walls of various rooms. Now that a goodly number of patients had obviously taken to the opportunities offered them for creative interests and useful occupations, the two original occupational therapy staff members (who were replaced some months later) responded warmly to the suggestions and undertook to bring them to fruition.

Under the then existing hierarchical staff structure, the responsibility to implement all such projects obviously belonged to the nurses in charge of the wards in cooperation with the appropriate departments. As it became apparent with the passing of time that no steps were being made to realize the plans, we repeatedly brought the matter to the seminar group but achieved little in the way of tangible results. The matter either drew a silence or reasons were offered as to why the projects had not been set in motion. In our capacity as visiting consultant, we considered it inappropriate to interfere with the work and authority of the staff in whose area of responsibility it was. Because of staff turnover and the crowding of innumerable other details, these matters passed into limbo to be revived and partially consummated some years later.

Some pictures had been acquired for ward B and remained hanging on the walls. However, the few pictures on ward A were destroyed at that time by the more disturbed patients, as were the indigenous works of patients which had also been on display. Much later, pictures hung out of reach remained intact on ward A, but the project for making curtains, which had great possibilities for group participation and evoking communal feelings and interests, has never been realized.

4. The Staff

While the patients were exposed to consistent discipline, the discipline imposed on attendants by their superiors was even more rigid and more demanding. The attendants were required, or so they thought, to be constantly and visibly in action and occupied. They averred that to be found sitting or seemingly relaxed evoked a demerit and, therefore, when caught in the act of relaxing by a superior, they would immediately propel themselves into action, becoming busily involved with anything at hand, in the belief that even sitting down to chat with a patient was an act of malingering which could militate against their promotion.

However, the staff interrelationships, although behaviorally less obvious, were more malevolent in their effect upon the living climate of the patients. The then existing caste system and the resulting "pecking order" had a constraining effect upon individuals and seriously contaminated the climate as a whole. Initiative was frowned upon and in most cases definitely disapproved of. It was particularly true of attendants—staff members on the lowest rung in the system—that they never dared to make a step, as imperative as it may have been, which was outside or beyond traditional practices. One of the psychiatrists was as much impressed as we were with the militaristic subservience to authority of this group of women. "The attendants," he said, referring to one of the wards, "do nothing on their own. They wait for orders from the nurse and when she is not there [which occurred quite frequently], they feel helpless and lost." This psychiatrist's reaction was particularly significant as it took place even more than a year after the inauguration of the project, the aim of which was freeing the staff as it did the patients.

Departmentalism and segmented authority made themselves intensely felt when the new plan was to be put into operation. Whereas the dynamics of a humane communal or creative life required flexibility and richness in resources, the constraints of bureaucracy and the conservatism would have greatly hampered our progress and negated achievement were it not for the supportive and meliorating attitude and help from the hospital's director. The elimination of differentials in caste attitudes, therefore, received major attention in our reconstructive efforts at creating a therapeutic climate on the two wards.

Escalated authority in hospitals with its characteristic dominance-subservience patterns was not the only factor that operated among the hospital staffs. There also existed simultaneously the two contradictory attitudes of rivalry and a uniquely intense solidarity. Although rivalry was not so much in evidence among the attendants, it was rather prevalent among a few members of the upper echelon involved in our project. They seemed consistently vigilant against inroads into their specific fields of authority, while at the same time seeking to extend it. This, too, was not unique in our hospital, for these attitudes are widespread in all mental hospitals, as well as in other areas of our culture. This rivalry and mutual antipathy of supervisors whose work should have been complementary for the benefit of patients, was particularly damaging.

There prevailed at the same time, intense loyalty among the lower staffs to each other. Thus, the attendants, the ancillary therapists, the psychiatrists, etc., each formed a self-protective phalanx, but all were also bound together by a defensive tie against the administration. In fact, it was with considerable consternation that we witnessed a statement at one of our attendants' seminar sessions by a State medical inspector justifying these sectarian phenomena among the staff as essential to their "protection," adding the information that it exists in hospitals among psychiatrists as well as in the lower echelons. Even more disturbing was this statement because it was made during a heated discussion centered around a particularly critical situation in which the blind solidarity of the attendants proved detrimental to patients.

However, despite the prevalent intense mutual protectiveness, there was also a singular absence of communication among the staff in the "lower" categories. While communications among the top staff were always guarded, in this group it was altogether lacking. We were unable to testify to the prevalence of this relation in other parts of the hospital, but it was definitely the case with our attendants and only to a lesser extent in others. Discussion of an untoward event or a serious error in judgment or an accident was tacitly avoided. The occurrence appeared to be erased from memory. This practice, which was of long standing, militated against "learning from experience," so important for personal development and even more essential to professional growth and appropriate functioning. Minor unpleasant occurrences were withheld from the administration, though happenings that could prove legally damaging were duly recorded as required by regulations.

This climate of secrecy and cover-up prevented emergence of professional judgment and skills that would have avoided repetitions of errors in dealing with patients. It was these considerations that were instrumental in our decision to bring up in our seminars all events and acts—good and bad—for discussion. It was the traditionally accepted and rigidly applied practice on the part of the staff, in all categories, not to correct or criticize each other's dealing with patients. The routines, timetables, cleanliness and the like were scrupulously carried out and each was left to his own devices, judgments and acts where patients were involved. One could not elicit information on the genesis of an untoward event on a ward if it involved a member of their coterie: the blame seemed always laid at the feet of patients. Causes emanating from patients were stressed, but the part played by a fellow staff member, even from another department than their own, was concealed or underplayed.

When this situation was brought forth in a private conversation with one of the top staff members who was intimately acquainted with staff's personal problems, he had the following to say:

When you think of their background, Mr. Slavson. I never realized this until several times I'd been down to where they had a death in their family. And I suddenly found myself in their environment. I can now easily understand why it's very difficult to get Mary Jane to complain about Mary Brown, because they live right in the same area and who knows but they might find a knife in their back when they go up the stairs at night. They talk amongst themselves about squealers or stupids or whatever it happens to be. Going down into the area where they live and working there with a visiting nurse, I found out many things that I didn't know before. I can easily understand why they have such cohesion between themselves [taped].

On the conviction that personal and professional growth can take place only in the fertile soil of benevolent mutual self-criticism and objectivity, we emphasized these and attempted to demonstrate their virtues. In the first instance we factually and objectively called attention to specific instances of conduct we had observed by attendants anonymously and led the weekly seminar participants (to the extent they were capable of doing so) to recognize the unsuitability of the reactions or measures taken by staff in dealing with patients. We then helped them formulate procedures more consonant with the therapeutic and humane intents of our demonstration project. The second strategy—that of encouraging self-criticism—was the freedom and ease with which we called attention to our own errors and limitations, by the hospitality with which we accepted the staff's criticism of our performance, and by the acceptance of valid suggestions that came from them.

The widespread solidarity from which stemmed avoidance of communication and criticism was obviously a self-protective device. Since promotion and the consequent increase in pay was dependent upon periodic "evaluations" of the performance of each staff member by supervisory personnel, it was understandable why each had striven to prevent any reflections that might influence the evaluations negatively. Thus, mutual cover-up was a logical outcome and an inevitable practice. "Tattling" was an unforgivable transgression against the mutually protective survival and security. Thus, inquiry of an unfavorable occurrence was met with silence or evasion, for the informer stood the risk of becoming the object of vengeful persecution and of calumny that could injure status and promotion.

As was clear from the attitudes of staff and from their remarks, the insecurity in relation to promotion and hierarchical structure prevalent in hospitals, perhaps unavoidably so, was the most sensitive source of resistance to change, equalled only by habit and tradition. It was enough, for example, for the unfriendly attitude of one supervisory member to the changes we sought to introduce to render all the subordinates to inflexibly adhere to traditional roles and functions.

Another factor that supported staff in their resistance was the legal job tenure of civil servants. Lurking behind their fear of authority was also the awareness that they could not be deprived of their jobs. [The process of terminating the employment of a civil servant is very involved and unpleasant, requiring hearings and substantiation by witnesses. Such problems were solved instead by a transfer of the offending employee to another station.] In our case, no transfers were contemplated or executed. This, despite the fact that the vast majority of our attendants and other staff were by training and temperament initially ill-disposed toward the new practices. Nor were the intellectual and educational equipment of the majority equal to the new tasks, though a few were emotionally disposed to accept the more humane approach toward patients. But they, too, were at first skeptical of its value or effectiveness.

We were constrained by the basic plan—or assumption—to carry on in the existing setting and with the staff as we found them. The hospital director's intent was to test whether a program such as we contemplated could be assimilated in a typical state hospital (in the United States) and with the staff commonly available. Despite our requests during the tenure of the project, he eschewed shifting or substituting staff. To mitigate or to idealize the situation, he insisted, would not prove anything. What he wished was to ascertain whether a humane and creative climate could be integrated in ordinary, not in ideal conditions which, though desirable, were illusory from the practical standpoint. He said that these were the reasons for his selection of the most disturbed two locked women's wards for the experiment.

At the initiation of our ward program in the middle of October 1964, the staff consisted of eight attendants on one of the wards and 10 on the other,[1] one "charge nurse," one occupational therapist, and one recreational therapist on each of the wards.[2] There was one social worker who carried the responsibility for and was available to the patients on all of the eight wards in the "service" (building holding about 520 patients) and, therefore, could not fully meet the demands on her from patients or staff. (Her office was located on the ground floor of the building, whereas our wards occupied the top, fourth, floor.) The two psychiatric interns had ended their terms, while the resident in charge was drafted into the armed forces. We were thus left with no permanent psychiatric services and had to rely in emergencies on the supervising psychiatrist of the "service." Contrary to our expectations, we operated for several months without the benefit of continuous or readily available psychiatric guidance. However, we did not find this a particular handicap, since our program was geared to creating a wholesome ward climate and to activation of patients through a *milieu* approach and ward-community participation.

One of the nurses had served a long term on her ward and was familiar with the operational patterns of each of her patients. This resource, coupled with our own observations and

[1] One of these attendants retired soon after and another passed a promotion examination and was transferred.
[2] The nurse on Ward A was removed during the early stages of the program and was in charge of a series of attendants.

78

conclusions seemed, after several weeks, to be adequate guides for our approach to individuals and to the group as a whole. The attendants, nearly all of whom had served on the same wards for some years, also had a substantial knowledge of the backgrounds, behavioral problems, and "quirks" of each of the patients, though the manner of dealing with them was entirely antiquated and unsuitable. The first two O.T. staff members, as well, displayed good understanding and responsiveness to the patients, in addition to a high degree of involvement in the dedication and loyalty to our program's aims.[3]

As is the case in all mental hospitals in the United States, we found our attendants to be the "men low on the (professional) totem pole," who were recruited, as is the case everywhere else, from the unskilled, marginally educated population. All our attendants were basically and primarily homemakers by background and mental orientation, whose responsibilities for homes, children, and husbands exposed them to all the anxieties inherent in these roles. We later learned that a surprising number of these women had serious personality and family problems.

They had been trained for their jobs in the hospital (as required by state regulations), in a program which was centered around the physical care and safety of patients with a brief and very superficial course in occupational therapy which they never utilized in their practice before our program was initiated. Their emphasis, preoccupations, and functions were geared to custodial care and completely devoid of helping patients toward better mental health. In fact, when this idea was presented to them, they reacted with surprise, disbelief and a degree of consternation. If the truth be told, with the exception of the hospital director, these attitudes permeated the staff in the higher professional and nonprofessional echelons as well.

The largest number of attendants by far bore expressions of impassivity, if not boredom, as they carried our their menial

[3] All the staff members had attended the 14 orientation seminar sessions conducted by us before the initiation of the ward program in October, 1964.

duties with detachment and automaticity. Observing them on our initial visits to the wards as they scurried about their "household" and custodial duties, we were impressed by their uninvolvement with patients. They exuded an air of messenger boys making deliveries of packages, the contents of which was not their concern.

Several were stony-faced, and some obviously also stony-hearted, though open cruelty was eschewed. Their responses were those of indifference to patients, manifesting no warmth or friendliness, though conscientious and meticulous in discharging duties as custodians. One woman in this category who hardly ever spoke, would sparingly greet one and only perfunctorily respond to a greeting by others. However, there were also a few attendants with strong maternal feelings who, though lacking the capacity or knowledge to identify deeply with patients' plights and inner suffering, were soft-spoken and gentle. Two of the latter were oversolicitous and patronizing, encouraging dependence and preventing the growth of ego strength, integration, and the patients' movement toward maturity and reality testing. One of these attendants had inordinate perceptiveness of psychic processes and a rare capacity to formulate them during our discussions. She contributed greatly to our seminars, but her intense emotionality and overinvolvement with patients rendered her much less effective than she could have been. As a result of our project, she had become aware of the change in herself and verbalized it openly at one of the sessions when she said, "I know I used to baby my patients, but now I know that it was wrong." The improvement reached beyond behavior, however. As our seminars and demonstrations progressed, her tearful emotionalism and former impetuosity disappeared and she improved both in appearance as well as in her relationship with staff. Even her exaggerated racial suspiciousness and sensitivity, which had been the cause of much tension among the staff, seemed no longer in evidence.

The entire staff would talk unreservedly, both critically and praisingly, about patients in their presence, as though they were noncomprehending little children. This kind of patronizing and condescension had, in our opinion, a markedly destructive effect on patients, for it perpetuated and encouraged immaturity and dependence. Since raising the level of self-regard in patients by dealing with them in an egalitarian manner commensurate with their age was the essential aim of our project, this subject, sensitive as it was, served as the substance of many of our seminar sessions.

The traditional and deeply entrenched attitude on the part of the staff toward patients was what is commonly called "baby-nursing," which we found most difficult to eradicate. Whereas, our aim was to encourage patients' self-dependence and responsible participation in their own lives and that of the ward, the attendants constantly reverted to doing all the chores themselves, leaving their charges to sit or mill about aimlessly. They dashed about with strained expressions on their faces, anxious to complete the cleaning, washing of floors, sorting of clothes for the laundry, showering, grooming, calming of patients, in addition to the numerous other chores incidental to a congregate life of a large group of helpless, disturbed women.

Even after months of repeated reiteration at the seminars that preceded the inauguration of the ward program, and after, of the need for change, and later actual demonstration by us, all attendants without exception would be found swinging mops, washing floors, and (when the kitchen had been installed) preparing coffee, washing dishes, cleaning the stove and cupboards —only to blush, smile guiltily, and look meekly when surprised at these occupations. It was understandably easier to do a job oneself than to encourage patients such as ours were to participate. One's housewifely standards are better met by oneself than by accepting patients' performances.

We reiterated time and again the refrain that what helps patients toward mental health and social adjustment is not the *quality* of performance—which would automatically improve in time anyway—but rather the awakening of patients' interest in their environment and stimulating in them the outward flow of energies (i.e., centrifugal flow of libido) to counteract their encapsulation and withdrawal from reality (or centripetal libido flow). Furthermore, we have repeatedly observed and called attention to how participation of patients, even in the simplest activities and responsibilities, had significant potentials in normalizing their personalities. As we shall see elsewhere in this volume, we have designed procedures that generated *spontaneous* participation and responsibilities, willingly chosen by patients, not ordered, delegated, or staff-planned. This required careful group planning involving patients, rather than traditional methods of scheduling and assigning.

The first part-time psychiatrist, whose tenure was short-lived, could not implement these plans at the beginning because of the distraught state of the patients at that stage. It was highly improbable that any kind of group discussion could have born fruit. It was clear that we first had to bring to the patients some inner tranquility (in which our project proved eminently successful) before such meetings could be attempted.

Ward meetings were introduced almost a year later by another female psychiatrist who replaced the first (after months without benefit of psychiatry altogether) on a once-a-week basis. However, her didactic emphasis during the discussions was on "attitudes" rather than the realities of the daily affairs on the ward that should have constituted the content with patients such as ours initially were. Because of other responsibilities, this psychiatrist came to the wards only infrequently and would spend ten to fifteen minutes on each. She was, therefore, unacquainted with the needs of the patients, the matters that occupied their minds, or the needs of the staff.

As already indicated, the attendants kept reverting to their custodial role, in which they apparently felt more comfortable through habit and training. A striking illustration of this regressive propensity was constant interference by attendants in the management of the mid-morning coffee break when it had been introduced after many months of delay (due to labor shortage and especially serious constructional difficulties). The intent of having a coffee break, we repeated numerous times, was not to feed the patients (though this alone had favorable psychologic meaning and was of great value), but rather to give them an opportunity for self-reliance and responsibility in a normal homelike situation and as an exercise in reality testing.

A striking example is the following incident of the ineptitude of the most sympathetic and cooperative attendants, as we found them, in applying knowledge acquired at the seminars. We had discussed on a number of occasions employing the eating situation in fostering self-reliance in patients, especially in the "problem eaters" who were fed separately on the wards (instead of in the dining hall) ahead of the others. Many of these patients were hand-fed by other patients, but mostly by staff. [We later succeeded in including *all* the patients—the most regressed, the mental defectives, and the idiots—at meals in the dining hall.]

Before we had accomplished this, I was once walking with one of the friendlier attendants through Ward A where the "problem eaters" were still fed separately. At the time, one patient was standing over another feeding her. Recalling our discussions and obviously abashed by my presence, the attendant ran over and impetuously grabbed the standing patient's arm, screaming, "Don't do that! She can feed herself! You mustn't do it!" and pulled the spoon from her hand, handing it to the abashed and frightened patient, who haltingly attempted to spoon up a plum from the plate without success. The first patient looked startled and puzzled, and shaking her head in complete nonunderstanding quietly walked away. As we left, I said calmly, "What you meant to do was right, but. . ." "I did it too abruptly, didn't I?" interrupted the attendant. "Exactly. What you should have done was to quietly go over to the feeding patient and explain to her that the other could really feed herself." The attendant then told me that the patient who was fed was a catatonic and in a constant state of semicoma. This was obvious from the way she handled the food: she had attempted to spoon up the plum, but did not succeed. (She was one of three patients who required assistance with food, the other two being physically incapable of handling the table utensils.)

It was evident that in all their dealings with the patients, the women attendants reenacted their own family patterns: they treated the patients as they had been treated by their mothers and as they had treated their own children. Their seeming callousness reflected their indigenous family and neighborhood cultures that had failed to enable them to sublimate and refine their native primitivism.

In order to prevent dislocation in the accustomed conduct of the hospital and the various services, it was our strict policy not to interfere with the work and practices of the various specialists and department heads. We therefore took no measures to prevent punishments of patients of which we did not approve. [Punishments automatically withered away later as they became unnecessary.] In line with this policy, we took no action when we found unsuitable to our project the second batch of O. T. personnel assigned to us, beyond calling this fact to the attention of the department head. This attitude on our part may have been a grave error for it later led to much unpleasantness and disadvantage (though we found it imperative to eliminate on-the-ward recreation of a type too stimulating for our patients). We also desisted from directly interfering with the role played by psychiatrists on the wards and in our program. Instead, we later arranged a four-hour conference to clarify the subject.

Patients had been consistently blamed for outbursts of aggression but it never occurred to anyone on the staff that their own conduct may have provoked such behavior. It is not unusual for parents to blame children for their troublesome conduct, and see themselves as entirely blameless. These attitudes prevailed among our staff on *all levels*. Perhaps one dramatic event may illustrate this.

In the early period of our project, an otherwise withdrawn and quiet patient with a clean, dignified appearance, who was not known to create any difficulties, was somehow embroiled in a quarrel with a fellow-patient, and was placed in a camisole. This occurred on a Saturday when I was not scheduled to come to the ward, but did so to "spot check" the staff's activities when they did not expect to be observed. I found the patient quietly sitting on a chair. She shortly shifted to an adjoining chair, leaving a quantity of fecal matter which seemed to ooze through

84

the thin nightgown in which she was clad. None of the attendants had observed this and I called it to the attention of one of them. Obviously, because I was present, she did not remonstrate with, or attempt to punish the patient, but rather, placing a hand on her asked her to come along. Another attendant forthwith rushed over to "help," which seemed to be the accepted practice: two attendants against one patient. When the patient rose, more fecal matter was revealed on the second chair. The two attendants marched off the offender in military fashion between them to the showering room.

Thus what had passed for an act of "incontinence" was actually an act of retaliation and anger, though not displayed in a usual temper tantrum, and in accordance with our practice, we described the occurrence at our next seminar session. Refraining from naming the persons involved, we submitted it to free discussion by the attendants. (The auditors who sat apart in an arenalike arrangement, had been asked to refrain from participating in all discussions since they were apt to prevent the less trained attendants to think through, on their own level, problems they faced in their daily work.) None of the attendants recognized the connection between the patient's deed and her punishment. We were able on numerous occasions to relate patients' disturbances, outbursts, and violence, as well as withdrawal, to insensitive slighting by, and callousness at the hands of, a staff member, a relative, or a fellow patient.

Such causal relationships were not always evident or easy to establish insofar as the destructive behavior of staff or relatives often escaped observation. Patients typically delay reactions to a real or imagined slight, but explode later, thus obscuring the cause of their disturbances. The tendency was always to consider them as stemming from the "evil" nature of the patient, not from his illness, the conditions of his life on the ward, or as the result of an act by another person. These discussions were aimed at fixing in the minds of the staff *the law of cause and effect*, to implant the habit of seeking out causes for every occurrence in the hope of preventing impulsive retaliatory or resentful responses from them.

We pressed on our seminar participants the theme of cause

and effect, not only in relation to behavioral manifestations, but also their sources in the peculiar psyches of individual patients. Therefore, one two-hour session of the four each month was devoted to intensive studies in depth of the more troublesome patients by a case presentation. Our lone social worker summarized the anamnesis and the current family setting. The charge nurse or attendant described the conduct and adjustment of the patient on the ward, her relations with patients and staff, and all other related information. This material was amplified by the psychiatrist's findings, and descriptions from the O.T., recreation, and other personnel. The discussion was then thrown open to the attendants who always had numerous additional incidents to narrate about the patient and her relatives, while offering additional background and current details.

After considerable disclosures about the patients' adjustment, inquiry was made into why the patient behaves the way she does. What is she attempting to achieve by her deviant acts? It was obvious that this step toward understanding rather than blaming and fault-finding was alien to the experience of *all* the participants and the professional auditors. However, once a question was raised, a number of the more thoughtful in the group usually attempted to explain the patient's behavior and motives in fairly psychodynamic terms.

The following instance will serve to illustrate the educational process we were attempting to achieve by these means:

On one of the early preprogram visits to the wards with a senior psychiatrist at the time of the midday meal, we heard a sudden ear-splitting scream coming from the porch. This disturbance emanated from a rather attractive, clean-looking and well-dressed young girl who jumped up with the speed of a rabbit from the three chairs, strung up couch-fashion, on which she had been outstretched while apparently dozing. She ran back and forth screeching at the top of her lungs, cursing someone. Efforts at pacifying her by an attendant failed. She paid no attention to her, keeping up the shouting and curses. The psychiatrist, as well, attempted to soothe her, but she paid no attention to him either. In his effort to communicate with her more effectively, he put his hand on her shoulder. The girl sprang away as though she were wounded, screaming, "Get away from me! Don't touch me! I know what happens when a man touches you!" As she said this, she clasped the thumbs and first fingers of her hands, forming an elipse, and in what appeared to be an unconscious gesture, placed the symbol on her crotch.

This situation was brought to the seminar for discussion. We inquired as to why the patient behaved so violently when she arose from her improvised couch. Insofar as there was no discernible reason, the conclusion was drawn that it was a spontaneous act of "defective brain." However, while on the ward, I observed that an attendant had gone up to the patient who had lain with eyes closed and shook her rather violently and told her to go to dinner. This act seemed to have escaped the notice of the attendants and the psychiatrist. Not to embarrass the offending attendant, I withheld comment on the event at the time of the occurrence, but when it was discussed at the seminar, we reported it, again withholding the identity of the attendant, which as indicated was always our practice.

In the light of this new information, the discussion assumed a different turn. The suddenness and violence with which the attendant shook the patient could not but arouse rage in anyone, let alone in persons as unstable as was this patient. [In fact, we urged that when a patient chose to skip a meal, the attendants should not urge her to eat, for there are always a few on each ward who refrained from partaking in a meal occasionally, as is also the case in ordinary life.]

The gesture and statement to the psychiatrist when he soothingly touched her assumed meaning when the social worker informed the group that this patient's sister was shot to death by her husband. This brought on the patient's breakdown and hospitalization. The severity of her reaction to being awakened became even more understandable when it was disclosed that she had an epileptoid personality. The group became so interested in the case that it was decided to continue the study in depth at the next seminar session.

In line with the accusative stance of the ward staff, any

transgressions by a patient or patients were maximized to the extreme. If one or two patients transgressed, it was reported as "the patients" (just as the average mother speaks of her troubles with "my children," when only one or two of the offspring are involved). For example, when we had thrown the dormitory doors open which had been kept firmly locked during the day hours, the attendants reported at the seminars that "the patients" spent their time lying on their beds. When questioned how many did so, they could not give a specific number. We, therefore, made a point of counting the number of such patients during every visit to the wards. In the mornings this number never exceeded three or four out of the sixty-five. Seven or eight patients took a nap after lunch. The attendants' annoyance with this confirmed their basic, though probably unconscious, hostile attitudes toward their charges. We pointed out in this connection that at least a similar percentage of housewives nap during the day in the general community.

A similar situation devolved around the dining hall. As part of normalizing the life of the patients and nurturing their self-respect, we eliminated the militarylike line formation on their way from the wards to the dining hall. In the past, when the doors to the wards were kept locked, patients of each ward would gather in a mass 15 to 20 minutes before the doors would be unlocked, standing about like cattle, in front of the glass paneled doors in the two oppositional wards, staring at each other across the foyer. When the doors were unlocked by an attendant at the appointed time, first one, then the other ward group, the latter being made to wait until the first was in the dining room, would follow in single file formation.

When later the ward doors were kept unlocked, the patients persisted in their accustomed gathering at the doors, but now they were allowed to proceed individually to the dining room at random. As a matter of habit as well as of necessity, since the food was taken up on trays by each patient cafeteria style, the patients formed a single file, not by wards, but indiscriminately as members of the same community.

At one of the seminars, attendants complained that the

88

THE STAFF

"patients" broke the line and pushed themselves ahead of others. When this complaint was repeated on several occasions, we asked for specific names of patients who committed these infractions. Three were named (out of 130). We later made it a point to observe the "line" on a number of occasions. The chief miscreant was a husky young girl, a deaf-mute mental defective, who would sail through toward the head of the line like a steam roller as she pushed her way up. Another one took her place out of turn quietly, apparently unaware of the others' presence, and a third would do so spitefully and trying to provoke a fight. The interesting feature of this phenomenon was that never did patients register resentment at these intruders or resist the intrusions. The attendants, however, did.

Our suggestion for dealing with the situation, although it seemed to us like a minor matter that could have been easily overlooked, was to discuss it at the ward meetings, that were now held, not in terms of the offenders, but as a matter of a group routine. This would bring to patients' awareness the importance of waiting for one's turn in a congregate situation. Another approach suggested was to hold a few sessions with the three offending patients to make them aware of the unsuitability of their behavior.

Apparently the problem was not broached at the ward meetings and one of the officials of the hospital who once happened to observe this mild infraction and was annoyed by it, *issued an order* that on alternate weeks the patients of one ward only should be allowed to go to the dining room at a given time. This would have required restraining the patients of the other ward three times a day for seven days, thus generating anxiety and anger. When this was communicated to me by telephone by one of the staff, I suggested that if such an unsuitable regimen had to be instituted, turns should be taken daily (and not weekly) thereby reducing tension among the waiting patients. This was the only time I countered or modified an *ukase* of a hospital official, upon whom its success in a great measure depended, so as not to jeopardize the project.

The propensity to issue orders from above with the expec-

89

tation of submissive conformity by subordinates raised its ugly head on many occasions during the life of our project. Our activities on the wards with various materials and the emphasis on cooperative working with patients and on relationships could be expected to tarnish the antiseptic appearance characteristic of hospitals. As far as we were concerned, *tolerable* cleanliness consistent with health requirements was all that would have been required. The excessive lustration on which public institutions insist was, in our view, absurd. The residents of mental hospitals have not been accustomed to such cleanliness in their homes and neighborhoods and will not find it upon their return.[4]

However, instead of discussing it with the attendants as a group and suggesting that the matter be taken up with the patients at a ward meeting[5] and form committees to carry out the project, the same official whom we quoted above *issued a peremptory order* to the ward charges that the wards be "cleaned up." The attendants forthwith proceeded to do so, which created a great deal of tension among the patients that lasted several days. It was particularly surprising to me in view of the fact that this official had attended regularly our seminars and seemed to admiringly concur, verbally at least, in our emphasis on involving staff and patients in planning and carrying out the routines of the ward communities.

The "command attitude" extant in mental hospitals was demonstrated in a somewhat more serious episode. The act of unlocking the doors of the wards as a symbol of freedom and confidence in the patients was an event of singular significance to them and to the more empathetic members of our ward staff. It was a source of evident gratification to Dr. Beckenstein, for it confirmed his unwavering faith in the patients. To us, it represented hope for further improvements in the future. After six months of this event, one morning I found the door on ward A

[4] We have faced this problem in another institution and dealt with it on a realistic basis. See Slavson, S.R. (1954), *Re-Educating the Delinquent.* New York: Harper and Brothers, 1954, and Collier (paperback) Books, 1962.

[5] Ward meetings had by now been introduced.

(our most disturbed ward) locked. Upon inquiry, I was informed that the supervising psychiatrist "ordered" it locked because one of the patients had absconded, and when she was brought back, he ordered the door locked. I withheld my indignation, but when, on my next visit, I found the door still locked, I decided to act. But not wishing to enter into conflict with an "official," I enlisted the intercession of the hospital director who affected the unbolting of the door. It was, and still is, difficult for me to understand how one could deprive sixty-four humans of their freedom and self-respect because of a transgression of one, unless such a step was arrived at democratically and approved by common consent of the patients.

A few of the attendants did demur at the incursions upon their newly found status. They chafed under these peremptory orders, but felt helpless and too frightened for their professional advancement not to obey or to openly disagree. Most, however, were too indifferent to care one way or another. Having been consistently exposed for long periods to the militarylike character of a hospital regime with its rigid staff caste system, submission and indifference became ingrained and could not be easily given up. Added to this conditioning, these attitudes were perpetuated by promotion insecurity, though at the moment, perhaps without justification. When we achieved a degree of mutual trust and an attendant would confide her demurral to us for having to carry out instructions that did not conform to the new spirit in the ward life, we would ask, "Why did you do it then?" She would respond with a mien of helplessness and a shrug. "What could I do? I was told to do it." And when pursued by the inquiry, "Why didn't you say something?" we were met by an expression of trepidation and the meek rejoinder, "Oh, you can't do that!"

As part of the list of procedures for management of patients we had suggested at the seminar sessions the immediate unforced removal of one who had become disturbed and was thus disturbing the others. We suggested that patients in that state be accompanied by an attendant to the quiet room at the far end of the ward which had been set up for this purpose and for small ward staff conferences (the "Conference Room"). This consisted of quietly asking the patient to withdraw so that she and the staff member could talk over her problem. By actual demonstration, we have shown that patients, with no exception, never refused to accompany the staff member when asked gently, with the suggestion, "Come, let's talk about it." Even patients in extreme agitation responded to this special attention and never refused to withdraw from the crowd.

We explained to the staff that patients in such a state actually feel uncomfortable and often guilty, and would welcome relief from the tensions were it offered them. Whenever this subject was discussed, and this occurred in many sessions, we helped the attendants to recognize that most often agitation and screaming flowed from the patient's fears which typically arise from memories as well as fantasies and distortions of past events that come to their minds as they sit idly and ruminate. Their screams are calls for help and protection. Hence, what was needed was reassurance. After we had provided patients with evocative occupations, social interests, and satisfying human relations, ruminations were prevented and phantasmagoric fantasies of danger seldom arose, much to the surprise of the staff.[6]

The effectiveness of withdrawing disturbed patients from the ward for a calming down period is further demonstrated by the following incident: I observed from a distance one of the more disturbed and wild-eyed patients, loud-mouthed and quarrelsome approaching the (male) psychiatrist and saying something complainingly to him. He answered her calmly, but she at once began to shout demands which I did not quite understand. As he prepared to answer her, her face reflected intense rage. She seemed prepared for a fight. I walked over toward them and said, "How about going to the conference room to talk it over?" They both walked along with me, and as I found the door bolt-

[6] After an absence of five years, during a visit to Ward A, one of the old attendants asked me with a broad smile of satisfaction (referring to the tranquil atmosphere of the ward and peaceful countenance of the patients), "Did you think this was going to be like this, Mr. Slavson, when you started the project?" "Yes," I replied. Still continuing in her happy, smiling mood, she said, "I didn't."

ed (which it should not have been) I unlocked it and the three of us entered. As we stepped in, the patient almost involuntarily said, "That's better." I at once walked out. Ten minutes later the two emerged, with the patient smiling broadly. This simple strategy avoided a possible serious disturbance to all the other patients, for this particular patient was very loud, aggressively persistent and unamenable to reason. The discouraging aspect of this incident was that even the psychiatrist had not thought of employing the procedure which we had repeatedly emphasized.

Completely ignoring or delaying response to patients' screams were common practice by the staff. Although screams and agitation of individuals were ignored, this was not true with fights that frequently flared up. These were expeditiously squelched, always by several of the attendants who would descend upon the combatants and forcefully subdue them. Three or four attendants would take hold of arms and bodies and lead their possessors off in camisoles, not infrequently to be locked in. Such expeditiousness was not forthcoming where individuals were concerned. Their agitation was largely ignored. Patients were left to their screaming until it would subside by itself or they would get into a fight. They would then receive attention.

At the seminars we pointed out time and again the therapeutic relationship and preventive values of turning immediate attention to a screaming patient. We emphasized that though patients (and staff) seemingly remained unaffected, in actuality screams by anyone induced covert anxiety in others which set off screaming as well as abreacting fights by the universal susceptibility to emotional contagion. The prevalence of this dynamic in all animals was illustrated with examples. Nonetheless, on many occasions when visiting wards one could find a screaming patient not receiving the attention from an attendant she required.

Detachment and indifference displayed to patients' screaming was evident also in other areas. We frequently found wards and other areas in semidarkness or suffocating heat, with no one appearing to be aware of these and similar conditions. Time after time on the wards we would call attention to these irritations, which were at once remedied by an attendant who would explain with a resigned air that a patient had turned off the lights, or that the hospital supplied too much heat (which was the case), but it did not occur to anyone to switch on the lights or turn off some of the radiators (or open windows where the radiators had no valves).

Lack of initiative was observable also with regard to patients' apparel and general appearance, in the incongruity and shabbiness of their dresses and footwear. This situation was ultimately corrected as the activities program on the wards progressed and the patients' self-images improved. But here, as well, distressing neglect gradually returned from time to time which went unnoticed by the staff until it was called to their attention.

Rising disturbances in patients also went unobserved and when noticed, no steps were taken to prevent outbursts of screaming, aggression, and violence. Such outbursts had most often been presaged in facial expressions and erratic conduct. In some instances these symptoms appeared days in advance of an outbreak. When these were called to the staff's attention, some of them revealed their awareness, but no steps were taken to avert the impending storm. This oversight can be laid at the feet of the psychiatrists since the awareness and the skills involved here were not altogether within the province of nonmedical personnel, though in most instances empathetic attention by a nurse or attendant would have sufficed. The need to *interrupt* rising agitation in patients was pointed out to the psychiatrists at our special session with them, as well as at our meetings with the attendants. I am not aware that this principle was put into operation by any of them throughout the life of our project. The following episode is an illustration of the efficacy of what can be termed the *interruption technique*.

One of our most disturbed and least accessible patients began a verbal attack on the O.T. worker for having been what she construed as slighted. Her rage was visibly rising as was her voice. The staff member did not respond, knowing the irascibili-

94

ty of this patient and the futility of attempting to reason with her. I happened to be nearby and asked the patient to come with me and talk the matter over. We went into the "conference room" and sat down at opposite sides of the table. I inquired as to her complaint.

At first she started to formulate some minor grudge, but in her characteristic manner soon drifted off into a word salad and thought confabulation. She presented herself as being at once eight or 10 of the leading female movie stars and even one male star. She then became Holy Mary who had given birth to Christ, switching to being Einstein, Edison, and a number of other prominent scientists. (This patient was widely read and a well-informed bright college student, later a school teacher, and in her confabulations drew on her rich store of information.)

I made one or two attempts at questioning the possibility of being such a multiple personality, but she ignored my questions, breathlessly continuing to rattle names, drowning out my voice by raising hers. After about 20 minutes of this delusional monologue, I calmly looked at my watch and said, "We have five more minutes? That's the trouble. You're always busy. I never have a chance to talk to you." Then she went on with her gibberish. As she talked, her face grew visibly calmer and a sly smile, as though she had become aware of the irrationality of her recital, appeared on her face. When the five minutes were up, I rose and she accompanied me from the room without protest, still talking, but now completely composed. We walked across the length of the activity room where the O.T. center was, and she cheerfully joined the patients silently working at the table.

As our ward program progressed, the need became apparent that in addition to our general seminar sessions, discussions with smaller groups of the specialized staff would be necessary. If the holistic approach was to be effective, each of the specialists would have to clearly understand their part in the total process and know how to integrate their specialties with all the others. Such sessions have, therefore, been arranged with the O.T. staffs, with the single music therapist and with the psychiatrists.

Only one session of four-hour duration was held with the latter, in which participated the hospital director, the consulting psychiatrist, the supervising psychiatrist, the part-time ward psychiatrist, the chief nurse and administrator and the present writer. After a review of the traditional functions of a ward psychiatrist that included supervision, training and support to staff and patients, the following functions of a specific nature had been formulated as a result of the conference:

a) *Preventive Therapy.* When a patient begins to show outward signs of disturbance either facially or behaviorally, the psychiatrist should turn his attention to her and train other ward staff to recognize the symptoms and methods for dealing with them, or at once report to the psychiatrist, who must respond to the call expeditiously. This process we termed *interruption technique,* i.e., interrupting the disturbance before it culminates into an outburst.

b) *Spot Therapy.* Patients who suddenly begin to act out their disturbances by withdrawal or physical aggression or conflict with others, display an extensive outburst of anger or rage, or show any other sign of psychological stress should be accompanied to the "conference room" and the psychiatrist called, or, if they agree to do so, should be taken to the doctor's office for a therapeutic interview. (Since no psychiatrist was available to us for much of the duration of the project, this function was carried out by attendants, and very successfully at that.)

c) *Sensitizing Attendants and Other Staff.* Work on an educational level with ward and administrative staffs to *sensitize* them to the problems, nature and needs of patients as a group and especially as individuals, would lead to a more humane and, hopefully, more sympathetic approach. This can be done in small group discussions and even more effectively with individual staff members as problems arise.

d) *Classification of Patients.* The psychiatrist should classify patients on the wards as to the nature and intensity of the illness, formulating diagnoses and a tentative prognosis for each,

96

indicate the intensity and nature of the medical and psychological treatment and convey this information to the ward staff in regularly scheduled seminar sessions.

e) *Participation in Determination of Patient Disposition.* Included here are the prescribing activities, the nature of the patient's participation in them, transference to other wards, allowing home visits, paroling and discharging. Decisions in these matters, as in others, should be arrived at in discussion with all the ward and ancillary staff at the regular seminar or supervisory group sessions. This would offer inestimable staff training opportunities.

f) *Responsibility for Total Case Care.* It is useless to make plans for patients unless they are carried out (which is unfortunately too often the case) and it should be the responsibility of the ward psychiatrist to follow up and see to it that they are implemented. [Through our experience in the project, we came to the decision that another full-time person specially trained as a "psychiatric group worker" or "social therapist" should be added to carry this responsibility. Of this later on.]

g) *Therapeutic Group Discussions.* Patients who become ready to participate in therapeutically oriented or other types of group discussions should be grouped by the psychiatrist, and either he or a qualified member of the staff (psychologist, social therapist or psychiatric caseworker) should conduct such discussions under his supervision.

h) *Individual Therapy.* A ward psychiatrist should carry as many specially selected patients as possible in continuous or group treatment and supervise members of his therapeutic staff to whom he would assign such patients.

i) *Staff Development.* Through individual contacts and a continuous series of discussions, the psychiatrist is to help develop the insights and professional excellence of *all* the personnel on the wards and encourage them to become self-motivated, independent individuals, capable of good judgment and of functioning adequately in helping patients toward health.

j) *Medication.* This responsibility is basic and essential to the treatment of psychotic patients and should be solely the responsibility of the psychiatrist.

Unfortunately we have not been able to put into operation most of the provisions of this plan during the life of our project, largely because of basic resistances to such innovations and the shortage and mobility of the psychiatric staff. Our psychiatrists worked on "a visiting basis" to the wards. They spent at most three quarters of an hour to an hour on each, at which time they would briefly speak to some patients who demanded their attention and ward off most of the others who surrounded them in eager droves. Instead they spent the remaining time in the ward office behind locked doors with the nurse or the attendant in charge on matters of management of particularly difficult patients and on medication. Sometimes a patient, through insistence would find her way to the doctor's office which was three floors below and was occupied by two psychiatrists at contiguous desks.[7] For many months on end we had to do without an assigned psychiatrist and were forced to rely on one called in in special emergencies as well as on the supervising psychiatrist. These latter also served short periods and as a result had little knowledge of the specific needs of individual patients.

The staff we have discussed so far was that which dealt largely with the living process on the wards to which we referred as "the Relationship Staff Group," as differentiated from specific activities. Another luncheon group consisted of the persons who either participated or were in charge of staff in the activity program. This group was known as "the Activity Staff Group." The largely artificial separation was employed in the early stages of the project, since the ancillary specialists had *specific* functions and needed *specific* help until the project got fully going. When this point was reached, the two groups met as one, thereby better serving the integration of the life and activities on the wards.

Several sessions were held at the early stages of the pro-

---

[7] Our repeated insistence that an office for the psychiatrist be provided on the fourth floor of W. Building was for some reason not acted upon. It did entail a major construction job, such as breaking through a thick wall to provide a door.

gram in conjunction with the Activity Staff Group with a view to helping them alter their practices from job-centeredness to patient-centeredness. We observed that particularly the occupational therapists were unduly concerned with the excellence of productions rather than their therapeutic meaning to the patients. This was even more true of the recreation workers. The first two O.T. workers very quickly understood and applied their newly acquired insights very effectively. This was not the case with the second set of workers who replaced them. One of them could not shed her abrasive and authoritarian manner, while the other was withdrawn and lacked leadership qualities.

At one of the sessions, at which were present the O.T. and the R.T. workers and their superiors, the music therapist, the nurse who served as the Remotivation director in the hospital, the chief nurse and administrator, and the ward psychiatrist, the inevitable struggle arose between the re-educationally oriented and the job-centered staff members. The phrase "I can show them" and "I can help them" (referring to the patients), constantly reappeared. The Remotivation director, on the other hand, promoted her own idea of staff-led group discussions. At one point she said, "Perhaps if the attendants are well enough versed in what we are doing—just what the *structure of the program* is—(and) if the patients are broken up into groups [which was not our intent], the attendants can in group discussions, as in remotivation, carry on as to what we hope to be doing."

When asked what the content of the discussions would be, she replied rather vaguely, "Well, that would depend on how you are actually going *to structure the program.*" Leader assertiveness and staff structuring were the dominant notes of the discussions. In the seminar approving the appearance of patients, one of the supervisors, for example, contributed the following: "Before you even get to those classes, perhaps the program that someone mentioned this morning is group discussion (seminar) at all levels. In other parts of the hospital we have attendants *who are active* in the groups. *They have* patients get together and talk about how they should look on the ward and

99

how they should look when they go out on the grounds, or how they should appear if they are going off the grounds. . . ."

The other supervisor described a project conducted by a volunteer who would station herself on the sunporch and *conduct a class* in self-beautification showing the patients who joined her how to apply make-up and fix their hair. No attention was given by either of the speakers to the ineffectiveness of these approaches to our patients in view of their bedraggled and unkempt appearance that resulted from these efforts.

We summarized the discussion by saying: "To balance our discussion, we should repeat what we said before. Our expectation, if we are right in our assumption, is that a lasting desire to look neat and be clean will come from a rise in patients' self-concepts, from an improved feeling about themselves and a better awareness of the world around them. They now feel worthless—garbage—and are living that feeling out. We see people in the community in evil-smelling clothes, piled one on the other. I recall a man who walked into a subway car and the odor he emanated was so offensive that most of the people moved to the adjoining cars. He had an inner need to feel low, like the vagrants who lie in the gutters because of their need to be as low as possible, to be filth.

"When our patients overcome these feelings of degradation through what we are attempting to do with and for them, when we build up their self-respect through our respect for them, their needs will change from being useless, filthy and worthless to self-respect and personal worth. Through our working together—from the approach from the emotional side and your approach from the activity side—we can rescue enough patients to make it worth the effort. But we must not forget that activities alone, without building up the patient's emotions is not going to be of much help. This may keep them going under our constant supervision, but they will not internalize feelings and attitudes for a better life. We found this to be true in the case of even healthy adolescent girls in underprivileged communities with experts in makeup. The girls were interested and carried out instructions for a few days, but then lapsed into their habitual manner and appearance which were part of their family and neighborhood cultures, and their feelings about themselves.''

5. *The Program*

Our original thought was to make available to the patients on the wards materials and tools for creative activities as we did to prepubertal children in activity group therapy, under the stimulation and guidance of suitable staff from the various departments in the hospital. However, after several visits to the wards it became clear that these "disturbed" patients were too disoriented and would not respond to free-choice creative activities; it was also apparent that such activities would have to be peripheral. Rather, what the patients required at the outset was a quieting environment and activation that would come from *actual needs* of life on the wards. We, therefore, designed a physical setting in which the life process itself demanded that the patients assume responsibilities and participate in the ward group life. To achieve this, activities and occupations were designed to flow from *realistic needs* rather than artificially created situations or "made work." The ward had to become a tangible *life setting* from which activity flowed as it does in an ordinary home and in the general community.

Since we were dealing with female adult patients, the setting had to be suitable for them. Accordingly we recommended at the next planning meeting with the hospital director and the psychiatric consultant that we supply two sewing machines for each of the wards. At first, attendants would actually be working at the machines in the hope that this would entice patients into activity. Materials would have to be provided for sewing aprons and dresses, knitting pot-holders, hats, sweaters, etc. The attendants, or perhaps outside volunteers,[1] could also be employed in stimulating patients to use washing machines, ironing boards, a modern electrical kitchen, table games, and "creative occupations" for which there were provided art materials such as crayons, water colors, drawing paper and brushes, materials for paper cutting, pasting, or folding; supplies for knitting, crocheting, claywork, tiling, etc.

Music was to be a *must* and would constitute a major ingredient in the life of the patients. We hoped to supply it by stereophonic equipment and suitable records as well as by group singing. As in the case of occupational therapy, specialists would be required in music as well who had been trained or were gifted in utilizing it in this setting. Dancing, rhythmic hand-clapping, and rhythm band were to be gradually introduced as part of the music program. For this, a moveable piano on wheels was made available to the two wards with a locking arrangement provided as a precaution against damage by patients.[2]

It was hoped that eventually, as they became more reality-oriented, patients would participate in dramatic endeavors. Real dialogue dealing with life conflicts was to be avoided for a long time, and only cautiously introduced much later to patients on an experimental basis.

Small group discussions for patients in good contact were to be considered for the future. The discussions could be held either on the wards or in off-ward locations. We thought that this might eventually lead to some form of therapeutic group

[1] The plan for employing volunteers was later abandoned for psychological reasons, as well as because of practical problems of recruitment.

[2] After observing the reaction of the women to these artificial and infantilizing procedures, we abandoned them and relied entirely on spontaneous responses to music, such as dancing in pairs and group singing under the stimulation of a gifted and dedicated recreation worker, Miss Kralides or "Miss Nicki," as she was affectionately called by the patients, who joined the project in its second year.

interaction and discussions, and that it should be allowed to grow out of the interests and capacities of selected, more intact patients.

Ward meetings were to be introduced as a degree of tranquility was achieved through activation, participation, and especially through interpersonal relations with staff and among patients; even then, their pattern and content should be pragmatically evolved.

We recommended that a small permanent library be established on the wards, starting with illustrated magazines of interest to women. The illustrations would help to bring outside reality into the monotonous life on the wards, activate the centrifugal flow of libido, and in some cases stimulate reading. Carefully selected, simple books were to be introduced experimentally as the project developed.[3] A 16 mm. movie projector and screen for suitable documentary shorts or other types of movies, especially those depicting the work of the world in industry and culture, would constitute the bulk of this repertoire. Both male and female residents from other wards would be invited as guests when, in the judgment of the staff, such interward visitations would be psychologically meaningful and appropriate. Although entertainment movies were shown in the hospital twice a week, very few patients from Wards A and B were allowed to attend, and only under the supervision of an attendant.

As the egos of our patients were strengthened, and better integrated, and as some degree of group cohesion was evidenced on the wards, parties, including dancing and refreshments (in the style of "social clubs"), would be of value. There was the possibility that individual patients as well as guests would offer entertainment, which later proved to be the case. Active participation of the audience would be encouraged. The parties would have to be carefully planned during the early period of the project and placed under the guidance of gifted and experienced

[3] During the first year of our project, the patients consistently tore up the books and magazines provided or threw them out onto the lawns.

staff members, who were skilled in preventing outbursts or dealing with them when they did occur. At first, patients in better contact and permanently or temporarily rational could be assisted by the attendants in the preparation and conducting of events, although eventually encouraged to progressively assume full responsibility for these affairs, as well as other activities on the wards. In time all of this actually came to pass.

When these plans were discussed with the attendants at the seminars, one of them suggested that a "beauty parlor" be provided on the wards, in addition to the well-staffed central one in another building, with professional beauticians, to which very few of our patients had ever been taken.[4] In this connection, the supervising psychiatrist stated in part, "One among our greatest problems on these wards has been the need to stimulate interest in personal appearance, and this would help."

It was obvious from the sallow appearance of many patients that walks and other outdoor activities were greatly needed. We, therefore, suggested a planned program of such activities to be carried out with regularity. Every ambulatory patient was to spend some time in the open air daily, in as active an occupation as possible or at least take a walk on, and possibly off, the campus grounds. The large hospital gym was to be employed in the interest of activation of withdrawn patients, who were in the majority, and the hospital recreation staff involved in this program. As patients became increasingly receptive, offground trips to centers in the community were planned to broaden their horizons and provide added contact with reality. Such a program was evolved for the first time in the summer of 1964 with the aid of the staff. The list included a neighborhood milk-bottling works, some factories, picnics in a nearby large park, a trip to the World's Fair held that year in New York, the Botanical Gardens, a printing plant, etc. However, perhaps because of Dr. Beckenstein's and my own absence from the country, none of these plans had been carried out, except for a select-

[4] Ours were the only female wards to which beauticians came to cut hair. An attendant was required to be present in the room with the beautician who worked in a small room off the day room. All other patients were free to go to the parlor on their own.

105

ed small number of patients who had been included with patients from other wards in a trip to the World's Fair.

The physical appearance, particularly the dresses, required
special consideration if we were to raise the self-esteem and
dignity of our patients as human beings. This involved many at
the time insuperable complications, and to prevent dislocation
among staff and the various hospital bureaus, no steps were tak-
en to remedy this condition until other, more pressing matters
had been arranged.

We recognized that too great deviations from routines and
practices would not be countenanced by the administrative staffs
and it was thus necessary that innovations be made gradually.
There were also fiscal, state, and many other regulations and
laws, to which our work had to conform. Therefore, before any
steps had been taken to implement our program, consultations
were held with each of the department heads involved, in addition to the protracted discussions with the ward personnel.

After several preliminary "planning meetings" with Dr.
Beckenstein, Dr. Lippman, and occasionally with the supervising psychiatrist on the service, we called an "introduction session" for a large group of the upper echelon staffs, in advance of
inaugurating the seminars for the "lower" staff.

Our proposals for the project, as submitted to the New
York State Department of Mental Hygiene, was read by the social worker to the assembled group of about 24 persons, who
were then asked to react to it. Each in turn took the opportunity
to indicate how his or her particular function in the hospital
could be utilized in our program as outlined. The most impressive element of these communications was the fact that despite
our emphasis on growth through spontaneous involvement by
patients, and their movement toward reality, each saw himself as
an *active* leader or teacher, rather than one to give freedom to
and allow spontaneity in patients.

This was true in the case with the specialists later on where
we asked each how the activities in their particular area—such
as recreation, art, music, occupational therapy, and so on—were
presently being introduced to patients. The answers uniformly

indicated that the specialists *initiated* activities by either assigning work or by cajoling, enticing, or even bribing patients to participate. When questioned to describe in greater detail how this was done, the language used and the tone of voice employed indicated that there has been little, if any, spontaneous response of free choice on the part of patients. Patients obediently submitted to staff's plans.

In further questioning, it was brought out that only a few of the patients who were "brought down" in groups to their special areas actually participated. Others remained indifferent observers, while most remained completely detached from what was going on, and a number always fell asleep. It was pointed out then that: "This means that only a few in the groups participate in the work which you present to them, the others are completely indifferent, and quite a number withdraw into their own introvertive brooding." The unanimous and simultaneous answer from a number of the staff was, "Yes, that is true."

The question was then raised as to how interest can be raised in all the patients, or at least a large number of them, thereby preventing indifference and withdrawal. Various suggestions were offered, but none dealt with the *inner* activation of patients toward interest and reality.

The three main themes that were re-emphasized in the initial orientation discussion with the "top staff" were first, that patients *must be helped to overcome their fears* against moving toward reality—the physical environment, activities, and people —through friendly and secure relationships in which benign attitudes on the part of the attendants and other staff members are the major ingredient. The second theme was the importance of dissolving the patients' murderous hostility which dominates the psychotic's psyche. The third indicated that life in the wards and in the hospital must evoke healthy interests and relations, as far as possible resembling those in a healthy civilized community.

From the very outset the attendants as well were engaged in a free discussion. Instead of our making proposals or formulating ideas for the project they were asked for suggestions "to improve the life on the ward." Suggestions had been offered freely by a number of the participants. One of the first was for music and "activities." Upon exploration it became apparent that "activities" referred to recreation and entertainment such as music and dancing. Trips off grounds was another suggestion. One attendant thought that the "aids" (attendants) ought to know more about the patients than they now do so that they could deal with them more appropriately; also that the "aids" should have more time to work with individual patients.

Another attendant thought that the patients should have "nicer clothes." Still another proposed that small group activities ought to be introduced, but admitted that only few in the groups participated in the past when small groups had been tried. One said that trips on and off the campus seemed gratifying to some patients and others felt there should be more of them. A few attendants complained that the chores on the wards were so numerous and pressing that "attendants had no time to talk to patients." There were a number of other suggestions for activities, but all of these seemed to be emanating from the staff and not what patients might desire.

The question was then asked: "In doing all these things, are you amusing the patients or are you 'curing' them?" This inquiry seemed to stop them short, and they looked thoughtful. The difference between being amused and *something happening internally in the patients which corrects their state of being* was pointed out. We also indicated that while the patients we are dealing with are chronologically adults, psychologically they are more like children. To this there was a spontaneous reaction of "yes" from a goodly number of those present and a nodding of heads from many others.

Having achieved this response, we then asked, "What do children need in order to develop into healthy adults?" Three or four in unison responded: "Love." "Is love enough?" we asked. "Would love alone satisfy a child?" There was a little fumbling on this point, but one or two finally came through with the statement, "Well, children have to have something to do." To this we heartily agreed and asked: "Would that apply to our patients, too?'' Several exclaimed, ''Yes,'' and the group was helped to apply this principle to our patients in addition to the affection which we must give them.

This was an appropriate time to explain that the psychotic isolates himself from the world and from people because he is afraid. When the word "afraid" was mentioned, a number of the staff immediately voiced agreement. We continued that we must therefore make the patients comfortable and trustful of us. This builds a bridge between patients and other human beings through us. First they discover that there are people who will not hurt them—these are originally the staff—then they will transfer this feeling to others. But we must furthermore remember that psychotic patients are generally harboring great hostility and murderous hate which we must transform into friendliness. When we give patients things, as is also the case with children— whether it be personal things or things through which they can get satisfaction, such as activities—they become aware that people can also be kind. Giving them things, therefore, builds a bridge between the staff member and the patient.

The group, under the guidance of the leader, then entered into a rather extensive elaboration on the themes of helplessness and dependency of psychotic patients (which, we pointed out, is also characteristic of children) and the hospital's responsibility to provide for such patients the opportunities to become as in- dependent as possible. Therefore *giving* things and pleasures is only one step. The fact that patients "love the trips," is only par- tially useful, for we must find a way of both satisfying them and making them self-reliant.

When we asked, "How can this be done?" one of the ward nurses said, "We should find out what interests patients had before they came to the hospital." An attendant, however, of- fered that we "Give them things to do on the ward."

Another suggested that there be a program of activities on the wards throughout the day. Some wondered whether all the activities would be confined exclusively to the wards, emphasiz- ing that outdoor activities and off-ground trips should be part of the program. We noted that no one activity or set of activities could appeal to all 65 residents on a ward. "What we must seek rather is activating each patient's inner interests which would lead her to move outward from withdrawal and thereby result in greater acceptance of reality and strengthening of egos to deal with reality."

The group was then asked, "What kind of activities do you think would be suitable for involving the patients?" A variety of creative activities was suggested, all of which were extremely pertinent and were actually later included in our program, including sewing machines for the wards. We later suggested, to the interest of all, washing machines, driers, ironing boards, and equipment for baking and cooking.

The next session was opened with the question:

Mr. S.: Have you any thoughts on last week's discussion?

Att.: I don't believe that most patients would be able to do things for themselves on the ward.

Mr. S.: Is there agreement on that?

Att.[5]: In time some could.

Mr. S.: Would you be willing to try, even though it sounds very difficult?

A number of voices: Yes.

Att.: About occupational therapy in wards—groups would be supervised and patients might do their laundry, but they have no place to put their belongings. There are no lockers and things get stolen. We could have occupational therapy in wards in the morning and go to recreational theapy in the afternoon. Sewing could also be done in the morning. We used to have occupational therapy in the morning, but they ran out of material and then patients sat around the tables and did nothing. Employees used to bring in some things and work with the patients, but the doctors didn't think this was a good idea. I think it gives more incentive to patients when employees work with them. *We used to just teach them to work and supervise them.*

Mr. S.: How do the rest of you feel about staff doing things other than just supervising?

Att. [who obviously incorporated as her own the previous week's discussion]: I feel that in some instances patients are able to do things by themselves . Other patients have to be led and assisted, helped to a point where they will want to knit, etc. [She then proceeded to agitate for a

[5] We had no facilities to identify the speakers in the recordings; hence the designation "Att." represents a number of participants.

variety of activities including washing machines for the patients who like to fix up their clothes, dress up.] They want to dress up, to be feminine, to have pride in ourselves. We have patients who, once they are shown, can do these things . . . Give them a single diet and they get bored. It should be divided: sewing, cooking, washing, ironing, housekeeping. For those who aren't able to, that's where the "mothers"[6] come in. Different employees can do different things.

    Att.: Some like washing, ironing, playing games.

Mr. S.: Do they do this on their own?

    Att.: Yes [This was not so.]

Mr. S.: How about patients who don't do things on their own? What do they do? ["They sit and do nothing."] Why? ["They like to do it."] Therefore, what can we do to arouse in them a liking to do things. People do what they like. It is very easy to sit through life and do nothing. . . .

    Att.: We have to find something that interests them.

Mr. S.: How would we find out?

    Att.: [Pursuing the traditional procedures]: *You have to* keep after the patients with different activities. If they refuse, you just can't let it go. You have to *keep asking them* until they have found something interesting.

Mr. S.: What if you have patients in your group who want to do different things; how would you take the group out?

    Att.: Do different things different days. If a patient wants to go to the movies, maybe one of the other girls [attendants] is going to the movies today and I can give her my patient who wants to go to the movies, and she can give me her patient who likes football.

Mr. S.: Very good. If we use our imagination, we can meet any problem.

    Att.: Our patients feel locked up. By keeping them closed in for so long, they became sicker, through not doing things, through not being active.

Mr. S.: Our point is, how would you approach patients on a ward without becoming teachers.

    Att.: *Get them* to do things.

Mr. S.: Wouldn't it be better to *draw* them in like you do children in a home, than making them do things. This can be done by exposure, by keeping materials out in the open, which we call visual stimulation. I am sure we can do this with our patients. Staff will have to work at these occupations to demonstrate to the patients. [Tells of his training

[6] This term which was later dropped, referred to the attendant in charge of a specific group of patients—obviously a term that reflected the nature of patient-staff relations, i.e., that of child and parent.

professionals by doing their "work" as do child-patients.] Another way is for a staff member to say, "Would you like to help me?" This means you are accepting her; you are building a bridge. It is not the *doing* of the thing that is important, but the *wanting* to do that comes from inside. It is the *desire* to work with you, to help.

Att.: [Tells of difference in response of a patient when she tells her to make her bed and when she tells her that she "needs" her help.]

Mr. S.: This is very important. It helps the patient's self-image if he feels that he is needed. What is the difference between the two approaches? [No answer.] The difference is that the second one contains an element of respect. Respect is really what people need even more than love. The expression of the fact that I need you means I respect you enough to need your help. . . .

The above abstract illustrates the participation of the attendants in their own re-education, as well as their resourcefulness and understandings that had been submerged by the traditional roles they had been forced to assume toward their jobs and patients.

As already stated, we followed up the "introductory meeting" with a series of orientation seminars for the attendants and the top staff, who were auditors, at luncheon meetings.

To introduce the ideas of the ward programs, we held separate ward meetings with the patients. At the seminar early in October, 1964, we had suggested to the attendants that such meetings be held, following their own planning discussions. We also suggested that chairs be arranged in two concentric circles to accommodate all of the 65 patients. We emphasized that patients were not to be coerced to join. Participation must be entirely voluntary. The ward nurses would announce the event a day or two before the meeting and again repeat the announcement on the morning when the sessions were to be held.

The attendants stood together in a cluster in the rear, apart from the patients. The psychiatrists, however, took places quite on their own among the patients, as did Dr. Beckenstein, who had entered a little late.

It was decided at the preceding luncheon meeting of the supervisory staff that the supervising psychiatrist conduct the meeting. In that he was in charge of the service, he was in a position to have more direct contact with the patients than was Dr. Beckenstein.

Initial Meeting with Ward A (the most disturbed ward).

When Dr. C. (supervising psychiatrist at the time) and I walked into Ward A at the appointed hour, 9:30 A.M., October 8, 1964, we were warmly greeted by some of the attendants who were standing at the door. There were about 50 out of the 65 patients already occupying chairs. The customary mass attack on Dr. C., with demands for various privileges and favors, did not materialize in this instance; only a few of the women approached him with their personal preoccupations. On the suggestion of the attendants, all of the women who were not as yet seated, but four, joined the assembled group. Two of these four remained in the "sun lounge," completely removed from the proceedings. The others were in the alcove which extended from the "day room." One of them, Hannah, shouted expletives, periodically emitting shrill screams. These were a distinct disturbance to the meeting.

Dr. C. stood (instead of sitting) in the middle of the circle. As soon as he said, "We want to plan in this ward things you would like to do and that you would like to have," pandemonium broke loose. Shouts came from all sides. One girl screamed, "We want to have men on the ward!" Another objected to having violent and nonviolent patients on the same ward. This was a new, rather attractive young girl, who had been transferred to the ward only a few weeks before because of her agitated state. Others made a variety of demands for privileges. When some semblance of order was achieved, a patient suggested a record player be supplied for the ward; another wanted a "place like a table where we can fold things" (apparently meaning folding clothes); still another wished that there be a kitchen on the ward. Among the other numerous shouted suggestions were: telephones "on the floor from which patients could call their families"; ice cream and drinking machines (obviously coin-operated machines).[7] All this against considerable noise and shouts that had no connection with the intended discussion, but rather reflected patients' personal involvements and delusional ramblings.

Whatever interpersonal conversation took place against the chaos was mostly between an individual patient and Dr. C., who, in order to hear what was said, would walk up to each and talk about her suggestion or question, most of which were essentially irrelevant to the intent of the meeting. Because of the tumult, the rest of the group heard nothing of these conversations. Dr. C. did not make a direct attempt to quiet the group. However, as the session progressed, some semblance of order gradually settled upon the assemblage so that one could hear *some* of these ongoing diadic conversations. One of the first utterances we heard was a statement by a new patient who said that she was "frightened of these women."

Shortly thereafter some relevant recommendations were made by some of the more intact patients, such as having window curtains for the dormitory. However, the most frequently heard demand was: "I want to go home!"

As all this was going on, I was approached by a rather loquacious and aggressive woman who proceeded to introduce herself and inform me about her sister, who promised every week to take her out of the hospital—four-and-a-half years had already elapsed without her doing so. Not waiting for a response, she abruptly stood up and made a long speech that patients should be "treated like human beings" in the hospital. "They are treated like things that are worth only 99 cents. They are not even worth a dollar." She elaborated on this subject rather extensively and then entered upon a loud complaint about her sister's neglect.

Dr. C. explained that the meeting was not held for solving individual problems, but for "the things which concern everybody." By now most of the patients were listening, though some

114

[7] Candy and cigarette vending machines were available in the rather wide hallway between the two wards.

mumbled to themselves, while a few talked to each other. Hannah, still in the alcove, was screaming at the top of her voice, attempting to make fun of the proceedings. Meanwhile, some more suggestions had been made, one of them being that there should be dancing sessions on the ward and arrangements for people to go to church on Sundays.

It was clear that the patients were hardly responsive to the oft repeated requests for quiet and that most paid no attention or probably never heard Dr. C.'s bidding for order. Dr. C.'s naturally quiet voice of low timbre was easily drowned out. (A bell would have served well to bring the patients to attention.) At this point, Dr. Beckenstein came in and at my suggestion took over. He entered the circle and, smilingly, in a loud voice said that, "We were to talk now only of how we could make things better for the patients on the ward." The same girl who spoke up before again repeated that she wanted to go to church and light a candle. She now began to cry. Another wanted Jewish services on Saturdays. Still another contributed that "there were not enough activities," and one woman wanted to have refreshments served "every day," but immediately reduced it to "every Monday."

Entertainment was another suggestion. Yet another said, "We had a lot of suggestions before, but what did we do about them?" One patient wanted more visiting days (at the present time relatives could visit on two half days a week). Another demanded more "honor cards" (which gave patients freedom to move about in the hospital and off grounds). One patient, in a sort of confused manner that made it very difficult to understand her, wanted a committee of the hospital to provide the patients with refreshments every day and "have one candle." When one patient suggested that the door should be unlocked, another said, among other things, "We can't have doors open because we have unbearable patients." The question of telephones was brought up again and this time it was more concrete: two telephone booths should be placed in the foyer so that patients could call their families.

Egged on by Dr. Beckenstein, who in a masterful fashion

assumed control of the meeting, suggestions came for arrangements for better clothing, while Hannah, who remained screaming from the alcove (and was from time to time told directly by Dr. Beckenstein to stop), emerged and walked back and forth in the day room, now with a companion, and talked about "shooting each other up," as she pointed to the television in the wall.

A suggestion came from one of the patients that, "A social worker should help patients to go to school and prepare for a job," while others wanted to "work in a laundry." One of the Negro patients stood up, and talking in a rather clear voice, and reasonably, said that she wanted to get "schooling." When asked by Dr. Beckenstein what schooling she wanted, she said that she wanted to learn to write the alphabet "legibly" and to go to high school. Dr. Beckenstein asked at this point what we could do to organize the ward. No answers were forthcoming. However, one of the patients offered the observation that the weakest and quietest patients sometimes became "most violent and more so" than ordinarily aggressive patients. Dr. Beckenstein suggested having small groups. At this the patients broke out in hand-clapping. Many voices seconded the suggestion of having smaller groups.

Then Dr. Beckenstein brought up the issue of improving personal appearances. (The patients were singularly dilapidated!) Among the various suggestions it was entertained that there be "more soap and nicer dresses." Dr. Beckenstein asked, "How can we get nicer dresses?" Some of the answers were that relatives should bring patients better clothes. Another demurred: "How can you take care of better clothes?" which brought the response from many voices, "Lockers!" As lockers were mentioned, widespread applause and shouting of approval broke out. Dr. Beckenstein, at this point suggested that the patients could also make their own clothes, and that there would be sewing machines for this purpose.

In connection with the improvement in appearance, the matter of showers was raised by some of the patients, several suggesting showering every day and "having more combs." Another offered a long dissertation, in a rather confused manner,

116

on the fact that patients throw their own shoes from the balcony and then take the shoes of other patients and throw them out, too.

In order to observe her, I had intentionally taken a seat next to a stuporous middle-aged woman, whom I had seen on my two or three previous visits to the ward in the same state, once in a fully frozen catatonia standing with her arms across her chest. She now appeared to be in a sleeplike stupor and did not respond when addressed. Apparently the attendants had placed her in a chair and she sat there in her characteristic slumped posture, lifeless, with her eyes closed. When I came up to sit in the vacant chair next to her, one of the attendants wanted to remove her. I motioned that she be left where she was.

For at least through half of the hour-long session, she remained in her stuporous state. Gradually, she opened her eyes slightly and looked straight ahead of her, apparently focussing upon the leader of the discussion. Her eyes slowly opened wider and she seemed to become observably aware of her surroundings. First she observed me as I was making notes of the proceedings, but when I glanced at her, she turned away. When she seemed to be following the proceedings, I asked her how she liked the meeting. She half turned toward me and mumbled something which I could not understand. Having requested that she repeat what she said, she repeated her unintelligible mumbling monotone. I gave up the effort to get her to talk more distinctly. (On inquiry, an attendant later told me that the patient had probably told me her name, which is her usual response to any question.) By the end of the session she sat upright with her eyes again shut, but appeared interested in what was going on.

When Dr. Beckenstein closed the session and the patients quickly dispersed, our patient instantaneously slumped again in the chair to a semireclining position and went to sleep.

Of interest is the fact that despite the obvious disorganization and lack of focus, individual patients displayed awareness of their needs and made some suggestions that were practical and useful. Of interest were their suggestions for a kitchen (and a laundry on Ward B), more suitable clothing and refreshments —all of which we had planned for them. Of even greater import was that when the attendants had been asked at one of our seminars for suggestions for carrying out our program, after the basic principles had been presented, they did not think of including a kitchen or a laundry or mid-morning snacks while some of the patients did. All of us have been impressed with the skill with which Dr. Beckenstein conducted the meeting in most strenuous conditions, interruptions, irrelevancies and delusional outbreaks.

The episode with the catatonic woman is illustrative of how important personal attention is even for most regressed patients and how sensitively one has to approach them so as not to frighten them into retreat. My inept scrutiny of her caused her to turn away, and my speaking to her drove her back into withdrawal. At the same time, barring direct communication at the beginning, at least, impersonal stimuli, such as the meeting in this case, activates even a catatonic patient to involve herself, though passively, in the world of reality.

Immediately after the conclusion of the hour-session on Ward A, one was introduced on Ward B, across the foyer.

Initial Meeting with Ward B

Here we found a much more orderly, better organized, better controlled group. They were seated in three much tighter and smaller concentric circles with a table in the middle which helped greatly in keeping the group under control. The patients made a more presentable appearance. There were fewer with body distortions among them than on Ward A. They seemed much brighter as a group and in better contact. There was less irrationality in their conversation, and they were better directed and more purposeful. Their suggestions, though less numerous, were more rational and easier to understand.

Dr. Beckenstein opened the session by introducing some of the strangers present. A number of the top staff and activity directors were present here, as they had been also at the meeting on Ward A. They also stood in the rear of the room with the attendants, away from the gathered patients. The ward psychiatrist, however, sat with the group, as did I, taking notes. Dr. Beckenstein asked, "What do you think we ought to do to organize this ward?" Several patients screamed challengingly in response, "What do *you* think?" After a brief silence, a middle-aged woman with staring eyes stood up and made a little speech to the effect that there should be more "recreation" so that patients would be "knocked out" at the end of the day and would sleep better. Another patient suggested that there should be dances. Still another complained that when she watches television the staff threaten her with putting her in a straitjacket. She wanted to know if this was right. Another suggested several times during the meeting that there be more fresh air (which was not inappropriate at the moment, since the room was becoming rather stuffy, what with the doors and windows closed).

Another patient asked for more activities and coupled it with the complaint that there was no activity going on, to which her fellow patient added that more walks should be allowed because, she complained, "No one goes out for walks." A third added to this list "off-ground trips," and still another requested parties with men. One was very vociferous that the "honor card" patients should be allowed to go to entertainments at night which are prohibited to them at the present time. Dr. Beckenstein wondered about the meaning of an honor card. The forthcoming response was that it meant, "that you are trusted." Now there was demurral from one of the patients against the idea of honor cards. What she wanted was more activities on the ward itself.

There followed suggestions for lockers, better clothes, and combs. One of the patients came through with a suggestion for a washing machine to wash the clothes and to iron them, and this set off one of the participants to suggest arrangements to "bake cookies and make coffee."

When the matter of lockers was brought up, Dr. Beckenstein asked, "What would you do with a locker?" One lonely answer was, "I would change my clothes every day."

Dr. B.: "How often would you like to have ward

meetings?" There were varying ideas: once a week, twice a week, and every day.

Dr. B.: "Who should conduct the meetings?" Answer from several of the patients: "You." Dr. Beckenstein asked, "Should it be the ward psychiatrist or the ward nurse?" No response to this. However, a complaint was voiced about the attendants being abusive to the patients. Obviously realizing the orderliness and good control of the patients in this ward, Dr. Beckenstein asked what they thought about their ward being an "open ward." The patients in great surprise asked, "How can you have that?" There was some discussion about some staff people having to stand at the door and check upon patients who may want to go out. One patient suggested, "Let us have a meeting like this every day and have strolling musicians come in" (obviously to combine the meetings with entertainment). [It evolved later that such meetings were held once a week with Dr. S. who was in charge the preceding year, and were followed by parties.] A patient asked for a dollar a week allowance. Dr. Beckenstein said, "What would you do for the dollar?" The patient answered that she would mop the floor and scrub the tables.

This meeting lasted about half an hour and ended in a constructive and organized manner.

After the conclusion of the ward meetings, the top staff who observed them and the leader met for an hour to react to what had transpired. It was decided to postpone having such meetings until the patients had improved and the discussion could be more reality oriented and less desultory. [We reached such a point some months later when rather orderly and constructive ward meetings were held under the guidance of a ward psychiatrist.] The most important decision arrived at at the sessions was that the ward activity program be inaugurated at once, before the patients forgot about it and to prevent disappointment. We learned that staff had made plans and promises to patients on many occasions before that had not been carried out. We were determined that this should not be repeated in our case.

After this discussion the hospital director, the psychiatrists involved, the two ward nurses, the director of the school of nursing, the chief administrator, and the present writer repaired to one of the hospital's dining rooms to consider the steps for implementing the program. The questions of individualizing apparel by marking it, separate meetings for the staffs of the wards (which was postponed), small group meetings with attendants led by psychiatrists (this was disapproved because of possible conflicting ideas with the larger seminar), and details of inaugurating the ward activity program were considered. Because of unavoidable delays in construction and obtaining equipment, only rudimentary occupations could be started, such as simple arts and crafts and some indoor recreation. It was decided to begin the program October 13th so as not to keep the patients in suspense.

Walking up to Ward B that morning, we were struck by the quiet which was in such striking contrast to the turmoil we had always encountered in the past. For a moment it suggested that the patients may have all been taken to some off-ward activity. But upon entering, we beheld the usual contingent of about a dozen of the older long-term patients quietly sitting in the day room (formerly "sun room") and two or three walking about in the passageway. However, on entering what was now the "activity room," one beheld a rather pleasant scene indeed.

Seated around tables were patients with either an attendant or one of the professional staff absorbed in various activities and games. About 18 patients at one center played checkers or were interestedly observing the game. At another table, in the charge of a recreation worker, patients were deeply absorbed in knitting and sewing by hand. At another "center," a smaller group played cards. At a fourth, patients with crayons and pencils were making crude drawings. Absolute quiet prevailed, and *only one patient* was lying on the floor. There were none of the usual outcries or screaming. Although the O.T. worker who was to inaugurate activities was not present, other staff members took the initiative and got things going.

No semblance of interaction among the patients around the tables was in evidence, however. Probably because of its novelty, the absorption in work seemed to isolate patients and staff while physically still in a group. Because of the importance of social interaction, this matter formed one of the topics for discussion at the next seminar session where it was concluded that if it does not interfere with the necessary concentration on games, conversation would be initiated by the staff with a view toward drawing in as many patient-participants as possible.

Another point that needed clarification at this staff session was the psychiatrist's circulating around the room observing patients at their occupations. We therefore suggested that *everyone* in the room be occupied. Patients were not to be made to feel that they were in any way being supervised.

A visit to Ward A similarly revealed absolute quiet, though there was a larger number of nonparticipants. Three centers of quiet activities were in action. My attention was particularly attracted to an elderly woman who was sitting by herself but near one of the groups, absorbed in sewing a dress. I looked at her with interest and as she looked up she smiled at me. Here, too, the attendants had taken the initiative in introducing the program without any professional staff present. [Inquiry later from the O.T. office elicited the explanation that they had "to make preparations" in terms of materials and other plans.] Inquiry from the ward staff brought the information that not one untoward act or outburst occurred on either ward that morning. Even Hannah refrained from screeching.

A visit to the wards several days later found them quiet and the patients absorbed in their work and games with incomparably more cheerful expressions on their faces. Even the older women, most of whom sat idly in the day room, or those who observed the activities in the activity room seemed impressively more relaxed. A few women in the day room were reading the magazines which we had left lying about.

There was now some conversation among the patients, particularly at the table in charge of one of the older attendants, about which 14 patients were engaged in drawing with crayons. Fourteen more were quietly absorbed in either playing or watching games of checkers. Others were grouped around the two other "centers of activity," while still others were occupied with individual projects. In their accustomed pattern, two or three approached me with complaints and requests which I warded off, explaining that I was in no way involved in discharging patients from the hospital or granting privileges. When asked again what my function was, I said that I was a teacher, and when asked whom I taught, I responded that I was teaching the staff. [I felt that it was best to be frank with the patients.]

The recreation department contributed to our program activities such as soft rubber ball, medicine ball, shuffle board, darts and target. The patients did not take to these spontaneously and when enticed by staff to play these games they did so with little enthusiasm. The games were always of short duration, which was not the case with the more feminine occupations such as cooking, sewing, knitting and crocheting. The two sewing machines supplied to us by the O.T. department on each ward were a source of considerable frustration as they were second hand, very old, and constantly breaking down, requiring the attention of a mechanic, who was not readily available. We always had to wait our turn, whenever services of the skilled workers were needed, so that the machines were ultimately of limited value.

Twice a week a duo or sometimes a trio of "strolling musicians" would appear routinely, as in the past, on each of the wards for a half hour and play popular songs. Usually four or five patients would break into dance and a larger number would accompany the music by singing. The instruments consisted of a piano (on wheels), a drum, and sometimes a cornet. Some of the better known popular songs with "catchy" tunes and stimulating lilt appealed to a fairly large number of the patients, but not to the older patients, the "sitters," who remained inert throughout. Once a month the traditional mid-morning party was held on each ward. The program included the strolling musicians, followed by coffee and cookies. These affairs were initiated and managed entirely by the recreation department with no participation from the patients.

About two weeks after the initiation of the activity program, the staff decided to hold the usual Thanksgiving Day party for the two wards. Our patients had by this time noticeably quieted down, and the climate grew increasingly less tense. But, having observed the effects on the patients of the other parties, we did not feel that they could as yet sustain the inevitable tensions and overstimulation of such mass affairs. Accordingly, we suggested that meetings be held on each of the wards to discuss plans with the patients. This was a major departure from the past.

Dr. B. opened the meeting by reading a draft of a letter written by one of the patients, on her own initiative, to the Ivy League (who had helped the hospital financially and had supplied funds for the equipment for our project, including the kitchen and lockers), inviting its members to the party. For the first time the patients voted whether they wanted a party or not. The vote having been unanimously affirmative, the sending of the letter was approved.

Dr. B. suggested that five committees be formed. He then called for volunteers for the decorations committee. On Ward B, five patients volunteered. When an arrangements committee was suggested, none of the patients knew what that meant. After explaining the committee's duties, he asked for volunteers. There were four responses. Fewer volunteered for the refreshments committee, and less spontaneously. This was the case also with the other committees, probably because the more activated patients had already offered their services. Dr. B. then suggested the need for a "clean-up" committee and the patients more or less unanimously suggested that the members of all committees would act in this capacity. Similar committees were chosen on Ward A, where more urging from Dr. B. was necessary.

During the preparations for the party, however, the recreation worker was found putting up the bunting herself, while the members of her "committee" were standing about or sitting watching her. It was called to her attention unobtrusively that the intention was that patients should begin to take on responsibilities, giving the reasons for this policy. The worker claimed that she had not understood this. But a half-hour later she was found again engaged in the project with the patients idling. Our admonition was repeated. When the subject was raised at the seminar without identifying the staff member involved, she found it necessary to defend herself for her act on the grounds that as a member of the recreation staff, it was her "responsibility" *to get the job done.* Besides, she claimed, she could not trust a patient on a ladder lest she fall down. This, despite the fact that a patient had taken over the job and performed it without incident.

The effect of this episode, and the movement toward health of even such regressed patients as ours were, were evidenced in a development a few weeks later. As Dr. Beckenstein visited the dining hall which was being decorated for a similar party for Halloween, a member of the "arrangements committee" told the same recreation worker, who again attempted to interfere with the committee's activities, to "sit down." The patients then took over all the tasks and did an excellent job completely on their own, even though some of the bunting was a bit askew and not quite symmetrical. "At the party," Dr. Beckenstein reported, "there was the largest number of patients that had ever attended, and there was absolute quiet during the bingo game, which was one of the activities. The only voice heard was that of the announcer, or a patient who would get a 'Bingo.' One of the patients remarked to me in passing: 'Respectable, isn't it?' When the president and some members of the Ivy League who had been invited by the patients entirely on their initiative arrived, they were asked, 'How do you like the decorations? We did it.' Three different staff members have independently told me that this party was quieter than any other they ever had before."

Further evidence of the quieting effect of the program was observable even though no physical changes had as yet been made on the wards and only a small part of the activities had been introduced. We faced months of delay in obtaining equipment for sewing, kitchen work, washing, ironing, clothes lockers and in installing the partitions in the toilets.[8] One day about three weeks after our ward program started (which was preceded by three months of orientation), the psychiatrist who was quite new walked up to me as I came on the ward and said, "Things are going very well. The resistance on the part of the staff is decreasing. I had a meeting with them last week and they seem to be beginning to see the value of this project."

The changed attitude of patients and their cooperation is well illustrated by the following episode. About a month after the initiation of the program, a patient on Ward A *asked to be put in restraint* because she began to feel "tense and afraid of what I might do." Some time later, she asked an attendant to remove the camisole, for she now felt better, she said.

We noted at one point that there was again no longer any conversation going on at the work tables as in the past. Apparently the attendants who had initiated conversation as suggested during the seminars must have forgotten to do so until their attention was called again to this matter. However, in time, the practice of encouraging interchange by and with patients was almost completely abandoned; nor did we press the point, having realized that the backgrounds of the staff did not favor such conversational interchange. To create a source of communication on the wards, we suggested at this time holding instead at least one ward meeting a week where patients and staff could make suggestions and decisions and express opinions.

One morning during the second month of the program, an attendant on Ward A volunteered the comment to me that the ward appeared "much better than it ever was. Things are quieter," she said and proceeded to explain that there was resistance to the changes because the attendants "did not understand; now they are beginning to understand what the program is about." In a patronizing way, she told me that the "kitchen things," "lockers," beauty parlor equipment, etc., were "on the

8 It was this observation that led us to conclude that the attitude of the staff and their warm and respectful treatment of patients was the core of the project, even though these could not have been effective without engaging the patients in self-initiated occupations, as limited as they were.

way and will soon be installed." On meeting me in an alcove of the ward, another attendant, who substituted for the absent nurse that day, said, "The ward is very quiet now and it is easier for us than it used to be."

When I entered the office of the supervisor of the O.T. department, I found her elated with what she had observed on the wards the previous day. She was particularly impressed with the fact that the "problem eaters" who were fed separately on the wards, and many of whom were spoon-fed, now ate in the dining hall with the other patients.

When the sewing machines arrived, they attracted much interest and were frequently seen operated with gusto even by the younger patients who seemed absorbed in what they were doing. They smiled when they saw me, as though gratefully acknowledging the opportunity for this type of work. However, as already indicated, the condition of the machines and the consequent interruptions discouraged this activity later on.

One day on Ward A, we perceived underlying tension, even though the large majority were quietly occupied at tables. Three patients were walking around, angrily hallucinating, which always occurred in a climate of tension. In the past, outbursts of screaming and violence would have been the result, but in a climate of comparative quiet, and because the majority were occupied, the patients contained themselves. [9] Another contributing factor in keeping the patients in control may have been the soothing background of music being played.

It was quite a struggle to introduce music, other than jazz, via the radio and phonograph. To do this we conferred with the sole music therapist and the recreation worker who was in charge of this part of the program. She, the part-time male music therapist and I listened to about 50 samplings of music which we evaluated as to suitability for our patients in various conditions. Despite the violent recriminations and quarrels be-

[9] We later traced the tension to a particularly violent outburst by one of the patients earlier in the morning involving patients and staff, who was now pacing back and forth on the porch in a rage, hallucinating.

tween the two as they misunderstood each other or disagreed on a piece of music, we succeeded in classifying the compositions under three categories: *concert*, *dance*, and *mood-setting* music. The guiding principles laid down for our purpose were that music was to be characterized by rhythm which stirs muscular as well as emotional responses. We drew illustrations of animal reactions to sounds and music, such as the wailing of a dog when high notes are played and the increase in milk productivity of cows when exposed to soothing music. The rhythm in dance music we considered from the point of view of its being raucous, such as the staccato rhythm in rock-and-roll and jazz, and eliminated it from our regular repertoire at this time. The cadence rhythm of a two-step or fox-trot and the flowing melody in waltz music seemed more suitable for our patients. Because rock-and-roll and jazz appealed to the small number of the younger patients, we decided to try them with caution, experimentally, and observe reactions.

For concerts in which the listeners remain quiescent and interested, popular songs and semi-classical music we considered as the most suitable. For background (mood) music, however, the compositions would be pleasant, with fluidity and consistent, continuous repetition of the central phrases. These should have a quieting effect. We pointed out that rhythms produce varying results because of their concurrence with inherent body rhythm and the conditioned responses to sounds of the nervous system. The recreation worker left the session with two lists of records that were chosen, one for "dance" and the other for "background."

Conflicts among staff, such as the one that arose in the music studio, had been replete and are to a certain extent inevitable in an active social process. During one of my visits to Ward A, for example, the O.T. worker said that she wanted to ask me something that bothered her. We went off to a corner where we could talk in privacy and she told me the following. Some days ago, one of the disturbed patients had asked her to take her down for a walk, which the worker, in her youthful enthusiasm and dedication, did. They went to the "community store" and then spent some time walking around the grounds. When the time came to go back to the ward, the patient hesitated about returning, but finally did so. The O.T. supervisor told the worker that this was improper behavior on her part: she acted outside the scope of her function as an occupational therapist. The therapist disagreed with her superior and seemed to expect me to support her in her stand. However, I agreed with the supervisor, stating that her function was to work with patients *on the ward*, in all the occupations in and outside of her specialty, but dealing with *behavior* and the *life* of patients required special training, experience and competence.

While we have emphasized in the seminars and other meetings that the staffs engaged in the program on the wards should function interchangeably as to their specialties and be flexible in their roles to meet needs of patients, they ought not to transcend each other's *boundaries of responsibility*. It would be wrong for attendants to take over the running of the O.T. and recreational program, although they should participate in these activities. It would also be wrong for an occupational therapist to take over the *conduct of the living process* of patients. Despite her disappointment, the worker seemed to understand this principle and accepted it.

One morning, after the seminar session in the middle of November, instead of meeting at lunch with the "auditors" I visited the wards, mainly to see how the mealtime was managed. I first called on Ward B and found the patients in a quiet mood. The ward looked much like the lobby of a hotel. Some of the patients were reading magazines, others sat quietly. The O.T. activities had been concluded shortly before. I later learned that the strolling musicians had made their weekly visit there for about half an hour. They gave another 30 minutes to Ward A. This appeared to be a good arrangement. It occurred to me that it might be advisable, as an experiment, to give this form of release to the patients every day, if it could be arranged. The musicales could be alternated with walks in the afternoon or with suitable gymnasium activities in inclement weather.

While I was observing the music on Ward A, a very attrac-

129

tive, matronly, patient came up and asked me, "Would you like to sit down? I will get you a chair." Without waiting for an answer, she brought up a chair for me, which I gratefully accepted. After lunch, a patient on Ward B came up to me and said, "We had such a wonderful lunch! The steak tasted so good. Thank you for arranging it for us." The patients seemed to have become aware for some time now that I was instrumental in arranging the program of activities and frequently would come up and tell me how much they liked the "new program," and "how smart" I was, and to thank me for arranging it.

When later I went to Ward B to look at the shower room which we had discussed at the seminar, one of the friendlier attendants enlightened me on its layout. Next to the two shower stalls was a door which she unlocked with the same key that fitted also the door to the room. This door opened on to a very wide shaft through which the laundry was dropped to the basement. In the past, patients used the shaft to commit suicide by throwing themselves down the four floors. I suggested that a Yale lock be put on this door, a key for which would not be available to patients. This would preclude the need to keep the shower room always locked as a precaution. The arrangement of the showering facilities was such that patients had to undress in the presence of each other and shower in each other's view. Only one long metal bench was available on which patients had to sit near each other as they dressed and undressed. By a simple arrangement of curtains between the shower cubicles and individual chairs in front of them, privacy, which the patients greatly appreciated, was later attained.

When I re-entered the ward, I found the patients with no occupation available sitting quietly, some watching television or reading magazines. Only a few strollers paced the floors. In recent weeks the number of strollers had greatly diminished. According to the program, the O.T. people should have been on the wards at this time, which was one o'clock. However, I later discovered they were scheduled for 1:30 P.M. This gave the patients an hour for relaxation and a nap, of which a rather large number of patients took advantage, lying on the floors of the toilet vestibule, the wards, or on tables. Some were asleep.

The question of the after-lunch rest was, therefore, brought up at the next seminar session and the suggestion was approved by the staff that the dormitories be left open all day and patients be free to use them at will. While the suggestion was not openly opposed, one felt a subsurface shock at such liberalism. Dormitories with their beds made up in perfect rows and neat folds are kept sacrosanct in all institutions.

The derelictions and regressions on the part of attendants, noted in the preceding pages, had occurred during the so-called theoretic period of our program; that is, during the months before activities on the wards had been introduced. During the first month, the seminar discussions were largely directed toward an overview of the nature of psychosis and the basic content of the schizophrenic mind. During this period we did not visit the wards, beyond the few times we dropped in in the company of Dr. Beckenstein before the seminar was inaugurated.

During the subsequent two months, brief visitations were made regularly twice a week to observe how the ward staff—attendants and nurses—applied some of the learnings in the seminars. Finding no alteration whatever in attitudes, functions, and in the treatment of patients, we based the seminar content on observations made during our brief visits. This turned the seminar sessions from being theoretic into what we termed "practicum seminars."

However, as preceding pages made it clear, these seminars as well, were not effective. The failure must be attributed to the nurses in charge of the wards who were, under the existing setting, responsible for the activities on the wards and especially for the conduct of the attendants. Whether this failure to translate theory into practice was due to natural resistance to change, inability or unwillingness to find procedures suitable to the new understandings, doubts of the possible validity of the ideas, resentment against the incursion upon their authority or discomfort or fear to correct the conduct of their subordinates, would be difficult to assess. But John Dewey's adage that "ideas cannot be translated into experience; only experience can be translated into experience," needs to be kept in mind in any educational enterprise. And it was this principle that convinced us to spend more time on the wards and "demonstrate" dealing with patients in accord with the teachings.

However, much of the doubt or unwillingness that may have impeded the program had disappeared, though never entirely, when the "activities program" for the patients got under way, especially as the climate on the wards grew progressively quieter. As could be expected, there were regressions from time to time but they were short-lived. The patients became more tranquil, screaming outbursts now seldom occurred and fights among patients grew infrequent. The latter, however, still constituted a problem, since the temperamentally combative and assaultive patients remained on the wards when our populations had been stabilized, i.e., when intransigent patients from all over the hospital were no longer brought to Wards A and B for quieting down. The combative propensities were a continuation of a few patients' characteristic patterns which stemmed from organic sources and former life experiences, which is the case also in the general community. However, even in these few, combativeness diminished and they became more amenable to self-control as tensions and resentments were reduced and the treatment of patients improved.

In discussing incidents of infractions, attendants would rattle off one patient after another who in the past had been a "holy terror," or that "you would be afraid to pass by her," or "she used to fight at the drop of a hat," who had now either given up their former irascibility or were better controlled. Many of them actually seemed to us quite mild and were friendly, though as in the case of the general population outside hospitals, were subject to mood swings. Staff gradually learned to respect these moods and avoided increasing irritations by inconsiderateness, scoldings and punishments. As the total climate became tranquil, the frequency of the mood swings also automatically diminished, and for periods entirely vanished. Absorption in activities and external preoccupation greatly diminished the likelihood for manifest aggressiveness.

Through the discussions at the seminars, the attendants gradually accepted the fact that in many psychotics, agitation reappears in cyclical sequences probably due to accumulation of toxins which could be counteracted by appropriate medication; also that irritations impinge upon patients from many sources: the noxious treatment and neglect at the hands of relatives; monotony of hospital life; frustrated sex urges; delusional dangers; slights from staff and fellow patients; menstrual disturbances and innumerable other circumstances, feelings and events. When ward staffs are not attuned properly, these conditions and malignant states add to patients' psychic loads and bring on outbursts of violence and regression.

The evening and night staffs on the wards were very small numerically and no activities were available to the patients. They knew of our project's aims by hearsay but continued their anachronistic practices of restrictions and authoritarianism in the denuded ward environment. This caused great resentment in the patients, who tended to react with rebelliousness against what seemed to them rejection and thus frustrated them. Rumors of violence by attendants against patients and vice-versa, filtered through to us from time to time, and news that an evening nurse once absented herself for three weeks due to injuries she had received at the hands of our otherwise manageable patients during the day hours did not come as a surprise. The day staff would find patients in camisoles upon arrival in the mornings. However, in time, even these incidents grew progressively less and less frequent.

Two weeks before Christmas (and two months after the program on the ward started), meetings with patients on each of the wards were held to plan for the holiday. The improvement in the patients' behavior and general climate of the ward that occurred since the last ward meetings held two months before is noteworthy. Dr. Beckenstein again conducted the sessions.

On Ward A the chairs were arranged in two concentric circles. About half of the patients were seated; the others were quietly sitting in other parts of the room. Three patients were walking about and several were still lying on the floor either sleeping or watching the proceedings. Dr. B. posed the question, "What season of the year is it?" One patient said, "It's the celebration of your birthday." ("Why my birthday?") "Well, you are Jesus Christ." ("What does that mean?") "Jesus Christ was the Savior." Several patients laughed. Finally a number of patients said, "Christmas." Then, "What should we do for this occasion?" A number of suggestions were made by various patients:

> We should decorate the ward.
> We should have music. [What kind?] Carols.
> We should have a party.
> [When would that be?] December 25th in the afternoon.
> [Anything else? What about Christmas Day?] Christmas dinner—turkey.
> [What should we do to make the dining room more attractive?] Tablecloths; Christmas napkins; fruit.

Dr. Beckenstein suggested the need of committees to arrange the holiday celebration. The patients suggested and selected the following committees: decoration committee; a serving committee for the food at the party; a committee to attend to the decorating of the tables on Christmas Day.

On both wards, when asked what else, the patients finally came up with "a Christmas tree." Asked why it would not be advisable to have a natural tree, many patients responded, "Because of fire." "What kind of tree should we have?" Some suggested a large artificial tree; others suggested the decorative type of artificial tree. (Large trees, which two patients on each ward offered to decorate, were provided.)

The question of personal appearance was then taken up. All agreed that they should make a special effort to look well-groomed on the holiday. One of the patients remarked about having curtains put up. Questioned why curtains could not be put up at this time, some replied, "Fire hazard"; others said that they were not available. One said that it was a "violent ward" and they "couldn't take a chance with curtains." When asked,

"What are they doing on the wards nowadays?", as if she suddenly saw the light, one patient replied, "They are painting!" "Would you hang up curtains before the painting was finished?" A chorus of voices answered, "No."

There was some disturbance on Ward A from the several strollers, especially from Hannah's periodic screeching, but much less than during the earlier meeting. Two patients kept jumping up to speak out of turn. The group as a whole, however, seemed much more relaxed, much less restless and better focussed in the discussion.

The same procedure was repeated on Ward B with substantially the same results. However, as expected, the meeting here was more orderly. The patients exercised better control of themselves and waited to be called upon after they raised their hands. They were more reality-oriented and a larger number participated. Each meeting was of about 20 minutes duration.

We repeatedly emphasized during our seminars the importance for regressed patients to be allowed to do things their own way, and refrained from imposing standards of achievement as symbols of *unconditional acceptance*. This principle is palpably illustrated by one of many similar incidents. One bright sunny morning the patients went to a large tree-covered enclosure on the campus. This parklike area was equipped for outdoor activities and for repose. I observed a tall, burly male recreation worker, not part of our staff, who was playing shuffleboard with one of our patients. Being mentally deficient and completely disorganized she could not play the game according to the rules. Her interest in the game obviously stemmed from the fact that she had the attention of a person, especially a male, and probably also from the physical release the game may have provided for her.

However, the staff member, being professionally rather than patient-oriented, persisted in instructing this obviously confused woman in the proper way of playing. On six different occasions I saw him walking over to her end of the board after her plays to explain the proper *modus operandi*. The patient

135

seemed to listen impassively. Finally, after the sixth "lesson," she pushed the putt with all her might, making it fly about 100 feet beyond the board's limits, threw down the stick and walked away. This same patient was seen a number of times smiling as she played shuffleboard with one of our own staff members on her ward. She seemed to enjoy the game when her performance was not criticized.

On the basis of observations of the individual staff members and their attitudes toward themselves, their responsibilities, and toward patients, we devoted one of the seminar discussions to clarifying their roles. When the unyielding preoccupations of the attendants with housekeeping chores and the specialists' concern with excellence of jobs done by patients at the neglect of their psychological needs came under purview, we suggested that attitudes toward work can be *self-centered, job-centered* or *patient-centered*. If for no other reason than that they laid bare the attendants' and other staff's biases and defenses, these concepts seemed to elicit one of the most interesting and fruitful discussions in our series and could not but lead to newer and broader understandings. A number of illustrations were drawn from observations of staff conduct on our and on other wards of job-centeredness as against patient-centeredness. The shuffleboard incident served well to illustrate where perfection in performance overshadowed patients' needs.

The difficulty was the staff's traditionalized image of themselves as caretakers, instructors, foreladies, disciplinarians, custodians, child-nurses. Until the inauguration of our program, none saw herself as a nurturer, developer of personality, stimulator of mind and spirit, and benevolent leader. When these matters were discussed, we tried to show that when we accepted even patients' inactivity, we were still helpful. *Just to be allowed to be* what one must be, is a great comfort and a lift to patients' spirits. But, our attendants, ancillary therapists and nurses, and sometimes even psychiatrists, would persist in passing uncomplimentary and critical remarks (at times humorously) about patients' dishevelled appearance, criticizing them for a divergent act or nonactivity, and the quality of their performances.

Attendants never said "please" or "thank you" to patients. We discussed these matters, too, at a number of sessions, but on this score, to little avail. Staff seemed completely unable to alter the deeply ingrained attitude toward patients as inferiors.

Nonetheless, our taped records of the seminars revealed increased acceptance of the new procedures and attitudes by the attendants. The attendants on Ward A, especially, began to perceive their functions as being other than custodial housekeeping and baby-nursing. The feedback definitely began to reflect awareness of wider responsibilities as educators and quasi-therapists. This could not but make them anxious and they began to verbalize resistances to the new role by complaints against low salaries, but more so in gripes among themselves. The discontent came to the ears of the administration and the matter was discussed at a number of our luncheon meetings, at which Dr. Beckenstein indicated that as attendants demonstrated their ability to function in a quasitherapeutic role, rather than merely as custodians, the State Department of Mental Hygiene would make salary adjustments. Another complaint that was often reiterated was the inadequate number of staff to man the new program, and the problem of being overworked.

Since we felt that these complaints had their roots more in insecurity than in justified claims, we had to step very gingerly in this area. It was my feeling, which I expressed at the luncheon discussions, that this was normal insecurity about abandoning the comfort of custom and would be particularly true in the case of culturally and economically limited persons. Defensive rigidities are stronger among persons who, like our attendants, had been traditionally regimented in details and who are now required to assume self-directed responsibilities.

Luck was with us in this respect. At about this time a new classification for attendants was established by the State Department of Mental Hygiene, which carried with it a substantial rise in salary for our attendants' grade. As to shortage of personnel, the chief administrator, who in a study of manpower needs came up with a recommendation for the presence of eight daytime attendants for each ward, raised the question with us. We told him that, "When the attendants did what we taught them to do, they would not feel the shortage." By this we meant that when the patients calmed down and could take over many of the chores, they would not command so much of the attendants' attention and time. This prognostication was entirely fulfilled in the course of time and complaints about overwork completely disappeared. In fact wards functioned adequately at times in the presence of two or three attendants and one O. T. worker.

The growing consideration of patients as persons—not as custodial objects—was gradually taking root, and was poignantly verbalized by one of the professional staff members who attended some of our seminars in the absence of his chief. We once met on the campus and stopped to talk. At one point in our conversation, tears welled up in the eyes of this heavy-set, somewhat rough-looking man, as he said, "What you are doing here is wonderful. Now the staff see the patients as human beings, people who had parents and who had relatives and grew up under conditions which had affected them. Before, we looked at them only as patients who needed to be supervised."

Because of these and similar events, the conduct of and the many remarks made by attendants along the same lines, we felt that the seminarians had an attitudinal and apperceptive readiness for an additional concept that would throw light on and give a *raison d'etre* for the basic aims of our plan. This was the concept of *respect*. From time to time we brought to the sessions for discussion inappropriate acts of the ward staff toward patients. These acts did not, for the most part, stem from cruelty or even callousness. They rather stemmed from a basic lack of respect for the dignity of *the person* characteristic of certain cultural segments of society. It now seemed appropriate to indicate that above love and compassion is *respect* for the individual's dignity and the right to his being what he is, whatever he is. We may not be able to love some people, nor even like them, but we must respect their right *to be*, and not expect submission from them and thereby avoid forcing people to behave as we wish, or respond to us as automatons rather than free independent persons.

It now became clear that all the innovations in our program could be viewed within the context of respect for the individual. Providing privacy in toileting and showering, improving the appearance of the wards (painting walls, etc.), supplying more appropriate clothing, preventing begging (by making available tobacco and paper for rolling cigarettes), abolishing unnecessary control of patients in the dining hall, stopping the practice of counting patients aloud on trips to determine whether some strayed away, creating opportunities for participation in activities, taking part in planning ward life, opening the dormitories for rest on beds (instead of lying on floors), unlocking the doors to the wards, providing freedom to leave wards by merely registering, employing the words "please" and "thank you," etc. —these were all steps to increase the dignity and self-respect of patients by displaying our respect for them.

Letting patients take initiative and leadership at every opportunity is part of the respect syndrome and even if such freedom of action may be inadvisable at times, the form of address used by a staff member should not demean patients. Condescension as well as domination are part of disrespect. Other, more subtle means of showing respect were enumerated as the discussion progressed. Among these were listening to patients instead of cutting them short because of real or fancied "pressures" of duties. We all recognized that no matter how important a routine may be, except, of course, in cases of emergency, patients must get preferred attention. We discussed techniques of engaging patients in participating in the work on the wards without peremptorily ordering them about (as was the case in the past). We suggested the importance of smiling when talking with patients, and elaborated on the negative effects of a stony-faced mien, which many of our staff wore.

It now became clear that serving patients and taking care of them as though they were helpless beings only entrenched their helplessness, and at the same time conveyed nonrespect for their powers and capacities. Even the phrase, "I *let* her [the patient]" do this or that, which came into use instead of "I gave her" or "I told her," which was universally employed by attendants, came under criticism as detrimental to personality growth.[10] The traditional practice of dragging or leading patients by the wrist or walking ahead of them instead of walking abreast as equals, also came under criticism. These practices were viewed as demeaning to patients. However, so ingrained were these habits that it was necessary to bring them to the attention of the staff on innumerable occasions before they were abandoned, but never quite completely.

Another matter that claimed our attention, in line with the emphasis on respect for patients, was addressing them by their first names. It was ludicrous to hear a 19- or 20-year-old attendant, and even those in their 30's and 40's address a gray old woman by her first name, while the patient on her part had to address the much younger attendant by her family name with the prefix of Miss or Mrs. We realized the difficulties that would be met with in any effort at changing this long-term practice which reflected the respective statuses.

This matter was not raised before the second year in our program and we warned the staff that because this might well be the most difficult change we had as yet attempted, it should be inaugurated with care. As a transitional step, we suggested that the staff might start by addressing patients by their first and second names, without using the appellations of Mrs. or Miss. Later, when the patients become used to it, we could drop the first names and substitute for them the appellations. The hesitancy with which these suggestions were met was considerable and we dropped the subject. At a later session one of the nurses reported that she did attempt to introduce the new form of addressing a patient. The patient turned on her and asked, "What's the matter, don't you like me any more?" Since we had so many more important changes to consider, we closed this chapter in our campaign.

To concretize our discussions of the mental processes of

---

[10] After many repetitions of this point, attendants compromised by saying, "I *let* her choose her [the patient's] dress," with an air of great liberality and progressivism, actually missing the spirit and intent of the change suggested.

our patients from which their behavior stemmed, we showed several films as part of our seminar sessions. One of these, a French film entitled "A Day in the Life of a Schizophrenic" depicted with startling authenticity the phantasmagoric, bloodcurdling scenes that pass through the schizophrenic's mind. Their effectiveness was especially stark for they were re-enactments of phantoms that obsessed the minds of *actual* schizophrenics who supplied them to the producers of the film. As a result, the film conveyed authenticity and conviction. In fact, according to the accompanying resume of the film, both the psychiatrist who produced the film and the young man who depicted the patient, sustained mental breaks following the production.

Some of the scenes required explanations and answers to the meager questions from the attendants and others present. The psychiatrist who acted as resource during our seminars took an active part in this discussion. During these transactions we asked, "When do ordinary people see such distortions and find themselves driven to such anxiety as we have seen in the life of the patient on the film?" A few of the attendants promptly said, "In dreams." "What do we call such dreams?" "Nightmares." "Well, can we call these 'nightmares' that occur in the minds of patients in their wakeful state 'daymares'?" We then recalled our earlier explanation of the outbursts of screaming and violence in our patients as a consequence of "daymares" which we had seen on the screen.

Two other films were shown in the course of our seminars. One was a British film of a mental hospital in which patients were depicted in many occupations including gardening and chicken-raising. Emphasis in this film was laid upon the diligence of the "aids" in fostering activities and helping patients with their work. The special pertinence of the film to our project was the stress on the importance of the aids' devotion to and involvement in the activities program. In the early stages of the educational program we also projected our own film on "Activity Group Therapy" with latency boys where the entire therapeutic vehicle is the free-choice arts and crafts projects, free mobility, and unrestricted interaction among the patients.

This procedure had special relevance to our project. The two programs were essentially identical in process, though at variance in setting and content because of the varying conditions of the patients, the psychodynamics of their disturbances, and the age and sex differentials. Each showing of the three films was followed by free discussion in which the psychiatrists actively participated.

It was obviously necessary for the success of our efforts that we extend attention to conditions beyond our wards that affected our patients. The impact of some of these could not be overlooked since they intimately and strongly shaped feelings and responses. Many had to be altered to varying degrees, while others that seemed not as important we overlooked to prevent conflict with other specialties, their vested interests and traditions.

One of the matters that required special and immediate attention was the application of shock treatment three times a week on Wards A and B, not only to residents of these two wards, but to all the female patients in the hospital. Our patients were required in groups of four to six to hold down patients under treatment, and see the contortions and convulsive spasms of those who were being treated. To allow this traumatic exposure is a measure of the degree of indifference toward the welfare of the residents of the two disturbed wards. Upon our recommendation the locale of shock treatment was transferred to a more suitable location in another building.

6. *Extensions of the Program*

A hospital ward is not an isolated, independent entity. It is part of a larger culture that impinges upon it. Just as the culture of a society and its values invade even the miniscule family unit by innumerable overt and imperceptible demands, pressures and mores, so do the ward practices and staff attitudes adopt the character and content of the larger social body—the hospital. To attempt altering the culture and values in a segment of the whole—the hospital with its culture, its aims and values—is like swimming against a strong tide with resulting exhaustion, and often inevitable collapse.

It was with a considerable naïveté that we tackled the subtle but nevertheless powerful currents that battered the ship of change. Fortunately, because of our cautious approach we did not generate over-intense conflicting head-winds and engulfing waves, the corrosive effects of overt and disguised opposition, imperceptible sabotage, misunderstanding, neglect, and studied passivity. However, they all became increasingly recognizable as we grew acclimated and our work progressed. It was not easy to penetrate the phalanx of the numerous covert interfering strategies that arose from many quarters.

The discovery that reasonableness of a theory and even undeniably beneficial pragmatic benefits to patients could not dissolve the reigning traditionalism was indeed disappointing to

143

the point of frustration. Of all the people in the different professional and nonprofessional strata and expertise, barring none, there was only one who truly understood the intent of our project. Hers was not the intellectual-mechanistic understanding. Rather it was the empathic amplitude of the total personality—intellectual, emotional and physical. This was the attendant who was so emotionally involved and identified with the patients' plight that she at times broke into tears. That some of her personality traits militated against better effectiveness in putting her resources to use was disappointing. But she genuinely perceived and understood the potentials of our plans and practices. Her effectiveness was further curtailed by the pressure and criticism of her colleagues who could not possibly understand the inner life of this good woman, despite her serious and often disturbing shortcomings.

Staff Egalitarian Status

Our insistence on egalitarian status among all staff could not but threaten the members of the hierarchy in the professional pecking order. While the director readily accepted this principle—largely due to philosophical orientation—others were less so disposed. Being less inwardly secure, they could not adapt themselves to the nondifferential level and the consequent new self-images. While fear of constituted authority prevented outspoken rebellion, the path of disguised noncooperation and sabotage proved a safer instrument and even more effective.

In my own conduct, I have attempted—as did also the director of the hospital—to demonstrate the egalitarian principles in staff relations. Not only were these verbalized (which is at best a fairly ineffective tool in human relations), but we put them into practice. We welcomed and even encouraged well-intentioned disagreement and honest criticism of ourselves and our procedures. We never introduced new equipment, activities, projects or methods without first submitting the plans for deliberation by the attendants at the seminars and by the professional staff at the luncheon meetings. At one of the latter, for example, a supervisor of one of the specialties reported that she had introduced, on her own, a new activity on the ward which *did* prove beneficial. It was called to her attention, however, that while her idea was an excellent one, the error she had made was in failing to submit it first for consideration by this group, which in turn would have brought it to the attendants' seminar. It was also pointed out, as had been done on numerous previous occasions, that we could not count on cooperation of the staff unless they were actively involved in the planning. Actually the failure of thinking through the plan with the others involved, created a problem for this woman, for she had come to an impasse that led her to seek the help of the luncheon group later on.

The first step toward eliminating differential status among our staff was made during a seminar session. When at the first session, Dr. Beckenstein and I entered the large, many-windowed sunny board room where the sessions were held, all those who had assembled—about 40 persons including attendants, psychiatrists, and nurses, who sat around the long, oblong, highly polished table, as well as the heads of departments, supervisors and ancillary therapists (the latter joined the group at the table later) who were seated on rows of chairs on the periphery—rose as one man (out of "respect" for the director, as I subsequently learned). It seemed that this Prussian-like deference to authority was the practice in all state mental hospitals, a practice that ran counter to the intent of our project (as well as our personal sense of values).

In order to terminate this traditional pattern, I entered alone the following week and sat down at the head of the table, the adjacent two chairs being reserved for the psychiatric consultant and the director. When the latter entered a few minutes later, I studiously remained seated and following the example, so did the rest of the assemblage. This demonstration put a final halt to the symbolic subservience of one class of employees to another. It is to the director's credit for having accepted this abrogation of an age-old universal practice with grace. In fact, he seemed to welcome the change.

Another empirical means of demonstrating the egalitarian status among the staff was the coffee break during the two-hour sessions of the seminar. At our suggestion, the administration arranged for a large coffee urn with the necessary equipment—cups, saucers, spoons, sugar, milk and cookies—to be brought in by the staff kitchen employees and left near the door midway during the seminar. The coffee was poured and served to the attendants and the others present usually by members of the professional and administrative staff who happened to be sitting nearest to the side table on which refreshments had been left. Occasionally an attendant or two, who had sat nearby, would help with this chore. Most often, however, it was performed by members of the upper echelon, including the present writer.

THE DINING HALL

We were presented with a vastly more difficult situation in relation to the prevailing practices in the dining hall, especially in the feeding of "backward" patients. Feeding and retiring are usually occasions fraught with difficulties. They are usually crucial daily landmarks for children living in typical family situations, but this is also the case in congregate living in institutions, especially with psychotic patients whose regressive behavior and reactions are largely analogous to those of children.

Great progress had been made in dining room management in mental hospitals since the days when knives and forks had been withheld from patients as potentially dangerous weapons. Along with other liberalizing reforms instituted in our hospital in the past years, these "dangerous" utensils, so essential to civilized living, were released to the patients—and without untoward results from this source in our or in any other mental institution. However, such steps have not obliterated other manifestations of the anxiety that food induces in immature people, particularly for the mercurial psychotic personalities who have been made to feel even more insecure by the deeply ingrained mistrust their keepers have for them. Dining halls in most mental hospitals are strictly supervised and with great vigilance by staff against violence, screaming and hallucinatory quarreling with phantom adversaries, attacks on dining neighbors and flinging of food. Movement is, therefore, strictly controlled and restricted and in some instances military-like formations and lineups are employed.

Routines in the dining hall, situated on the same floor with our two wards, were comparatively mildly applied, though the patients on each ward were required to take turns filing in a single line behind those of the other ward. When the glass ward doors had been kept locked, the patients in their respective wards crowded around them eyeing each other jealously across the foyer. The line-ups and their progress were rigidly supervised by attendants in their starched shining white uniforms towering over them as the patients moved from the wards through the long foyer and into the even longer, cheerful, sunlit, many-windowed dining hall. They then moved on toward the counters in the rear where the food was dispensed by a kitchen staff assisted by attendants, onto the trays which the patients had secured as they passed them and the cylinders containing the tableware. This phase was comparatively orderly, if one overlooked an occasional episode of pushing ahead of others which usually resulted in screaming or a transient altercation. These were speedily nipped in the bud by the vigilant attendants who were spaced at intervals on the sidelines.

Turmoil, noise, hallucinatory screaming and violent outbreaks appeared with greater frequency and intensity after patients seated themselves, six to each table, to partake of meals. It was seldom that a meal passed without some kind of disturbance requiring staff intervention. Incidents that invariably disturbed the atmosphere in the room may have been a fight for the possession of a seat, a quarrel concerning a real or imaginary interference in seating, grabbing each others' food, longstanding antipathy against a neighbor, or completely inexplicable outbursts of screaming and vituperations. Not infrequently a patient would suddenly, without any visible reason, go into a rage, throw the utensils or the food to the floor and stalk out of the room angrily muttering incomprehensible expletives, probably recalling in her ruminations some traumatic incident of the past which was reactivated by the eating situation. Perhaps the inappropriate behavior was her way of giving vent to anger accumulated through unpleasant encounters on the wards in the preceding hours or days, or of discharging rage generated by the vigilant aspect of the attendants who toweringly and conspicuously walked back and forth, the full length of the aisles, ready to spring at the first sign of an eruption.

More significantly impressive than these incidents was the less tangible "atmosphere" that reflected the emotional state of the diners *en masse*. Viewing from the open wide door into the dining hall, one felt tension in the air, not unlike that before an outbreak of a storm, punctuated by an isolated outcry, a scream, and sometimes even a wailing. The relaxed feelings of persons free of excessive tension can always be felt in the intangible "climate" that prevails. Similarly, where persons are under great tension *en masse*, where hostility and intrapsychic disturbances prevail, or where there is expectation of a hostile outbreak, the atmosphere is tense. This was the case in the dining hall occupied by wards A and B.

It was obvious that naught could be done directly to alter both the climate and the patients' conduct. Apart from minor changes in routines, improvement had to come as a consequence of inner changes in the patients. Gatherings of benign families, and all people in repose, create a sanguine and quieting atmosphere. In our situation this would have to arise as the result of inner quiet and a degree of ego integration. This assumption was fully justified in time and the dining hall climate served us at any given time as a barometer of the emotional state of our patients as a unit.

As our program took root, the patients would enter the dining hall with progressively diminished residues of tension and hostility from their lives on the wards. This rendered them less susceptible to irritation and explosiveness, which became unmistakably evident to every observer including the few visitors whom we allowed on our wards and to view the dining hall. These observers would invariably express their surprise at the order and calm that prevailed in a room peopled by almost 130 "disturbed" patients.

148

Before the program made inroads, my presence in the dining hall was, to varying degrees, disturbing to some of the women. There were those among them who displayed unmistaken self-consciousness, while the attention of others would be diverted from their meal and riveted on me as though they expected comment or criticism. The faces of others registered resentment at the intrusion, while still others grew hostile, openly expressing it by becoming verbally abusive, and one or two would in shrill voices peremptorily order me out. The patient whom we described as the most irascible in the hospital (Geraldine) was by far the most vociferous. She would invariably burst forth at the sight of me in an angry scream and a torrent of abuse, at times standing up as she did so. After several early visits I, therefore, made it a practice not to enter the precincts during meals and instead made fleeting observations from time to time through the door which was now kept open and fully ajar.[1] This was quite sufficient, as one could readily register the mood of the patients from the climate that prevailed. Later I was able to spend much time in the dining hall during meals without arousing interest; in fact, many patients would greet me cordially with smiles, while others would address me as I passed them.

In time, the aspect in the dining hall grew to be similar to a gathering of dignified women in the community. In fact more so, for the room was much too quiet for the usual gatherings of so large a number of women. This we considered an inadequacy insofar as we had hoped for more spontaneous communication among our patients. At meals, the attention of most of the patients was centered upon the food. Some did have atrocious table manners, which in part reflected the cultural level of early home training and practices.

We have made some small adjustments, however, in line with the general intent of our program. When the doors to the ward had been left open, patients were at first allowed to go to

[1] The door of the dining hall had been kept locked in the past both between and during meals and was opened only to let patients in and out at mealtimes.

the dining hall as individuals rather than as total ward groups. This eliminated regimentation and lining up, but the arrangement was found awkward due to shortage of staff, and after a brief try the attendants decided against it at one of the seminar sessions. We therefore returned to alternating the ward groups on a daily basis in their migrations to the dining room. We have failed to eliminate the crowding by patients at the doors in anticipation of the mealtimes even when the doors were open. They would still gather at the thresholds in large numbers to await the signal from an attendant before venturing out through the doorways. Deeply ingrained habits died as hard among patients as they did among staff, in our small world. We could have eliminated these unaesthetic practices, but it would have involved the use of pressure and generating resentments, which we scrupulously eschewed.

It was an established practice for four attendants—two from each ward—to march up and down the four aisles between the rows of tables through the mealtimes. The patients of the two wards were ranged at different sides of the room and were monitored by attendants of their respective wards. The functions of the latter consisted primarily as inhibitors of violence among patients, putting down outbreaks, helping patients who may have needed help with their food or utensils, or who had become emotionally upset or broke into weeping or wailing. Their other function was to serve "seconds" to those patients who asked for them, if extra portions were available. This practice was aimed at eliminating movement in the dining hall.

The aspect that this arrangement presented to the uninitiated was that of a prison messhall with guards on the alert for a jail break. The monitoring by our rather bulky staff members attired in crisply starched and dazzling white uniforms that made them stand out as they marched stiffly back and forth, was a far cry from the homelike friendly atmosphere for which we had striven. This order of events was accordingly brought to the consideration of the attendants at one of the seminar sessions. With little opposition we decided that once the patients had seated themselves at the tables, the attendants, too, would sit down with the patients and attempt to initiate a conversation among the diners. The intention was that they would join two or three tables successively in the course of a meal. Or, if this was not possible, they could seat themselves at the door in the rear of the room, out of sight of most of the patients. In either case, they would not bear an expression of supervisory watchfulness and still be ready to act should their intervention be needed.

At the same time, we suggested that we would try to arrange for the various attendants on duty to have their lunches at the patients' tables so as to create a homey atmosphere. After many months of negotiations with various officials, this plan was vetoed as it ran counter to state *laws* which specified that food supplied by the hospital was to be consumed by patients only. [This in spite of the fact that there was an excess of food every day since there were always some patients who refrained from eating. Thus although the left-overs had to be disposed of in some way, they could not be used with the therapeutic aim we had in mind.]

Because we were unable to arrange for attendants to join the patients for meals at the tables, we suggested that the attendants could take a cup of coffee, which apparently they were allowed to do, sit with patients and attempt to strike up a conversation with them. We also suggested that they move to different tables during the course of a meal, or on different days.

At one point I raised the question of table napkins which had been conspicuous by their absence from the dinner trays. Inquiry from the dispensing "kitchen" staff brought the rejoinder that "there probably were napkins in the large cupboard in the room." A search did reveal large packages of paper napkins which remained tucked away unused for months and probably years. We at once laid them out alongside the utensils and trays. The alacrity and obvious pride and satisfaction with which all patients took them up, *on their own* as the first article for their trays were both startling and moving. It appeared as though they had always longed for them, but having been denied, they were afraid or had lost interest in requesting them.

It seemed that having napkins gave the patients a feeling of

151

normalcy, of being a part of the world in which they had lived and from which they had been sequestered. The napkins were a symbol of their new status as persons, being like other people (and not nonpersons or even minus-persons). We then consulted the hospital business manager who assured us that we always had a quota of napkins for the two wards. After checking the files he told us the number of the monthly allotment. This turned out to be enough for just one meal a day. The mid-day meal which was the heaviest of the three was chosen to be graced by napkins.

For about two months napkins had been made available to the patients, then they disappeared again. Inquiries revealed that requests for them had to be sent each month to the storehouse, but there was no one interested enough to do so after the first few tries. It was becoming clear from this and numerous other events that the details of the program we were introducing would vanish as soon as the iron hand of supervision was removed. I, therefore, limited myself to a few reminders to the kitchen staff, but feeling their indifference, I decided to drop the matter. The patients were thus denied this very important symbol of self-worth.

For many decades, food on the counters from which patients helped themselves or were served as they filed past, was arranged in such a way that desserts appeared as the first item. Patients would help themselves to these, then proceed on to the section where the meat or fish and two vegetables were served—each item dispensed by a different staff member. Further on, bread or rolls and glasses of milk were lined up to which patients again helped themselves. Some of the more regressed would eat the dessert as they waited to be served with the hot dishes. In many instances they would forget that they had already consumed it and would return for another helping, creating confusion and often conflict. We suggested that the areas for the bread and desserts be reversed. Our logic was that the trays, being full and heavy, and engaging both their hands, the patients could not eat the dessert on the way to the tables. Nonetheless, several of the most regressed patients still consumed their desserts, like small children do, ahead of the other victuals.

During one of the visits to the dining hall a nurse came up to ask me whether the patients should go up by themselves to get "seconds" or whether they should be served as was the practice in the past by attendants. We suggested that the first plan be adopted. As we were talking, the pleasant quiet was suddenly broken by a mass movement and clatter of utensils. When I saw the patients lining up with their trays, I asked what they were doing and was informed that they were returning them with the plates and utensils to the alcove in the rear to be washed. The women were orderly and efficient. Each patient brought up her tray, placed the silver into a huge bowl containing hot water and germicide, handed the plates to one of three patients, each of whom was performing a special duty—one scraping the plates, one stacking them, and the third stacking the trays. All proceeded very efficiently and everyone appeared to be thoroughly absorbed in her duties.

A visit following a seminar discussion of the new practices in the dining hall, which, by the way, was still locked after the patients had filed in, found three attendants from Ward A idly standing in a group at the head of the room overseeing the patients as the latter collected their utensils. We raised the question as to the purpose of their watching the patients, which must have made them uncomfortable and self-conscious. We also tried to establish why it was necessary to lock the patients in at mealtime. One of the attendants offered the explanation that some of the patients *may* leave the hall before putting away their dishes and some habitual run-aways may abscond (even though all egress from the floor was barred). [This conversation took place after I asked the three women to *sit down* with me in an unoccupied part of the alcove and out of sight of the patients.]

For the rest of the dining period we kept the attendants sitting removed from the patients, engaged in talking, thus demonstrating to them, without comment, that the patients did not require surveillance. We suggested that one of them (not three) sit on a chair in the rear of the hall where she could easily see her half of the dining hall without conveying to the patients that they were being watched. As to locking the door, we suggested that it need not be locked at all, but if they felt uncomfortable about patients' absconding, they could sit near the door (near the entrance to the dining hall) where they could have their own lunch if they should care to. Actually, as events proved later, none of these precautions was necessary.

The dining hall staff assisted by several attendants were extraordinarily efficient in the serving alcove and the room was meticulously clean. The counters, the utensils and all the other appurtenances used in the distribution of food were aseptic and well-kept, as were the tables, the chairs, the floor and the windows. One patient was either assigned or volunteered to clean the floors and tables at which she spent nearly all her wakeful hours, carrying on a hallucinatory conversation as she vigorously applied herself to her tasks. She was at the time sufficiently in contact to respond to my greetings and at times she would remember my name. Some mornings, however, she would be so engrossed in her delusional preoccupations that she would neither hear my greeting nor notice my presence.

The food served at the hospital was singularly good in all respects: content, preparation and service, and was served to the patients expeditiously. The fly in the ointment in this area of our patients' lives, however, was the hostile and contemptuous attitude of the kitchen staff. The women in question, particularly one of them, displayed physical aversion to their proximity. Their faces were distorted by a combination of disgust and rage while serving the dinner ingredients to patients as the latter filed by. They never looked directly at patients; their eyes were lowered and riveted on the trays as though these were presented to them by a belt conveyor. Fortunately, there was only one of them at any given time since they took turns at serving, and their destructive attitudes were diluted by the three attendants who participated alongside them and whose attitudes were vastly more friendly.

I spent some time with each of the women involved. In an effort to soften their feelings toward our patients and to evoke pity and sympathy for them, we explained the nature of the psychotic process and the need for kindly treatment. While the women listened deferentially, later observations revealed no alteration either in their facial expressions or actions.

For some months we waged a campaign for leaving the solid oak door to the dining hall unlocked and open between meals. This was an accepted practice on the other three floors of the building. Despite our efforts, the door, while kept unlocked, was still closed on the days when they knew I would make an appearance and locked on all other days, as the staff members would sit in the serving alcove having coffee and gossiping with visiting colleagues from other floors. It was rather important for our project that patients not be given a feeling that they were unwanted or untrusted in any part of our set-up. In addition, the brilliantly lighted room, with the sun streaming in from numerous windows on both sides of its full length, brightened up the view from the foyer and lifted spirits.

Whenever I found the doors locked on the days when I was not expected, as I made my way to the wards usually through the dining hall, I would routinely lock them behind me. In doing this I sought primarily to prevent enraging the staff members who would undoubtedly have vengefully acted it out against the patients. Another consideration was preventing incursion upon the domain of these specialists which as a policy we assiduously avoided.

In view of the unsuitability of the personalities of the two "kitchen" staff members, I pressed the administration for a change, which at first was considered favorably by the director, but apparently this set off the machinery of the institutional politics, and after months of hesitancy, the request was indefinitely shelved and died a natural death.

THE PROBLEM EATERS

During one of my preprogram visits to the wards in the company of Dr. Beckenstein, we were presented with a strange sight. On each of the wards were strung out tables at which sat a score or more patients in a row with attendants serving them trays of food. After placing these before each patient, the attendants, assisted by a few of the "better" patients, proceeded to feed them. Upon inquiring as to the meaning of this procedure, we were informed that those who were the "problem eaters"—slow eaters, regressed patients who could not feed themselves, and a few on special diets because of diabetes. These patients were fed in advance of the regular service in the dining room. Insofar as the situation seemed too bizarre, we raised the question at one of our seminars for discussion by the staff. The following is an abstract of the deliberations:

M r. S.: How do you feed your patients on the ward? Do you give them individual trays? Did you ever try to put them together at one of the large tables, as a group?

A tt.: We do put them together in a group.

M r. S.: They eat in a group?

A tt.: Yes.

M r. S.: Around, or just in a line?[2]

A tt.: Around.

M r. S.: And they accept that? They don't want to eat in the dining room?

A tt.: Some are diabetics, some are on diets. Others have to be fed, the catatonics. That type of thing. . . .

M r. S.: I'm speaking now about those who can sit around a table.

A tt.: [evasively]: Oh, they all go into the dining room.

M r. S.: I know. But there are those who don't go to the dining room.

A tt.: They're slow eaters and we have to see that they eat. And some won't eat at all. We have to feed them.

M r. S.: However, they don't eat separately. They eat together, those who eat on the ward. They *can* tolerate each other.

A tt.: That's correct.

M r. S.: But they cannot tolerate the large dining room? Is that correct? Well, we'll have to figure out what's going on here and try to get these patients to eat in the dining room. What is it that keeps them away from large groups?

---

2 Whenever I saw the so-called "problem eaters" on the ward, it was at tables which had been *strung out lengthwise*, with the patients sitting lined up at one side, facing the empty space of the ward.

156

EXTENSIONS OF THE PROGRAM

ATT.: Well I don't think there's anything that keeps them away. Some of them are not capable of feeding themselves. *We have to feed them* and some of them won't eat.

MR. S.: Right. How many of those? I mean those who feed themselves and sit around the table. You mean you sit with a group at the table and feed each patient separately?

ATT.: No, we have to feed some of them.

MR. S.: Separately. Away from the group.

ATT.: Oh, no. They're with the group. And some of them just stopped eating altogether and if you send them out to the dining room they won't eat at all.

MR. S.: Well, I just wanted to know whether they eat separately or together. We'll have to study those patients. It's our job to find out why it is and to try to get them to eat with the others, if at all possible. You see, the fact that they act that way does not mean that they have to be that way. They are here to be changed. They are not here to remain as they are. We, therefore, have to do something about making them more normal.

ATT.: Well we have some who mingle with the other patients just like the others, but they just stopped eating. They just won't eat.

MR. S.: [to psychiatrist]: What would happen if you let them starve?

PSYCHIATRIST: Well, it's possible that they could starve themselves, yes. It's possible.

MR. S.: Some of them. Not all that you have now on the wards. How many do have—12, 16?

ATT.: We have 20 [on one ward].

MR. S.: Would all of them starve themselves to death?

ATT.: Well, I believe some of them would really starve themselves to death.

MR. S.: All the 20, or only six or eight of them?

ATT.: Well I would say all the 20. They would find some way of not eating. They would not eat.

MR. S.: If you didn't give them any food for three or four days would they still continue not eating?

ATT.: I believe some of them would.

MR. S.: How many would and how many wouldn't? That's what we're trying to establish.

SUPERVISING PSYCHIATRIST: Of the 20, how many do you think would actually die?

ATT.: I would say about 15 out of the 20 would probably starve themselves to death.

MR. S.: Well, that's what we needed to know. Dr. F---, did you want to say something?

157

Dr. F. [psychiatrist on Ward B]: I don't know who these 20 patients are or who these 15 patients are, but if they are in the same state of overprotectiveness they could probably operate for a couple of days without eating. [Many excited voices talking at once in disagreement.]

Mr. S.: I beg your pardon. Would you repeat that please?

Dr. F.: I don't know about these patients, but I know there are some on the other wards who are put on what is known as a Duncan Diet. This is a diet for people who are extremely obese; they do not eat for seven, 15, 21, 30 or 50 days to lose weight. They lose about a pound a day, with no difficulties at all.

Mr. S.: Well, this would have to be done under the direction of physicians. We cannot become involved in that kind of thing. It will be up to you and the other doctors to decide. We'll have to decide which patients could be allowed to starve and which should not. But I would try to break through the whole thing. I mean, this business of feeding them. You see, they want to be babied. We're only helping them to continue being babies for the rest of their lives. It's ridiculous! They may as well die if they're going to live all their lives with somebody having to feed them. I think it would be more kindly to do this. But I think they refuse to eat because they get too much pleasure out of being treated as babies, and we ought not to play up to that. I think we ought to study this and do something about it.

Dr. F.: If you want to, you can try to say to the patients, "Either eat in the dining room or not at all." And they would say, "Well, I'm not going to eat." They may not eat for three or five or seven days. It's not going to hurt them.

Psychiatrist: Obviously not. There may be a very small segment who might actually fast to the point of starvation.

Mr. S.: This is something we have to work on.

Psychiatrist: Three or four days is no problem.

Mr. S.: This is a medical problem and it will be up to you people to make a decision. My position is that I am not going to continue keeping these people as babies. As a private citizen, not a hospital staff member, I'd rather see them dead than let them live and be fed like babies for the next 30 or 40 years.

Att.: You can't make a blanket statement that they're better off dead.

Mr. S.: Well, this is purely a personal reaction. It is not official or a suggestion for action. This is the way I feel about it. However, let's say we ought not to continue the way we did. It is obviously a misguided philosophy about hospital treatment of patients.

The outcome was that in about three weeks all the so-called problem and slow eaters joined the other patients in the dining room without missing even one meal. The exceptions were three patients who were physically unable to manage a tray and the table utensils. However, the steps taken and the process involved presented considerable difficulties, arising mostly from the attendants, which had to be overcome.

As a first step, the "special feeding problems" were moved to the dining room where they ate a half hour ahead of the other patients and would leave just about when the bulk of them would troop in. After a week or two, the "problem eaters" would start about 10 minutes before the others and would continue and finish their meal at about the same time. Gradually they were integrated and joined the regular line into the dining room, took up their trays, table utensils and the food as part of the general community. The three patients who had to be separated were fed in advance but they, too, remained in their seats so as not to feel apart, different and rejected. These three were Dorothy (Ward A), Shirley (Ward A), and the stuporous woman (Ward A). It was my feeling that if we could have sufficiently reassured our attendants—and I believe I could have done it if I were on the spot *every day*—this woman, too, could have been brought to the point where she would become self-dependent. The attendants could not bring themselves to apply the necessary pressure—starvation—and I felt it inadvisable to expose them to this anxiety unless I was there in person and assumed the responsibility. Nor was there a psychiatrist available for this task as this development occurred during one of the several long interims when we had none on our wards.

When the "feeding problem group" was first moved to the dining room, the attendants continued to bring them trays of food to the tables, but the patients now sat face to face in groups of six and four at tables nearest to the serving alcove on different sides of the room, according to their wards. Attendants of the respective ward hovered over or fed them. I realized that if we were to make progress on this not too simple project, I would have to take a hand in it, since the staff tended compulsively, either by force of habit, fear, or expediency, to continue in the old pattern. I, therefore, personally supervised and took an active role in the initial steps. I would walk along with the patients and instead of letting them sit down at tables expecting to be served as did the attendants, I directed those at the head of the line to the pile of trays and the adjoining eating utensils and then to the serving counters. Automatically, other patients would follow and attendants fell in to help with patients who still needed some help. At first some would break the line and sit down at a table before reaching the trays. These we approached after all the others had been taken care of and conducted individually to pick up their supplies and victuals.

I was stunned to discover that Shirley was able to carry her own tray, although she could not manage selecting utensils or directing her steps to where the food was dispensed. But once she was helped with this, she carried her own tray, selected a table and sat down to *devour* her food. Similarly Justina was at first unable to grasp the relation of obtaining food and eating it. When I led her for the first time to the table containing the trays, she did not know how to pick one up, and when I pointed to a utensil (since she was deaf and could not understand language) she still could not perceive what was intended. Instead of continuing on her way, she turned to the nearest table, not realizing that she needed food as well as a tray. When led back to the silver holders, she did not know what to do or how to pull out the eating utensils and place them on her tray. I then helped her with these things. She also had to be guided to the food dispensing counter where she required assistance in getting the food, as she did not recognize the relation of the objects around her. She had never been exposed to this experience in the many decades she had spent in the various hospitals, as it was assumed in advance that she would not learn and no one had evinced any interest in helping her expand her experiences and perceptions.

We were unsuccessful in making this patient fully independent in the dining situation for a long time, though she responded more appropriately as time went on. There were too many steps, the relations of which at first seemed beyond her limited capacities. We discussed this situation at the seminar where we indicated that one and the same person should be assigned *to train* Justina, and that the sequences of steps must be exactly the same and never vary or she would become confused and never learn. That is, in picking up the several eating utensils, the same order should be observed in the same sequence: fork, knife, spoon. A change in this order would interfere with establishing the necessary neuronal connections, for she was incapable of deriving perceptions or understanding relationships as do other people. The process we suggested was drawn from the training of animals and was an intensified form of habit conditioning with humans.

I had the opportunity to observe this patient on February 14, 1966, about 14 months subsequent to the events described, when a play was presented in the dining hall on the morning of that day. At the conclusion of the performance, entirely unassisted, she selected a tray and utensils, proceeded to the dispensing counter where she was given her food, after which she chose a table and proceeded to have her dinner. The limited improvement achieved by this patient was manifested by her remaining seemingly intensely interested throughout the performance, swinging her body in rhythm with the music. This behavior was in striking contrast to a similar situation at the 1964 Christmas play. At that time, she was led into the dining hall, the locale of the performance, by another patient who had taken her under her wing and made her sit down in a chair. When the performance began, Justina seemed to have gotten frightened and rose to leave. Her volunteer mentor, who had sat near by, pulled her down. A few moments later, Justina rose again to leave and again she was pulled down onto her chair. This occurred once more, whereupon she burst into weeping and determinedly left the room. Her sponsor was apparently too abashed to again apply force.

It was evident at the very first try that Dorothy, another imbecile, could never take part in this form of training for self-help in meals. She seemed completely confused and wore an expression of stubbornness and rising rage, which often proved very threatening and severe. In addition, the rigidity of her fingers made holding the eating tools impossible for her.

The nonverbal attractive woman who fixedly stared ahead of her with a Mona Lisa smile playing over her face was also a problem eater. Her problem, in our opinion, stemmed from an overwhelming spite, which was also the cause of her general rigidity and which resulted in her refusing to fetch her food. When she was given food, she ate leisurely and with good manners. She was the one who would break away from the line of the eating-problem patients, when one was introduced, and sit at the table with an air of imperious expectation that she be served. Her manner seemed to indicate that she expected individual attention. Some weeks later, as I stood in the dining room while the general line (not the problem eaters) was proceeding toward the kitchen above, she appeared in line with the others, whom she had joined voluntarily. I found her looking at me fixedly with her enigmatic smile for a long time as she approached where I stood, as though to show me that she could do it. From that time forward she ate with the bulk of the patients, though occasionally would revert to her old pattern, but quickly cooperated when asked to help herself. Perhaps it would be interesting to record how the change in this patient had come about.

One day she came in with the other "problem eaters," before they had finally joined the larger group, and sat down in her usual chair, studiously remaining immobile and looking straight ahead of her with a stony expression on her face. In the past a tray would have been prepared and brought to her. On this particular day we decided against the practice. Seeing that no one was paying attention to her, she impulsively rose from her chair, gathered up a tray and table utensils, passed on to the counter to get her food, then making back to her seat proceeded to quietly eat her dinner. On the same day an attendant began to feed our perpetually stuporous patient. At my whispered suggestion, she instead placed the fork in the patient's hand and walked away. The patient picked it up and proceeded to eat entirely on her own.

Within three weeks as the attendants stopped forming the secondary line, all but a few "problem eaters" automatically joined the bulk of the patients. Even the remaining few, who were physically handicapped, ate with the rest, though they received at first the individual attention and help that was essential for them. Not infrequently this help came from fellow patients. As soon as the few backward patients finished eating, attendants would hurriedly remove their plates and tableware and wipe up the tables for them. We discussed this detail, as well, at our seminar, pointing out that even these few markedly regressed patients were able to complete the cycle by returning their dishes to the assigned place in the kitchen alcove. This was easily accomplished, though these patients required reminding to do so for several days to break their habitual conduct.

In the past, patients who finished eating were required to remain in their seats until *all* were ready to line up the utensils and plates. Then they were told to line up. This, naturally, had potentialities for disturbances, as some of them had become bored after finishing their meals and wished to leave the room. We, therefore, suggested that the patients return their utensils to the kitchen alcove individually, upon finishing eating. There was strong demurral from the attendants on this score because they felt it would create "commotion." Their doubts were not justified by later events, for no difficulties whatever arose from this activity, which was ultimately therapeutic in that it fostered individual initiative rather than amorphous group action.

Perhaps the value of this innovation would be best illustrated by a situation that confronted us at the one visit at supper one evening. At the termination of the meal all the patients remained seated, and the night nurse in charge, who stood facing them, called up, in military fashion, each row of tables. The patients thereupon stood up, formed a line, and returned their utensils. When these patients were finished, the next row was called. Since there were six rows of tables, all the others sat immobilely and waited for their turn to be called up, a procedure that took a considerable amount of time.

163

The changes in the dining hall were not achieved without strong resistance from the attendants, the staff of Ward B being the most resistant of all, to all our efforts. The three cooperative attendants on Ward A responded to the changes with great alacrity, but were uncertain as to *modus operandi* to achieve the intended results, especially in making the so-called problem eaters more self-reliant. For a time they faltered and frequently reverted to the old procedures when a patient would become intractable or dawdled at her meal. This tendency to shortcuts required sharp vigilance on our part and frequent reinforcement of the new approach by many repetitions at the seminar sessions and in personal contacts. Perhaps only one of numerous instances of resistance would make the point palpable.

Our most stony-faced attendant, who was supposed to be in charge of the problem eaters on her ward, came in with an extremely withdrawn woman whom she led *by the wrist* to the supply table, and proceeded to prepare a tray for her. I whispered to her that she replace the tray and see what the patient would do. The latter remained standing perplexed. After about three minutes, I quietly suggested that the attendant tell the patient to take a tray and silver. Once told, the patient, almost with alacrity, gathered up a tray and utensils and proceeded to fetch her dinner entirely on her own. The patient had apparently been confused by a hitherto unaccustomed situation and all she needed was to be stirred into action rather than lulled into inertia by the attendant remaining completely passive. This is an apt demonstration of lack of judgment that was characteristic of almost every one on our staff in all categories.

Institutional Garb

The problem that defied our efforts more than any other was the bedraggled appearance our patients presented. The motley crumpled dresses that were available to all but a few, who had clothes supplied by their families, maximized and intensified the already strong feelings of worthlessness and unattractiveness that dominated the minds of the women, at the same time greatly detracting from the total aspect of the wards. In view of the many other pressing details in reorienting attitudes, making new arrangements for the ward life, and introducing activities, we were compelled to delay raising this question with the staff. When we came around to it, numerous and conflicting reactions and ideas ensued. We discovered that the laundry staff supplied dresses haphazardly. Sizes of the garments did not always conform to the sizes of the wearers and the resulting appearance did not favor "personal pride" or self-regard. Once the matter was raised, there was instantaneous and interested response. All the staff seemed to be aware of the problem, even if this awareness may have lain dormant, and we were puzzled as to why no steps had been taken to remedy the situation in the many past decades. The only explanation was indifference on everyone's part.

After a number of lengthy discussions we evolved a plan of coordinating with the laundry to supply dresses in sizes needed by the patients. This considerably alleviated the sordid situation but only for a short period, when gradual deterioration set in. After some months had passed the patients were to be seen with the selfsame aspect that they had before our efforts. We took the matter up again with the staff, always in the hope that the nurses, the older attendants or the chief administrator would become cognizant of the situation and follow through on the arrangements. This matter was actually outside of our jurisdiction and should have been in the hands of the administration. The attendants, too, could not have been held responsible for the nefarious condition, since their job was to carry out the details on the wards with the materials supplied them. It is contrary to the traditions of mental hospitals for the lower echelon to make demands, offer criticism or volunteer suggestions. Should anyone have the affrontery to do so, he is considered "difficult" and his job advancement is thereby impeded.

We, therefore, brought up the matter periodically at the seminar in the presence of the administrators, as a move to activate improvement in the garb supplied to our patients. Some changes had apparently been made with a second setback. At the third return to the subject, since the improvements that had been instituted for the second time had again not been maintained through neglect and indifference, we pressed the situation more vigorously. Finally, the chief administrator undertook to enter into the situation and informed us at a later session that, "according to the laundry people," if we wished to have the patients' dresses properly cared for, they would have to be sent down in special baskets ordinarily reserved for privately owned clothes of patients, instead of following the standard practice (which was to throw them down the chute). From this point on, we left the matter in the hands of the administrator and the personnel in charge of the wards.

The improved appearance of the patients and their expressions of gratification over it during the periods when their clothing was in a better state was indeed striking. Everyone who had known the wards in the past never failed to remark on the improvement. When the matter was discussed at the luncheon meeting with the supervisory staff, universal enthusiasm prevailed over the salutary physical appearance of the patients and its good effect upon their mood. This effect was produced in individuals not only by their own more attractive raiments, but at the sight of each other. The total outcome was a generally pleasing appearance which fitted the soothing climate of the wards and could not but raise spirits and calm turmoil within. However, despite all our efforts and the periodic recounting in great detail of the steps to be taken for continuing these (as well as most other) improvements, regressions began to set in, which were entirely due to the indifference of the persons responsible for the wards.

It was simpler to blame the laundry staff, who had no connection whatsoever with the ward life and were in no way involved with or concerned about the patients. It was obviously the responsibility of the "ward charges," specifically the nurses, to pursue the matter and press upon the laundry staff their various needs. However, no one was sufficiently interested or courageous enough to take up the patients' cause in this regard, so that to prevent a rift in our relation with the staff we finally had to accept this situation as inevitable.

The problem was not limited to dresses alone. The coats the patients were compelled to wear on their winter walks were a conglomerate of sizes, colors and styles that made our patients look like the proverbial Coxey's Army. In fact some of the women wore men's overcoats. Just where these garments came from was a mystery, though it was quite likely that some male patients or attendants had contributed them; not having anything else, patients would wear them against the cold. One very bright and rather attractive young woman in a man's overcoat once somewhat ostentatiously looked at me accusingly, as though to say, "See what they are doing to me." There were not enough coats to go around for all the patients and several had to take turns in using the same garment, a situation that provoked many conflicts and even physical fights over possession. This matter, too, we referred to the administration, but the situation was never fully remedied, possibly also because of limited funds.

The problem of shoes, as well, gave us reason for concern. To some extent it was caused by patients mislaying or throwing them through the outer porch grating to the lawn three flights below, where they were inevitably lost. Partially as a result of this, patients walked around the wards barefoot or in stockings, even during winter months, or wore unmatched shoes. At one point, at a seminar session, when we brought this situation up, the decision was made that all patients be supplied with labelled sneakers of the proper size. The staff were to "encourage" them to keep these in their lockers to prevent appropriation by others. Despite these precautions, losses and misplacements were reported and some patients continued to throw their footwear onto the lawns. At one of the discussions I suggested that wire mesh with smaller openings, such as chicken wire, be put up, that would prevent the tossing out of shoes. The attendants voted against this and we accepted their decision.

CHANGE IN VISITING LOCALE

We observed the inconvenience patients and their relatives experienced during visits to the wards, where they had to sit huddled in small groups in close proximity to other groups and endure the many distractions and disturbances of other patients moving about and talking, shouting and screaming. There was little opportunity for intimate conversation or affective closeness possible in such congestion, tumult and public exposure. Patients could be seen standing near the family groups either listening or breaking into their conversations. During visiting hours, particularly on Sundays, the wards were crowded with people and a motley array of pots and dishes laden with food, scattered paper bags and other debris, resembling a market-place. Only 10 steps away was the cheerful, well-lit, large dining room with small tables and chairs, unused at the time.

I raised the question of visitors at one of the seminars and the obvious tensions generated in the patients that often proved troublesome to the staff during and, even more so, after the visits and into the following day. I also pointed out that the patients who had no visitors (and these were in the majority) could not but be unhappy about their neglect and abreact to their feelings. During the ensuing discussion, it occurred to me that the dining room would be an ideal place in which patients and their relatives could visit together. The suggestion was unanimously accepted and proved a great boon, both for patients who were fortunate enough to have visitors and to their families, as well as to the patients who were "unvisited." The latter now had the wards to themselves and could engage in suitable activities and diversions which we later provided for them.

One of these which met with warm response was bingo, but instead of offering, as in the past, standard prizes of trinkets that were of no value to residents on a hospital ward, the prizes now consisted of small sums of money and cigarettes. These were greatly appreciated as almost all of our patients had very little financial resources and many none at all. Their winnings, therefore, had a tangible value for them. They verbalized their joy for now they had money to buy candy and precious cigarettes, which enhanced their enjoyment of the game. We also recommended the game be modified so that instead of the usual single winner, several would be allowed to win.[3]

When the dining hall was opened to them, each family quite automatically settled around a table, quietly conversing with the patient, partaking of the food which was invariably brought in. In the early period of the program and before the patients quieted down, outbursts of screaming and fights with their relatives continued to occur as they did on the wards. Much to the discomfiture of everyone present, patients would suddenly begin to scream at their parents, accusing them of indignities and neglect.

Two attendants from each ward were assigned to supervise the proceedings in the dining hall and we assumed that they would help quieting such outbreaks. However, they remained completely impassive when these outbursts occurred, permitting the disturbances to mount and spread by contagion. On a number of occasions I demonstrated ways of dealing with such incidents and briefly discussed them at the seminars. One of the techniques we found effective was to ask the patient and her visitors to withdraw to the conference room or another of the smaller rooms off the wards, where they could have privacy. In *all* instances, when this was tried, the conflicts instantaneously subsided.

In time, the dining hall remained perfectly tranquil during visiting hours and it became a subject for comment how all the 24 tables would be occupied by small family groups in quiet conversation, with the patients eating the food and goodies their relatives always brought for them. The privacy and quiet favored a degree of freedom among the patients and their relatives, who seemed to display greater warmth of feeling than they could when crowded and on public display on the wards. Part of

[3] This is one more instance of the adherence to traditionalism and lack of imagination by staff. We always wondered of what value trinkets, doodads, combs and purses could have to these confined women, beyond the infantile joy derived from the magic of winning.

the reason for these developments can undoubtedly be attributed to diminishing tensions and hostilities in the patients resulting from the more sanguine life-setting and the increased ego strengths to better control emotions. In fact, the dining hall presented the appearance of a friendly indoor picnic with the various family groups sharing food in friendly communion. Parents and relatives happily remarked on the patients' improved behavior and expressed their gratification at the changed location for their visitations.

In the past, a major source of friction between patients and their families was their demands that they be taken home. Some asked for brief visits, others wanted to leave the hospital for good. Because of the disturbance they created in their home, their requests were not met and much unpleasantness had arisen from this source. However, as the patients grew more content on the wards, these demands upon their families as well as on the psychiatrists, almost completely disappeared. This fact was commented on by the psychiatrists themselves and by state officials who had visited the wards.

The relatives' increased pleasure in visiting patients also increased their number and the frequency of visitations. Now that the unpleasant encounters diminished and in most cases completely disappeared, families frequented the hospital more often. Dr. Beckenstein, who usually dropped in on the wards during visiting hours, commented on the impressive changes in the climate, in the relationship among patients and their relatives, and on the vastly larger number of visitors. He had several times canvassed reactions to the changes and without exception the visitors were very gratified; many had voluntarily come up to him to express their pleasure. Because of the marked improvement in the patients, parents and other relatives began to evince greater willingness to take them home for weekends, and two years later, for sojourns for as long as three months and longer, and after three-and-one-half years, for permanent return home in a considerable number of cases. Whereas in the past the patients had been completely sequestered from their homes and communities, now, as their behavior was more normal and they grew more reality-oriented, they were given the opportunity to rejoin their families and neighborhoods.

One of the problems we attempted to solve, but with little success, was the relatives' practice of feeding heavy ethnic foods to the patients soon after a substantial mid-day meal, almost to the point of force-feeding them. On the few occasions when I was present during visiting hours, I attempted to explain to some of the parents the inadvisability of this practice, but found them to be completely unresponsive, stemming as they did, from cultures where food was a symbol of interest and love. Since the food ritual seemed to allay guilts, they were unable to accept or heed our demurral, but would refrain from force-feeding while I was within sight only to resume it as soon as my back was turned. On many occasions we discussed the merits of having meetings with parents after visiting hours, but these never materialized.

OFF-WARD ACTIVITIES

Gym Activities.

Before the activities on the wards were introduced, the patients were for the most part kept in the confinement of their locked wards. However, some diversions had been supplied from time to time to a select number, but even here they usually played only a spectator role. For entertainment, a band consisting of a piano, a drum and occasionally a cornet, would play popular songs once or twice a week for 30 minutes on each ward. As already indicated, the music was extremely loud, almost raucous. A few of the patients would burst forth for a brief interval in a dance—usually solo, unless a staff member, though never an attendant other than the two very young women, would join in. Irregularly a group of 10 to 20 patients, in better contact, would be taken for brief strolls on the grounds under the rigid and militarylike supervision of attendants. Some of the women were infrequently taken to the gym where they would try to toss a ball into the basket, never succeeding.

Holders of "honor cards"[4] were allowed to go on their own, but were restricted to the general store and the common lounge, in another building, where male and female patients congregated and sat impassively while some men (patients and staff) played pool.

A visit to the gym—which proved to be a very commodious bare conventional gymnasium containing only a basketball rack and rough-hewn benches strung alongside one long wall—revealed a dozen or so women from our wards sitting immobile in a row. The male instructor called upon each of the middle-aged and stout women who rose obediently and heavily. Each was handed the ball with instructions to toss it into the basket. This each one did mechanically once, without a word or a change in the bored expression on her face. Having done so, she as mechanically returned to her seat. Not one of the women had succeeded in placing the ball. The odd feature of this performance was that the instructor boasted of his ability to "activate patients."

In discussing the possibilities of the uses to which such a large and bright room could be put in our project, we suggested, among other things, music, and involving the overweight participants in dancing, specially designed calisthenics to musical accompaniment, and active group games that would, in addition to physical exercise, lift the spirits of these largely depressed women, and inject an element of gaiety into their morose lives. These suggestions, however, were accepted as criticism of the existing recreation practices and skills of its staff. All we got for our pains was increased enmity and resistance.

More than a year later and quite on her own, Miss Kralides ("Miss Nikki") initiated such a plan, when she was assigned to our project, a year after its initiation. Being uninformed of its aims at the time, she submitted a detailed traditional hourly schedule of recreational activities on and off the wards, suitable, as we told her, for "a girls' private school." We outlined

[4] These were issued on instruction from the psychiatrist to patients who were considered "trustworthy," and revoked in cases of infractions.

172

lined to her our approach in encouraging spontaneity and free choice by patients, emphasizing developmental and therapeutic values rather than just "busy work." Because of her educational and cultural background and. I believe, largely due to a personal disposition, she immediately grasped our intent, and scrapping the sheets on which her extensive program was outlined, she proceeded to follow the patients' interests and readiness as individuals and members of groups.

She arranged for once a week bowling and twice a week light exercises and sports in the gymnasium. These were conducted in cooperation with a member of the recreational personnel of which she had been a member for eight years. Patients were told when there would be bowling and "gymnastics." About 10 patients from each ward voluntarily joined the bowling group and about 15 from each ward chose the gym. An attendant accompanied patients to these activities in each case and remained with them. For a few sessions Miss K. observed the activities conducted by the recreation instructor and reported that there was very little participation on the part of patients. Some were pacing, others were looking for cigarettes, still others sat on the floor. At her suggestion the recreation instructor introduced music as the patients were doing their exercises. Miss K. played the piano for them and, being an advanced student of music, improvised according to the spontaneous movements, such as shaking, bouncing, swinging and swaying, pushing and pulling, bending and stretching. She reported that this particular recreation instructor grasped her intent and "was very good with the patients. He always had a pleasant smile and there was good rapport between them."

In December 1965, Miss K. described one of the typical bowling games in which eight patients from Ward A and ten from Ward B participated together. The patients from A were more active and took greater initiative. Teams of four patients from each of the two wards organized *themselves* into teams and played "against" each other. However, at our suggestion, the scores were purposely ignored by her, in an attempt to

173

avoid competition and the inevitable "defeat" of one or the other team.[5] Each play stood on its own merits and no criticism or unsolicited instruction was given the players. The fact that they were interested in voluntary participation and had the experience of cooperating with teammates and relating to residents of a different ward, held sufficient value in such games. The latter was particularly important since what appeared to us as enigmatic antagonism between the staffs of the two wards had been automatically communicated to the respective groups of patients.

These feelings had been somewhat diminished with the unlocking of the doors and resulting patients' visits to each others' wards. Otherwise they were strictly separated at all activities, in seating in the dining hall and all community affairs. Miss K., working as she did on both wards, and being convinced of the value of widening the perimeters of human relations for the patients, had done much to bridge the psychologic chasm that had been artificially created between the wards.

Unfortunately Miss K. could not continue with this offward work because she had to remain on the wards most of the time where the bulk of the patients needed her attention. The work was continued without her, however, and according to reports from the attendants, the patients were enjoying the gym activities more than they ever did before and much more so than the bowling.

During the ensuing four months on visits to the gym, Miss K. found more and more varied participation and greater enthusiasm. Patients were engaged in different activities. Some were throwing the ball into the basket, some were punching the punching bag, others were spontaneously marching to music. This part of the program had to be postponed for many months because of needed repairs to the floors of the rather ancient building where the gym was located.

[5] For a fuller discussion of the rationale and procedures, see S. R. Slavson (1937), *Creative Group Education*, New York Association Press, Ch. XV, "The Gymnasium and the Competitive Spirit." *Idem: Character Education in a Democracy*, New York Association Press, 1939, Ch. IX, "Education for Social Action: Group Co-Activity vs. Inter-Group Activity." *Idem: Recreation and the Total Personality*, 1948.

THE "RECREATION LOUNGE"

About three months after Miss K. joined the project, she was walking with a group of about 15 patients in the tunnel passage between buildings and dropped in to the small recreational lounge, which was unoccupied at the moment. This is a small, well-appointed room separated from the active part of the hospital. She had observed that the interest in activities on the wards was beginning to pall after 15 months. There was occupational therapy, but by now it engaged a smaller number of the patients, largely because of the stereotyped, unchanged materials and failure by unimaginative personnel to devise strategies for keeping interest alive.

By now the unchanged table games also began to recede in patients' interests, and the television occupied only one or two patients at a time. She, therefore, conceived the idea of introducing additional activities that would lend variety and thus activate interest. As a first step, she announced in January, 1966, on each of the wards, that there would be activities offered in the recreation lounge three mornings a week: Tuesday, Wednesday and Friday. (Thursday mornings were taken up with the staff seminar and Monday mornings with bowling.) When the announcement was made, some of the patients asked her what activities would be offered in the lounge. Miss K. enumerated light sports like horseshoes, bean bags, recorded music, and arts and crafts materials. (An additional reason for introducing this project was that due to the subway strike in New York during that month, most of the attendants were kept away from the hospital. Only a few were able to report to work and they had to be fetched by the hospital vehicles. The removal of patients from the wards was, therefore, helpful.)

As the project in the lounge continued, the number of patients who joined steadily increased until it was doubled, so that within a few weeks there were 30 patients who regularly came to the lounge. Whenever possible, an attendant would help Miss K. However, because of the dearth of staff, she usually took charge of the activities entirely by herself. The patients were at first rather fearful. Although they seemed to like the atmosphere, the free cigarettes and the coffee, they were frightened at being in a new environment as a result of their confinement to their wards for years and shied away from the activities offered them. After two weeks their apprehensions disappeared, however, and they participated freely from then on.

The typical picture in the room was as follows: a group of patients were listening to and singing familiar songs, sometimes played on the piano by Miss K., but most often by one of the patients. Another group was working with clay. A few women were painting with watercolors. The most regressed were tossing about the medicine ball and threw the horseshoes. Very few were attracted by table games, which they also had on the wards. There was considerable interest in bingo. The ordinary table games required the participation of a staff member, except for cards. This game patients initiated by themselves and continued playing on their own. Bingo, as well, was taken over entirely by the patients, as one of them called out the numbers without any mishaps or conflicts. Four patients who usually did nothing but pace the floors on the wards did so also in the recreation lounge, but they would occasionally stop to either watch a game or take part in one briefly, then resume their pacing. Patients would stop pacing long enough to help with the serving of coffee and cookies or setting up the cups and saucers. When a drama project was introduced about this time, most of the costumes had been made in the recreation lounge by these patients.

The procedure employed was to prepare the setting for the activities by exposing in advance the materials on tables, so that when the patients came in they would seat themselves at a table of their choosing on which specific materials had been laid out, and quietly continue to work. One of the stimuli was graphic art materials that were laid out on a table, consisting of water colors, crayons and paper, and construction paper for cutting and pasting. The development of one of the patients may illustrate this method which was also used on the wards: There were four patients who became particularly interested in art work. These women had never taken part in any of the occupations on the wards; they would withdraw, were always submissive, and to all intents and purposes were "good patients" and none of them ever made any contact with Miss K. on the wards. Being isolated and self-encapsulated they had nothing to do with her. Stimulated by the art materials in the new setting and a nonthreatening small group, one of them produced a very attractive and lively colored bunch of flowers in a vase—a sort of still life. The patient turned to Miss K. and asked her to look at it. Miss K. registered approval facially, and exhibiting the picture to the group said, "Look what a beautiful picture E— has made for us." Very pleased, E— asked Miss K. to display her drawing along with those hanging on the wall, produced by other patients. There was no scotch tape available for the purpose and E——, entirely by herself, devised a way of attaching her picture to another, thus displaying her artistic product.

Since this event E— became very friendly and attached to Miss K. Months later E— decided that Miss K. was her "psychiatrist" and asked her to give her permission to go home. When Miss K. said that she should talk to the psychiatrist about this, E—grew angry and said with emphasis, "You are my psychiatrist. I have no other psychiatrist." A similar development occurred with another patient of the lounge group.

The climate of the room was invariably one of quiet and placidity. Even the small number of patients who were not occupied with a specific activity sat, as was also their wont on the wards, but were obviously happy and relaxed. Some even smiled to themselves contentedly. Miss K. found that the concentration span of the patients was maximally about an hour. Their distractibility was indicated by the increased number of patients pacing the floor. This served Miss K. as a signal for suggesting a walk on the hospital grounds before returning to the wards, which all patients always enjoyed.

However, in view of the fact that our project directed itself toward demonstrating to ward staff a climate suitable for disturbed patients on wards with a large population, removing some from that locale was not in keeping with our aims. Our objective of having Miss K. on the wards was for her to demonstrate procedures with *all* the patients and involve attendants as far as possible, so that they might ultimately take over the work with the patients. We, therefore, regretfully decided that the project in the recreation lounge, invaluable as it was, should be terminated and Miss K. returned to the wards. An added factor in making this decision was an undercurrent of resentment against this project and against Miss K. on the part of the occupational therapy staff, who felt that they were placed in a less advantageous position by remaining on the wards. Soon after the termination of the reception lounge project, the occupational therapy people suggested that they, too, segregate small groups to work with in the conference room (which could have accommodated at most six patients) thereby depriving the larger number of these essential activities. Of this we shall speak later.

The significance of this short-lived enterprise lay in a number of directions. First is the fact that it confirmed our contention that 65 patients were excessive for creating a fully effective therapeutic working and living climate; it also confirmed the thesis that patients, as indeed most of us, participate better and enjoy activities more fully when these are self-chosen rather than assigned, or when persons are cajoled into doing them; it proved that creative and voluntary interests in a proper setting favor emergence not only of creative powers, but also of relationships as demonstrated by E—— and others not included in our report, and that ingenuity and problem-solving are stimulated under favorable circumstances, which have immense value in bringing patients to confront reality, thereby diminishing their psychotic state and arresting its process.

Walks, Trips and Excursions

An appropriate means for extending the narrow perimeter of the world in which residents of an institution live, and helping them toward more reality testing, are trips and excursions. It was with this conviction that we urged upon the staff such outings for patients the first summer (1964) before we had begun the ward activities program. But the list compiled by the staff in free discussion was relegated to the paper on which it was detailed, for due to our absence abroad, none had the interest or initiative to put it in operation. Perhaps there were some extenuating circumstances that may have contributed to this neglect, such as reduction of staff due to summer vacations. Our expectation, derived from predictions by staff members of various departments, including the different chauffeurs who had driven me to and from the hospital, that the patients on our two wards would be uncontrollable in the summer, as was always the case in the past, did not materialize. Nor had this occurred in the summer of 1965 when plans for off-ground trips had also been ignored and were limited to routine walks on the grounds and the streets in the vicinity of the hospital.

Our plan included visits by small groups to communal, natural or industrial centers of interest, and would be followed by discussions by the participants of observations and reactions. After not too long an interval, a visit to the same scenes would be made by the same group with another follow-up discussion so that patients could become aware of features they may have overlooked on the first visit. The aim of this procedure was to increase patients' awareness of physical reality and thereby heighten their interest in it.

During the latter summer (1965) we had utilized to great advantage "area nine" where patients could enjoy the outdoors in pleasant, sunny surroundings, and in relaxed leisurely activities. "Area nine" was a large enclosure on the hospital grounds with tables and benches under shady trees and a concrete walk that could be used for such games as shuffleboard. Entire ward populations with their full complement of staff were encouraged to spend a good part of the sunny mornings in this pleasant retreat. Patients were free to spend the time as befitted their fancies with attendants and recreationists in readiness to help them with whatever activity they chose. Thus some patients played cards, others read newspapers or magazines, a few indulged in light sports, and a number lay on benches dozing. On the whole, the spectacle struck one that, if it were not for their shab-

179

by dresses, this was an outing of an ordinary group of women on a summer day.

The striking effectiveness of an outdoor trip of a large group of patients was demonstrated on Ward A which, one morning before our first Christmas holiday (about six weeks after the start of the program), seemed restless and could not settle down to work. There was a tense atmosphere and much milling around. A number of patients were being noisy, making strange sounds. We therefore suggested to the attendant in charge that the patients who were not engaged in activities at the tables should be taken out for a walk. When they returned they seemed much quieter, and when seen during and after lunch that followed they behaved in an exemplary manner. They acted in a fully responsible manner when it came to getting food or returning dishes and trays, and seemed relaxed and quiet afterwards. This technique we have described as "Interruption Technique," but instead of applying it with individuals, in this case it proved effective with a rather large group. The changes in self-control and social development are reflected in the following telling entry in our diary a year later, recorded under the date of December 6, 1965: "Patients on both wards now form their own groups of four and six and go on walks unsupervised."

Trips and excursions took on quite a different character under Miss Kralides's dedicated guidance. During her first summer's incumbency, she made the trips a joyous experience for the patients. While it seemed impossible to carry out the full program we designed, the walks in the neighborhood and the weekly outings by small groups of about 12 patients to a large municipal park a considerable distance from the hospital, the picnic lunches, the ball tossing and playing, the singing she had introduced, and the freedom of moving about unrestricted by apprehensive, untrusting attendants, all served to evoke a character hitherto unknown to our deprived, denigrated, oversuspicious, infantilized patients. No wonder, therefore, that incidents such as the following occurred.

One morning when I stepped out of the elevator, I encountered a group of patients waiting to descend on their way for a trip. Among them was Hannah (the patient with the most typical and classical psychotic face, who endlessly paced back and forth the full length of Ward A—that is, when she was not lying on the floor asleep or out of contact, periodically emitting ear-splitting screeches). Hannah had not left the hospital grounds for years and only very seldom could she be induced to take a turn around the hospital campus. Her preoccupied facial expression, which was always seedy, disgruntled and angry, was now shining with an inner light, and on seeing me she exclaimed, "I'm in heaven! I am going for a walk!" Miss K. later reported that not once had she had any difficulty with any patient on these walks and outings in almost two years, after which time she left the hospital for another job. The relationships she had established with the patients, her smiling kindness and affection were recognized by them and they responded in kind.

The following saga of a trip to Coney Island, the famous New York playground on the beaches of the Atlantic Ocean, would make tangible the possibilities an activity holds in the hands of a resourceful, devoted guide. As the variety of trips expanded, the patients grew more courageous and more enterprising. One dramatic by-product of ward activities was that one of our extremely difficult patients, who had heretofore been indiscriminately assaultive and a frequent runaway, became our talented "poet laureate". It was she who suggested a "Trip to Coney Island," a former hangout of hers, where she had lived as a derelict and had become pregnant.

One morning in talking to Miss Kralides, she suggested a "small number of patients" be taken to the beach. Miss K. responded by saying that the idea was wonderful and that she would do her best to arrange it. Following the practice we suggested, Miss K. introduced the idea to the staffs of both wards. Ward meetings were then held and the patients welcomed the idea.

During the meetings there were many who impulsively expressed a desire to go along. However, Miss K. suggested that the number be limited for each trip and that two attendants would accompany the group. She assumed the responsibility for arranging suitable garb for the entire group, and each patient undertook to prepare her own picnic lunch. Of the many who at first expressed a desire to join the group, only the more intact, who successfully could carry out the various responsibilities remained. The final group comprised 22 women, consisting of about an equal number from each of the two wards. One of the patients from Ward B had baked, on her own initiative, a large cake for the occasion.

The group who left at 11:00 a.m. on the hospital bus was described as looking "very attractive in their clean and ironed dresses and all appeared happy." During the trip, the patients were singing under the direction of the most assertive patient in the group. [This patient also directed the chorus in one of the plays given by the patients.]

The patients on their own began planning a program of activities when they arrived at the beach. Some of the suggestions were ball playing, buying drinks (each with her own money) to which the hospital added 25 cents), going swimming. Some had no bathing suits and planned to rent them. However, upon arrival they discovered that there were none available. Only eight patients had bathing suits and were able to go into the surf. Four of these had brought their own, and four were supplied by Miss K. Only those who fitted into the suits were, therefore, able to go into the water. [The suits had been tried on by the patients before they had left the hospital.] Our most irascible patient from Ward A could not fit into any of them and plunged into the surf up to her neck with all her clothes on. The staff refrained from commenting on her act.

When she emerged from the water, the wind was blowing and skies grew cloudy making the temperature chilly. The patient complained of feeling cold and the staff wrapped her in the blankets which were brought along, while patients volunteered to hold her clothes up in the wind to accelerate drying. Withal there was a mood of hilarity, joking, and laughing while this was going on. Miss K. was the only one of the staff in a bathing suit. While the bathers frolicked in the water with Miss K., the other patients played cards by themselves, some helping with the preparations for lunch. A few went off to "explore the neighborhood." Before they left, Miss K. told them that lunch would be served at one o'clock and all returned punctually. The return home was one of cheer, fun and good fellowship with the patients asking for a repetition, which was arranged some time later.

The good fellowship, feeling of belonging and the relationships the patients experienced on an outing such as this, when repeated frequently, could become a basis for psychosocial development. But it must be kept in mind that this effect cannot be created when the humanizing elements are omitted, such as self-initiation, participation and sharing which always flow from the leader, in this case the staff member in charge. Another type of "trip," by another kind of leader will illustrate this point.

Walking trips in the neighborhood were usually peaceful affairs, though at times a disturbed patient would create difficulties, although never one that could not be managed. The trip on which we shall report was suggested and undertaken by a professionally trained staff member. *She* suggested the trip; *she* determined its direction and its objective, which in this case was a five-and-ten cent store. We shall describe the developments in her own words as recorded on tape.

Well, it wasn't too much shopping, more window shopping, but it was a good experience for them because they saw the prices of things and they were so surprised how expensive clothes were. We did go to the five-and-ten because K— wanted some shoe dye, and she is one of the girls [sic] who can go shopping on her own, but really does not know how to buy. She had the experience of having the things that she bought at the five-and-ten shrink. And I had suggested to her that *she ask for permission* to either go downtown or to New York [Manhattan]. She has been to New York, but she has not gone shopping. She will not talk very much about the trip. But they [the patients] were glad to see the five-and-ten.

I suggested that they look around, you know, look at the various things in the five-and-ten, but they were interested in the candy counter. They had candy on sale. So *I bought* a bag of candy for them and they shared it. And they started to have a little argument in the five-and-ten because Y— told E— that she owns it [the candy]; it did not belong to all of them.

183

So *I said*, "Ladies, let's not draw attention to ourselves, and let's quiet down." And then we left. And we went around on C— Avenue. Well, one of the problems I found is that they wanted to pick up the long cigarette butts on the street. *I explained* that it's not quite sanitary. And of course *I gave out* my cigarettes. I think that with the next group *I'll suggest* that they make cigarettes before we go, so that they'll each have enough to last them.

"Now C— wanted to leave soon after she bought the shoe dye and she read the directions and she said that she needed to remove the old color of the shoes. This wasn't right. And I began *to be a little worried* about her because she gets a very sick look in her eyes and they tell me that when she gets this look there's trouble. So I suggested, *I said,* "Well I have dyed many shoes," and *I said* "Let's try it a little bit on one section of the shoe where it won't show too much." And she said, "Well I think I'll go back. I have an honor card." And *I said,* "Well *you signed out with me*." She said, "But I have an honor card." *I said,* "Well, all right, then go back." So the group said to her, "We're going back anyway, so why don't you come with us?" So we walked down to 46th Street, and then they decided they wanted to walk that street back.

Well, N— wanted to go further down but the group objected so we started back. Now, E—, a girl in this group that occasionally runs away and goes home but she comes back soon after . . . and she got very tired and complained that it was very warm, and *I said* to her, *"What do you want to go back to that stinky* [!] *old ward for?"* And she said, "It's not stinky and I wear a coat up there. There's a lot of fresh air blowing back and forth." And she insisted, "Let's go back." So we walked back and when we got to the . . . oh, along the way they wanted to help themselves to the various roses and flowers belonging to the public, you know, to the people in the block, so *I said,* "No, this is private property, you can't touch it, just look at it and enjoy it."

So when we got back to the hospital, *I said,* "Well let's sit out a little bit longer under one of the trees." They still wanted to come upstairs. Well, they got very thirsty, and a few of them went in for a drink of water.

One of the amazing things to me was that G—, now she is one of the women who gets involved with the wine and the [alcohol] drinking and I didn't think she would want to go with this group, and she said yes, she would go along, but when we started she said, "Well, I'll leave you at 49th Street in the hospital area." *I said,* "Oh no you won't, because *you signed out with me* and I'm responsible." So she went along, and she didn't want to come back up. She sat on the ground, and sat there for a little while and they [the patients] continued saying, "Well, let's go upstairs."

Then C— finally left. She said, "I have my honor card." And she went up. So after about 10 more minutes of this, *I said*, "Well let's take a vote on it." And they voted on whether the group should go up or not. And they voted to go up, so we all went up. And I had promised them that *they could go again* on Friday.

And another thing that stimulated interest was that Miss B— [one of the few dedicated attendants] suggested that I go downstairs and get the proper clothing for them, dresses, so a few girls [patients] who weren't going on the walk also went down for clothes and so that they all looked nice, and *I suggested* that they keep these dresses for Friday's outing and that perhaps we could go to F—Avenue and stop and have pizza and a soda. So a few of the girls asked me if we were really going, and C—again now, who has her honor card [and therefore could go out by herself] but it seems like she's interested in going with the group. She asked me again this morning [Thursday] if we'd go tomorrow.

The psychiatrist's reaction to this narration is equally revealing. He said:

Now this is very instructive because it reveals the fact, which we've mentioned before, that the patients find for many reasons that the hospital is a very secure place for them. And it isn't that we're keeping them prisoners. They are. They don't want to leave. As bad as the ward may seem to us, or as bad as it may seem to us if we put ourself in their place, to them it represents security and they don't want to leave. So here they have an opportunity to go a short distance from the hospital where they don't have any responsibility, and it's not very complicated from our point of view, and they wanted to get back to the ward as soon as possible. And they'll give you all kinds of rationalizations why they want to get back.

The episodes occurred, unbelievably, in the third summer of our project—almost two years after it was initiated—and reveals how tenacious a mental set and an ingrained habit can be. The leader of this outing was a person who was professionally trained to "supervise" activity and to "get results." To her a patient was an individual who had to work and produce in her (the staff member's) particular speciality; only then did everything go well with the patient. Patients' inner lives and growth did not seem to concern her. [It was this woman who was elated when a new psychiatrist once revoked all (humanizing) "privileges" unless patients participated in occupational ("therapy.") In addition, her conduct had a destructive effect on patients. Of this she was completely unaware. The project from beginning to end disregarded the autonomy of the individual and lack of respect for human beings, which would be unsuitable even in a custodial agency.

Perhaps the best way one could characterize this humorless, perpetually angry woman is by the fact that in the year of our association I have never, nor has anyone else, seen her smile while on the job. Unfortunately, she held a central position in our activity program, and through her power and assertiveness managed to cause the ultimate decline of our program.

The psychiatrist's reaction to this woman's conduct with the group is equally nonunderstandable. It is quite possible that to some of the patients—especially the long-term aged residents—the hospital may represent security. But he missed the point when he failed to recognize that the group had been in rebellion against their "leader" who took over all their functions as thinking, willing human beings. She constantly "told them," made decisions, admonished for what she considered as "bad" behavior, disapproved of their conduct, determined the destination and route of the trip and opposed their desire to return to the hospital and to the ward until she was defeated by them. The doctor failed to recognize even that the only time the staff member could get some cohesiveness and group action was when she permitted self-determination to the group in voting on their preference between sitting vacuously on a bench outdoors, or returning to some of the occupations that may have been going on, on the ward.

The fact that she volunteered the suggestion to have another walk indicates that she had not become aware of the patients' antagonism toward her throughout the trip, which culminated in her being rejected when the group voted against her and returned to the ward. Nor did she become aware—and the traditionally trained and practicing psychiatrist did not help her with this—that had she used a democratic, participatory approach from the outset, as did Miss K., with whom she was acquainted, she may not have had as much trouble with the patients.

The validity as a living and therapeutic instrumentality of the democratic-humanistic approach in contradistinction to that employed in the above episode will become even more palpable through the following section dealing with "playmaking."

PLAYMAKING

The first play was given by Miss Kralides in March of 1965, about five months after the ward activity program was initiated, and before she was assigned to our two wards. [6] It grew out of the patients' own suggestions during the time when she visited the wards once a week for an hour on Tuesday mornings. She introduced her work through a group of seven patients who voluntarily joined in singing. These seven had known her before from another building.

Miss K. had been described to us as "a person of many talents and facilities," who could give one hour a week to our project. As the first step in introducing her program, she had a moveable piano brought in and at times used an auto-harp and a victrola, the latter being a very cheap, ill-sounding affair. As she played these instruments unobtrusively, patients gradually gravitated toward her, the number of which grew to between 12 and 15 on each ward. As she made a point of playing commonly known popular songs with "catchy" melodies and lilt, the patients spontaneously burst into singing. After a time they have shown a sustaining interest in these musical hours and some displayed real enthusiasm. Miss K. then suggested that they might form a singing group and asked for volunteers. The same

[6] An incident illustrative of the reputation of our wards occurred at a discussion conducted by Miss K. with a group of about 40 actively participating patients from other wards on "Mental Illness," in an astonishingly frank treatment of the subject. During the interchange, she asked whether some of the patients would care to take part in a play she was planning to rehearse with Wards A and B. They refused, stating that they found "visiting on those wards very depressing." The opinion of these wards was later changed as the "most interesting" in the hospital to which patients from other wards asked to be transferred.

seven patients who had known her previously joined at once, the others still remained wary of her and too frightened at this stage of making direct contact with a "strange" person.

After some weeks, one member of the singing group suggested that they give a play which she had seen Miss K. direct in the other building (with fairly healthy patients). Others joined this nucleus of the project after scheduled rehearsals began on the wards. At the behest of the instructor, the central theme of the play was chosen by the patients themselves, which was "spring," the season during which the play was to be presented, and was an adaptation of a one-act children's play. This was gradually revised and elaborated as rehearsals proceeded. In its final context, the play included elves, snow drops, flowers of the year, to be personified by members of the group, and several songs about spring. The story dealt with the seasons: "when spring comes the winds and the snow drops disappear, giving way to warmth and sunshine."

By the time the play was ready for presentation, the number of participating patients rose to 24. However, because of the condition of the patients at the time, the central roles, requiring understanding of the subject matter and consistent carrying through of a part, Miss K. found it necessary to bring in a few patients in better contact from another building.

Because of the size of the group and its many activities, the rehearsal locale was now transferred to the smaller recreation lounge. In addition to a piano and other necessary equipment, this sunny room also had a private lavatory, a matter of great importance to our patients at that time, before the stalls had been built on our wards.

One day the R.T. worker on a walk with 10 patients, unaware of the progress of the rehearsals, dropped in at the lounge. The patients became profoundly interested in what was going on and remained throughout the rehearsal. As a result, some of them asked to be included in the play. Others joined later. Miss K. continued giving the one hour a week of singing and music on the wards, in addition to the three weekly rehearsals. During one of the musical sessions on Ward A, a patient who had joined the cast asked Miss K. if she would like to have two more recruits. It seemed that she had talked up the play to fellow patients on her ward.

By this time there were 19 of our own patients involved. A week before the presentation, five more patients asked to be included. Miss K. welcomed them and asked them to come down to the rehearsals. Arrangements were accordingly made for them to be "brought down" by an attendant to the lounge, which was four flights lower and involved a complicated walk through a maze of underground tunnels. An interesting phenomenon was that although they asked to be included, three of the five newcomers remained silent during the singing; they just sat there. Overlooking their diffidence, Miss K. treated them as though they were fully participating. She did not urge them to join, nor did she convey any feeling that she expected them to do so—she accepted them on their own terms. As we shall see presently, her strategy bore fruit.

The public performance was given in the dining hall. The patients from both wards sat at the tables with all the chairs turned toward the rear of the room which was cleared of furniture where the chorus was seated facing the audience. The soloists and ballet dancers stayed out of sight in the kitchen alcove before they made their appearance.

Miss K. played the piano which was turned in such a way that she could see the actors and the proceedings. Occasionally she would motion to the cast what to do. However, the patients were for the most part self-directed. They knew their cues and made their entrances on time. They remembered their lines, so that the performance went off without a hitch. Both the singers, the solo dancer and the "corps de ballet" knew when to go on and when to go off. Miss K. had intentionally made the performance brief, not to tax the concentration span of the audience and the participants.

The audience consisted of all the patients but one, Shirley, who remained completely alone on the ward tied to the bench as she always was. When I went through the two wards to see who stayed away, I found her in her usual position, oscillating her right arm in front and the left arm at the side of her face, salivating more profusely than usual with intense fear in her eyes (obviously at the sight of the empty ward and being abandoned) and highly flushed cheeks, which was extraordinary since her complexion always remained sallow and dingy.

The following poems were handed to Miss K. by different patients during the rehearsals: (The first poem was sung by the chorus and was used in the play.)

Snowflakes whirl and dance around, dance around;
Snowflakes fall upon the ground, through the winter.
Now the spring is coming fast, coming fast, coming fast;
Now we know they cannot last, for much longer.
Winter, you must go, your icy reign will soon be past.
Spring's at the window: she'll send you flying fast.
Streams wake with rush and roar, and foaming, race along,
And clear from the tree-tops rings the robin's song.
Winter you must go.
With seed astir on every hand, soft buds unfolding to charm the waiting
    land.

Clouds wander o'er the blue above the quiet plain.
What joys we shall have ere winter comes again.
Look, how the fields are changing: colors bright I see.
Love from the skies arranging. Flowers for you and me.
Shining lilies bless their Giver,
Harebells blue as rushing river.
Perfume and bows exchanging, nodding sweet and free.
Come, let us give them greeting: gladly march and sing,
Buds we are now entreating, generous bloom to bring.
Flower bells ringing, join in praises;
We are friends of pinks and daisies.
Joyfully all are meeting, thanking God for Spring.

The following composition[7] written by one patient and recited by another:

[7] This was written by the patient to whom we had referred as "our Poet Laureate." At this stage she was too frightened to appear even before the limited audience, the members of which she personally knew. As we shall see later, she had read one of her writings before a large general audience in the hospital's assembly hall. Before the project, this patient had been constantly hallucinating and was extremely withdrawn. She was also the one who had, in a rage, thrown the medicine in an attendant's face, coffee in the face of a clerk at the store, slapped the nurse, bit the O.T. worker and kicked me—all in one morning.

EXTENSIONS OF THE PROGRAM

The Kind of Person I Admire

by———

What I admire most in another is Hope, especially in an emotionally disturbed person here in the hospital. Since I've been here, I see so few patients smiling. They seem to have given up fighting or trying.

Without Hope & Love for one another, we are not really living. So few patients on my ward ever actually stop to look out the window at the Beauty of Nature especially at this time of year. Perhaps if they would do this it would have given them More Hope & Love. They would want to try to help themselves to get well.

Some of them feel the medicine will do all the work. But it definitely will not if they lose Hope, So keep Smiling.

The following poem was handed *after the play* to Miss K. (Miss "Nicky") by the author of the foregoing as a personal tribute:

To Miss Nicky

When I feel alone, near yet far from home
Her cheerful air helps me bear
Blue thoughts that that tend to roam
With a welcoming kiss so sweet
Warmed my lonely heart, helped dissolve the clutch of fear
That ensnared me from the start.
Lighting the darkened way
Somewhat every day, some light seeps,
Invades the inner core to stir
Dormant seeds of love which in harvest reaps.

Even before the play emerged, when Miss K. visited our wards on a once-a-week basis, she said that she found the patients "more secure, more outgoing and better related to reality" and to her. She had known the patients for six years through occasional visits and work with them on the wards in connection with various projects and knew some of the small number of the "better" patients who had been involved in the off-ward recreational program. She had made the above observation about two months after the ward activities program had begun

191

and before the various physical amenities had been introduced. Apparently the effects of finding activity interests, the improved attitudes of the attendants and the resulting feelings of self-regard affected the patients' personalities to a noticeable degree even in so short a period. As she worked with them on the play, Miss K. was greatly impressed with the comparative security and ease in relationships among themselves and with the staff.

The second play came into being after Miss K. had transferred from the recreation department and joined our staff full time in October, 1965. At the end of December "Miss Nicky," as she was affectionately known, was playing bingo with a group of patients on Ward B when they asked her if they could have a party. Miss Nicky had agreed with us that the parties that had been held *for* the patients on these wards in the past, and which we had eliminated, had proven overstimulating. The disturbing after-effects usually continued for hours and sometimes days, often resulting in disturbed behavior on the part of some patients. She wondered whether at this point the usual goings-on at a party—the preparing and serving of food and coffee with the loud music playing and the dancing—would not again prove overstimulating. In addition there usually was a shortage of staff during the Christmas and New Year's holidays, and this would make it difficult to manage groups of 65 patients. She felt that it would be better to arrange something that would be less exciting and perhaps more educational and constructive for the patients. She, therefore, suggested that they do something else which they could discuss after the holidays.

On January 3, 1966, during the subway strike, when there was no transportation for the personnel, Miss K. found herself alone on Ward A with two attendants who were busily engaged in household chores. In addition to the absence of the occupational therapist, there were no table games, the latter not having been supplied to us for some months due to some budgetary "mix-up."

The patients were rather subdued, sitting around at various tables and, since there were no materials or games, did nothing. Miss K., who was standing nearby, asked: "What would you like to do to make life happier on the ward today?" One of the older patients, an alcoholic, who had not participated in the first play, suggested a new one. Flinging her arms in her characteristic fashion, she said, "Why don't you do something different, Miss Nicky? You have so many talents." Miss K. agreed on the matter of the play and proposed that they start planning one. She suggested that this patient help her in the planning. In the presence of the others, the patient proceeded to recommend various people, enumerating what talents each had and what parts they could take in a play. She had mentioned seven patients; two patients included had not taken part in the first play. The other five who sat nearby asked that they proceed with the project at once. Thus, there were seven participants from Ward A.

When the news got around that there would be a play, patients from Ward B asked Miss K. if they could join.

In response to a question from her, stories for the play were suggested by several patients and one was accepted by the group. It was based on a story of the life of St. Valentine, who was known for "his kindness to people and his interest in the life of young people, especially." The basic idea of the play, as verbalized by some members of the group, was to impress on other patients the importance "of love and affection through love songs, poems and dancing."

On the afternoon of January 5th, 18 patients from both wards were on hand. Our "poet laureate" volunteered to tell the story of St. Valentine, stipulating that she would be very much afraid to face an audience, but that if Miss K. would stand where she could see her, then she would feel more secure. She said, "Your being in front of me would give me courage to talk to the audience." She also volunteered to write a "Love poem for St. Valentine's Day." The others enumerated titles of songs they would like to sing.

Another patient asked: "Miss Nicky, how can you direct the group while you are playing the piano?" Whereupon she offered to direct the singing during the performance, as well as during the rehearsals. This patient is an aggressive, quarrelsome, authoritarian, bright, middle-aged woman with a strident voice, habitually acting out her aggressiveness against groups. Her manner now aroused resentment in another patient and a quarrel ensued between the two. Miss K. stopped the rehearsal. After a brief interval, she said, without addressing anyone directly, that she and the group were waiting for the two to end the quarrel before they could continue. Another patient stood up and said it was "a shame to lose so much rehearsal time by quarreling," and turning to Miss K., said, "Don't bring these two any more to the rehearsals" (which were held in the small lounge).[8] After this declaration, both contestants apologized to Miss K. for the interruption.

Two of the group displayed their short concentration span and restlessness. For a while as the rehearsal was going on, they would rise every few minutes and briefly walk around the room, then sit down again in their respective chairs. Miss K. did not restrain them, recognizing that motoricity was important in maintaining psychologic equilibrium in these patients. All the others sat through the half hour until the break, which consisted of five to ten minutes for smoking and drinking coffee. At first there were three rehearsals a week of a half hour's duration. The length of the period was extended as time went on, to an hour. The play was presented on February 14, 1966.

There were altogether 18 rehearsals. Whenever Miss K. felt that the patients were becoming restless during the proceedings, she would relieve the tension by telling them jokes. Most of them consisted of memories of her own childhood in Greece, the locale of Miss K.'s early years. These activated considerable interest and lent enjoyment. The patients reacted by remaining very quiet during the telling and responded with laughter at *appropriate times.*

An example of this is Miss K.'s memories of her own school days when the class was in the process of preparing a play, and how strict her teacher was. A number of the patients responded to this with their experiences of teachers' strictness.

---

[8] By this time Miss K. would gather the participants in the play on the fourth floor of the building and go with them *alone* to the lounge without the assistance of attendants.

Miss K. would then reiterate the importance of cooperation, working together in producing something worthwhile, emphasizing the fact that the group was one family working for a common purpose. Most of the patients seemed to understand and responded to these ideas.

At the time when the patients discussed the outline of the play, she listed the characters as suggested by the patients and they chose their own parts. Because there were no major or subsidiary roles in this play, no conflicts arose as to preferences. Once the parts had been fixed, Miss K. asked what the participants would like to say in the context of the story, which she now summarized. There were only four speaking roles, the others were a chorus group and a dancing group. The four who had chosen the speaking roles had later written down their monologues and turned them over to Miss K. Out of these she constructed the play. However, as the rehearsals went on, all the patients—not only the four who had speaking roles—made suggestions for changes in the dialogues, which resulted in a rather well-constructed play sequence.

At one point, Miss K. said that the group ought to plan for costumes and suggested that the patients do so. The group discussed the details, and decided on white dresses—which were to be worn over their regular clothes—and large red hearts pinned over their chests. They then proceeded to make the costumes from materials supplied by Miss K., working on them during rehearsals in the lounge and later on the wards. Interestingly enough, patients who did not take part in the play helped in making costumes. As many as 15 from Ward A volunteered. Another interesting feature of this project was that the attendants, as well, were drawn into this bustling activity and voluntarily helped with the work, assisting the patients whenever needed. Thus, the staff were involved in the patients' project and became part of it.

This play was also given in the dining hall. It was introduced by one of the patients who volunteered to read the history of celebrations of the day in various periods of human development and the manner in which they were carried out according to the culture and content of each. This included, among others, Egyptian, Greek and Roman civilizations as well as modern celebrations symbolized by St. Valentine. The content for this essay was gathered by the patient with Miss K.'s help in a public library, off campus. Having discovered that the hospital library had no book dealing with holidays, the patient reported this fact to Miss K. who suggested a trip to a public library in the community. She, Miss K. and three others, who evinced an interest in a visit to a library, made the trip. While the others browsed, the prospective valedictorian found with Miss K.'s help a book of holidays and copied the material which she presented at the performance.

Contrary to her own expectation that she would be frightened by the audience unless Miss K. supportively faced her, the patient carried off the reading with flying colors. Miss K. remained seated on the side behind the piano and out of the patients' vision. The reading was followed by group singing directed by our aggressive friend. Because of the size of the cast, they sat in two rows facing the audience, while the M.C. announced to the audience the name of each song before it was rendered, improvising the form and content of her remarks. She would turn toward the audience to make the announcements and then turn back to the chorus to direct it. Following the singing, four of the actors rose and, walking toward the audience, presented the dialogue on "What is love?"

The dialogue itself evolved from the singing of the song during the rehearsals when the M.C. asked, "Girls, do you know what love is?" This question set the group off to formulate an answer. In introducing this number, the author asked the same question of the audience. After its conclusion, a song entitled "What is Love?" was rendered by the entire group with some of the audience joining in. The singing was followed by a square dance, then again by the singing of three more songs, again introduced by the M.C.

All but one of the residents on both wards and staff were present, and this time including Shirley who was freed from her bonds by now. The audience applauded heartily after each number and at the conclusion of the performance left the hall in a happy mood, particularly the actors. Dorothy, one of our "idiots," looked radiant. Her emerald-blue eyes shone with ecstasy. Hannah, who usually appeared unaware of her environment, was the only patient on the wards who stayed away. When I came upon her after the play, she said in her garbled speech, "I love you. I want to kiss you," and attempted to do so on the lips. As tactfully as possible, I turned my cheek, which she kissed and in her characteristic manner abruptly turned and walked away.

The conduct of Justina and Shirley, two of our most primitive and autistic patients, was symptomatic of the changes that occurred in their personalities during the first year of the Vita-Erg program. Justina, who could not sustain the action at the first performance, and sought to leave soon after it started (when restrained by a fellow patient, she burst out in tears), broke away from her mentor and left the room. She was now able to sit through the performance and took an active interest in what was going on, keeping her eyes rivetted on the actors and seemingly enjoying the spectacle. However, unlike the other patients, who smiled appreciatively, and some who sang along with the chorus, her face did not leave its bland expression. She nevertheless swayed with the rhythm of the music in a babylike fashion. [It was after this performance that we noted that she had taken a tray and table utensils entirely on her own, obtained her food, and settled down to her meal, which she continued to do thereafter.]

Shirley, who at the first performance remained tied to the bench on the ward in increased agitation, attended this performance. She sat in the last row with her back to the players, however, jabbering (instead of her usual gibberish) words to the four women sitting in front of her. This time—and it was the first and only time—she formed three or four complete, comprehensible but discrete words, which she kept repeating, but which conveyed no thought or sequence. This time she also looked straight at her table companions as though seeking to communicate with them. They, however, being absorbed in the action of the performers, gave her no heed. As soon as the play ended and the patients began to stir, she returned to her accustomed gibberish.

The foetal catatonic patient was led to the performance by one of the attendants who sat her down in a chair along with the other patients. She kept her eyes open throughout and appeared enlivened as though following the action of the play. As the audience broke up she walked back to her ward on her own.

With the approach of summer (1966) once more the thoughts of some of the patients turned to a play, and they again suggested that one be staged. As may have been anticipated, matters went more smoothly than before. Groups from the two wards formed much more quickly, and details were arranged more expeditiously. In the first discussion the title of the play chosen was "The Gate of Happiness," which was also the key to its content, and excerpted from a book in the hospital library. However, much of the material in the book was altered and simplified during the first two rehearsals. After the play was read aloud to the group by one of the prospective actors, they found the dialogue in the book unsuitable for their purpose and proceeded to write their own dialogue, which was arrived at in discussion in two sessions step by step, with a goodly number of the patients participating. A list of songs to be rendered by the 24 participants was compiled, again through group agreement. Since there were some eight songs, Miss K. had the words mimeographed and supplied them to all participants. One of the interesting developments was the request from a considerable number of patients who did not take part, to be allowed to watch the rehearsals, many of whom did so regularly.

Now competition for the various parts arose. The conflict was resolved by Miss K. by suggesting that contestants for the same role study the parts and read them, then the group could pass upon the one who was most suitable. The choices were made by vote and the one who received the highest vote had the part. There were eight main characters, but only three were contested. Two of the losers accepted the defeat without demurral, but one, the orally aggressive patient of the former "Siamese twins," who had not been able to memorize her dialogue, was angered. Set upon having that part she continued to argue.

Some of the patients indicated to her that she could not possibly read her lines from a paper at the public performance and since she could not memorize them, she could not have that part. After some struggle, she capitulated.

At one point when the patients came for rehearsals, three of them announced that they did not know the parts because they had lost the mimeographed sheets. Miss K. took this opportunity to point out the importance of taking care of materials, explaining that it was an extra burden on her to re-do the sheets. Since then there was no difficulty on that score. When the actors had finally gained control of their respective parts, rehearsals for the dancers were initiated. The members of the Corps de Ballet, which was introduced by the patients into the revamped play, resisted accepting Miss K.'s choreography and she suggested that they decide on the pattern of the dances themselves. The group worked them out together, making decisions on the basis of free discussions.

There was one soloist, a young, very intelligent and attractive girl. She was encouraged to improvise her own solo. At first she had sought assistance from Miss K., who, instead of giving it, suggested that she make up her own dance to the music played on the piano by Miss K. The week preceding the performance, rehearsals were held every day, instead of thrice weekly from 45 minutes to an hour duration on a real stage in the auditorium. The idea of giving the play in the large public auditorium in another building came from the patients themselves. I had some hesitancy as to their readiness to appear before a large audience on a regular stage with scenery. However, our doubts proved quite unfounded.

The play was introduced by a reading of a poem written by our poetess who, being inordinately frightened and shy, had gone through a period of extreme anxiety for some days before, seeking reassurance from everyone who would listen to her, including the office staff of the building. Nonetheless, once she faced the audience, she was under complete control and projected herself with remarkable poise and even with traces of humor. She was elated with her success afterwards and talked about it for days. She was not the only one of the actors who faced with apprehension the ordeal of appearing on a real stage with footlights and all. However, none of them had been as frightened as she, although she carried it off with flying colors.

When the performance was over, a number of patients turned to Miss K. and said to her, "Are you pleased, Miss Nicky?" Miss K. assured them that it was wonderful.

The scenario of the play follows:

Scene 1

The curtain opens with a song, "Oh What a Beautiful Morning," as the girls are out in a forest collecting flowers:

Gloria: Sit down, my friends.

Mary: Look, there is a cardinal!

Pauline: Look beyond, there is a bluebird.

Gloria: They are there because they like us, but they do not know that there is danger in the forest.

Mary: What danger, Gloria?

Gloria: The rich man.

Pauline: Can he harm our birds?

Gloria: If they do not hide well.

Pauline: He must be a very bad man. He is outside the "Kingdom of Happiness." Let us go, my friends. I hear his footsteps. I have an idea. Let us leave Margaret here. Maybe she can soften his heart. (They leave. Margaret, who found a bird's nest with eggs, holds the nest in her hands and sings, "I Talk to the Trees, but They Do Not Answer Me.")

Mr. Montgomery (the Rich Man): What have you there?

Margaret: A bluebird's nest.

Mr. Montgomery: Give me the eggs. I want them for my collection.

Margaret: I can't take the eggs from the bird.

Mr. Montgomery: Do you realize that you are talking to your superior! Let me by.

200

Margaret: You shall not have them.

Mr. Montgomery: You shall pay for this.

Margaret: As you will, my friend. At the present we be lass to lad and if you try to touch my eggs, I will knock you down.

Mr. Montgomery: I will not stand such insolence! Would that I had not lost my way. I will soon have you dragged from my path.

Margaret: A coward never feels safe when others are around.

Mr. Montgomery: You call me coward!

Margaret: Yes, I do. You will not dare to face me alone.

Mr. Montgomery: I am rich and powerful and you are a peasant lass. I will not involve myself by fighting you.

Margaret: Then leave the birds alone.

Mr. Montgomery: Am I not rich and powerful? Why should I not have my way?

Margaret: I pity you.

Mr. Montgomery: Pity me? Why?

Margaret: Because you are lonely.

Mr. Montgomery: Are not all people lonely?

Margaret: Not the poor. We have to help each other and we learn to love.

Mr. Montgomery: What is that, love?

Margaret: The greatest thing in all the world. The love of those who need us and whom we serve.

Mr. Montgomery: No one needs me.

Margaret: We need you.

Mr. Montgomery: (smiles) You really mean it? What's your name?

Margaret: My name is Margaret.

Mr. Montgomery: My name is Mr. Montgomery. Give me your hand, Margaret, I should like to know happiness.

Margaret: I would like to lead you to the Kingdom of Happiness. Come with me to the village. Throw aside your gun and let's enjoy the beautiful Springtime.

(They leave as the curtain closes)

201

Scene II—Village Square

Curtain opens. The girls are seen singing "Spring Is Here." At the conclusion of the song, the couple is seen coming to the festival, and the girls react with pleasure and surprise.

Margaret: My dear friends, I would like to introduce Mr. Montgomery. He wants to see how we celebrate spring.

Mr. Montgomery: I don't know how to say this, but Margaret made me realize what a lonely life I have.

Marion: Oh yes, Mr. Montgomery. We have so much fun here in the forest celebrating the spring.

Please continue.

(The girls sing the songs: "Welcome, Sweet Springtime," "When It's Springtime in the Rockies," "Younger than Springtime.")

Mr. Montgomery: Please, Margaret, dance for us.

Marion: (Margaret is dancing to the song, "The Flowers That Bloom in the Spring." At the end of the dance, Margaret hurts her leg and falls. Mr. Montgomery runs to her and helps her sit down. Then he sings the love song, "With a Song in My Heart." At the end of the song, he is kissing Margaret. The girls get enthusiastic and start dancing. Mr. Montgomery leads the square dance. At the end everybody sings, "Spring Is Here.")

The condition of these patients a year and a half after life on the ward had changed is a far cry from what we had seen it to be when we first started. In addition to their general improvement, they have become aware of the possibility of finding love. Though aware of their despair of the past, they now had hope. There was unquestionably evident a spark of joy and optimism in their involvement with the play. Their enterprise in doing research for the play without direction and their judgment in selecting and rejecting themes had surprised even the most skeptical, but confirmed our confidence in the growth capacity of most of our charges.

The content of this play was of a much higher order than the two others and has clearly revealed their impelling need for love and for human relationships. All their plays offered a channel for bringing this to their awareness, which was invaluable and would have been rendered even more so had time and staff permitted following it up with discussions where these points could have been brought more to their consciousness. Actually, in a patient-centered hospital, this should be the function of medical and nonmedical psychotherapists. The capacity for personal interrelationships was impressively demonstrated by the ease with which problems that used to give rise to violence had been resolved amicably. Even the most violent and truculent in the group recognized the inappropriateness of their behavior and apologized for it when it had appeared.

The point must again be emphasized that these results in reconstructing human personalities cannot be obtained by merely behavioristic conditioning or by imposed work. They must flow from benevolent relationships between staff and patients, from growth that can flourish only in the soil of human understanding and love, from activating dormant creative trends and a normalized milieu.

Ward Meetings

There was no situation more strenuous and more emotionally draining than was conducting ward meetings of our highly volatile and unstable patients. The difficulties of such a task are multiplied many times when disturbances and agitation are as great as they were among the patients on our two wards. The records of a few meetings elsewhere in this volume are bland compared with the intangible climate that prevailed. Patients of the order we were dealing with could not sustain an orderly aim-directed discussion even for very brief periods, nor arrive at a conclusion by any semblance of sustained mass action. In early sessions, interruptions came hot and heavy from the so-called participants—that is, the patients who sat around the leader—as well as from the strollers, stragglers and others who sat on the sidelines.

Irrelevant shouts such as "When can I go home?" or "When can we have a party?" or "I want to go for a walk!" came from individuals in all of these groups. The proceedings of the sessions were periodically punctuated by sudden outcries or screeching from patients, or sudden screams of rage, or loud irrelevant laughter.

Assemblies, large or small, evoke memories and reaction to past events in the primary group, the family. These events had been in most instances evocative of anger and were relived on the ward at the sight of an aggregation of people (the family). There was also the element of exhibitionism and attention-getting in the disturbing conduct of the patients. On the other hand, we had patients who had been so cowed by their families, school and other groups that they feared joining any assemblage and stayed in the periphery or removed themselves to another room.

Even at a much later period of our project an otherwise cooperative male psychiatric resident, for example, could endure the lesser disturbed conduct during these meetings on Ward B, but was completely incapable of dealing with the distress caused him by the turbulence on Ward A. He frankly declared at a seminar session, "On Ward A we conducted meetings for a period of only four weeks . . . and I found it necessary to discontinue them." Such difficulties were not in the specific domain of our "disturbed" wards only. I once observed a session on one of the "good" wards of the hospital that had been conducted on the open-door plan for 10 years, and where patients were free to come and go as they pleased.

The meeting was conducted by a calm, unruffled young resident who took the disturbances with admirable equanimity and seemed able to sustain an evenness of voice and facial expression throughout. Nonetheless, there was considerable diffusion of thoughts, irrelevant statements and frequent changes of subject —all of which he was able, through calm and great persistence, to cut through to some extent and keep the deliberations on a given course. One impediment, however, was in the person of a youngish woman patient, who all but defeated his efforts. She sat near him and in a loud voice refuted every statement made by patients, ending her tirade with the declaration that the psychiatrist was her husband. This declaration was repeated numerous times by her. At a consultative conference following the session, we suggested that means should be found to prevent this patient from attending the ward session, for her delusional *idee fixe* could not be dealt with in the ward group and her conduct was too detrimental to his efforts.

We have not, therefore, attempted ward meetings during the tenure of our first resident, beyond two or three attempts by Dr. Beckenstein (recorded elsewhere and in preceding pages) as a trial. The patients were obviously too distraught and enraged to muster sufficient self-control for any length of time or to take part in any kind of deliberation. It was only through the skill acquired from many years of experience and perhaps also through his authority status, that Dr. Beckenstein was able to carry off these meetings. Our patients had far to go before ward meetings would be a constructive experience for them. In fact, observations led to the conclusion that at the time they were detrimental. Patients and attendants would have a long road to travel before either would bring about the sanguine climate and attitudes necessary for such mass projects.

My persistent innuendoes that some psychiatric intervention must be introduced to reinforce our interpersonal and activities measures stirred our second female resident to introduce weekly meetings on each ward. By this time a considerable degree of intrapsychic and group tranquility had settled and the conduct of the patients was incomparably more propitious than before. Due to my own schedule, I was able to observe (from a hidden vantage point behind a column) only one session on Ward B. At this session there were two long periods of sustained, rational contributions from a goodly number of patients in the two concentric circles who were seriously grappling with practical details of life on the ward. About half of the population of the ward joined the circles, thus physically participating. Many others sat quietly on the periphery listening, while a small number were scattered in different parts of the ward and the accessory small rooms.

For ward discussions to be effective, the majority of the patients must be in a state of comparative tranquility; or rather they should not be in a condition of disturbance or agitation. If the latter condition exists, all group efforts are doomed to failure or, at least, will yield stressful outcomes. Meetings need to be, therefore, appropriately timed with a view to the state of patients as a group and their mood on a particular day. If, for any reason, the prevalent climate is one of tension, it may be advisable to delay sessions to a more opportune time. However, there may also be occasions when a meeting—for discussing a difficulty—may serve as a palliative for ragged feelings and bring about calm. In such eventualities, making refreshments available in conjunction with the session increases its soothing effect.

As already indicated, we had experimented with seating arrangements to ascertain their relation to attention span and orderliness. Three patterns had been observed: circular, scattered and rows of chairs. The first and third are self-explanatory. The second arrangement was to let the patients sit at the various tables where they had been working or playing games. This was the least satisfactory arrangement. Our *impression* is that the chairs set in rows is preferable. Although circular seating may be suitable under ordinary circumstances, psychotic patients seem to be overstimulated when facing each other, which favors acting out.

At one point in the program, the male resident psychiatrist terminated abruptly meetings on Ward A after three or four sessions as already reported, but he also complained of difficulties with Ward B, where the disturbances had been at a minimum in the past. At the seminar session where he presented his problem, various suggestions came from the staff and decisions were made, all involving *manipulative* procedures, rather than exploring patients' feelings and needs—and the total ward climate—which, when recognized and corrected, might have re-

206

moved the difficulties. The suggestions had a wide range: shortening the duration of meetings, *required* attendance from patients in better contact, removing disturbed and hallucinating patients from the wards during the sessions, meetings in the conference rooms with small groups of "better" patients, and orientation of small groups, preceding the ward meetings, who would presumably set the climate and carry continuity at the larger gatherings. The question of *the climate of the ward* at that particular time was raised by no one, however.

We had not introduced meetings before an atmosphere of tranquility was in unmistakable evidence. For the same reason we initially withheld off-ward activities from the patients. We wished to prevent counteraction or neutralization of patients' growing benign feelings in their early stages by callous staff members who might treat our patients not in consonance with our plan. It was only when the constructive feelings and attitudes had become more ingrained in the patients, the past injustices perhaps forgotten, and when awareness of our attitude toward patients took hold on other staffs, that we consented to have our patients handled by them.

Group meetings where free expression and spontaneous interaction is the rule are stressful situations for all, and would be particularly so to the fragile and volatile personalities that made up our ward populations. Careful consideration of the many conditions as well as their timing required careful evaluation. First and foremost was the general disposition of the patients. Other elements that operated in the situation were: a) the psychiatrists were newcomers to the project and had as yet not had time nor did they appear predisposed to establishing a favorable image of themselves with the patients; b) they made the error of at first acting in the customary authoritarian manner and assumed a depriving and punitive stance; c) attendants from other wards rotated as trainees in the "new" approaches to patients (to be described later), while most of our original personnel were being transferred to other wards "to spread the gospel," as it were, so that our patients were deprived of the favorable transferences and durable secure dependencies; d) the

207

impervious overemphasis on work as a requisite for patients, and subordination of interpersonal relationships and ward tranquility to this concept—all of these and perhaps other, less obvious dynamics added to the tensions and apprehensions of the already ego deficient and confused women that constituted our population.

An example of how a conductor of a ward meeting can contribute to tension and resentment is contained in the following verbatim description by a new psychiatrist of what had transpired:

"We tried to discuss problems that came up with cleaning . . . . There's always a group of patients on the ward who do most of the cleaning. Some don't do any at all. We wanted to encourage *everybody* to do a little bit . . . . Another was the management of the coffee breaks. . . . *We felt* that the coffee break was an activity in which *everybody* should participate; that the preparation of the coffee, the cleaning of dishes, the removal of dishes—*everybody* should participate . . . we explained . . . that if everybody didn't participate *we would discontinue the coffee breaks.* I really laid down the law . . . I threatened them with discontinuance of the coffee breaks at the top of my lungs, actually they understood . . . . If I recall, after we had that meeting, it had an effect in the sense that more people participated . . . ." Of course, for a short period a few of the patients who happened to be particularly interested did volunteer, but at what a price! As the session receded into limbo, their interest understandably waned.

It is obvious that the focus of interest in the leader's mind was to get "the jobs done" rather than to *evoke* favorable inner motivations toward their world in our agitated, self-encapsulated, completely detached patients. The aim seemed to have been to satisfy the staff's criterion that work is noble and that each must contribute to the common weal, an ethic that was still meaningless to the patients. The leader's immediate aim should have been to continue to generate the inner propulsion toward environment and reality which we had begun. One is at a loss to understand what value there was for disturbed psychotic patients still with all their fears, hostilities, resentments, hallucinations and resistances, to go through the motions of doing things without interest or a sense of their significance.

Pragmatism and existentialism supplement each other in the re-education and reintegration of the psychotic patient, as indeed they must also in the education and rearing of children. When either is omitted, the outcomes cannot be anything but barren.

In her second and last year before she left the hospital, Miss Kralides had taken over the responsibility of conducting weekly meetings on both wards with the cooperation of the ward nurse on Ward B and the attendant in charge on Ward A. The latter ward had been under the supervision of an attendant for almost three years, after the transfer of the nurse to other duties in the hospital.

I was not present at any of these meetings, but have consulted with Miss K. from time to time on her activities on the wards, including the ward sessions. The ward discussions centered, as they should have, on practical and often pressing problems of routines and follow-ups on previous decisions and on plans for new activities. A considerable number of patients took an active part in the deliberations; by far the largest number, while remaining nonparticipants, seemed to be interested listeners. Thus, they can be considered "passive participants." The former numerous interruptions by the "passive participants" and the interferences from the nonparticipants had almost disappeared.

There is little doubt these improvements emanated from the warm regard in which the patients held her and from her manner and skill in conducting groups and the uninterrupted relation she had had on a daily basis, with no absences, during the period of her association with the project.

SMALL GROUP MEETINGS AND PARTIES

Small group discussions that proved significant, in that they engaged patient interest, extended reality perimeters, and stimulated cooperative activity, were introduced about two years after the inauguration of the ward program. The delay in initiating them was partly due to the lack of suitable staff, but more so to our patients' unreadiness to participate in and gain from intimate discussions. Because of the personality states and intellectual level of our patients, group interactions had to deal with concrete matters that touched on, or had arisen from, their daily lives; they had to flow from pragmatic experience rather than ideational or abstract sources.

As Miss Kralides developed her work, she took advantage of the opportunity for expanding her activities in this direction, which had so far remained in the realm of plans and intentions. The first chance offered itself in connection with one of the holiday celebrations which were always welcome as enrichment against the monotony of ward life and, perhaps, also as recall of the pleasanter memories of the patients' past.

Two weeks before Halloween, soon after she joined our staff, Miss K. accompanied a group of about 20 patients to the playground of the hospital. As they were walking toward the field, they commented on the pleasant weather and mentioned the coming holiday. One of the patients asked if the "Recreation Department" was planning to give a dance for the entire hospital for Halloween. Miss K. said yes. The patient then asked if they could have a special party for the two wards instead. Miss K. agreed that it was a good idea and said, "Let me find out if we have money for the party and I will let you know."

She then consulted with the appropriate authorities and brought the matter, as required in all new projects, to the attendants' seminar session that week. All agreed to have such a party and to try to motivate as many patients as possible to participate in the preparations. Miss K. then called a meeting of all the patients first on Ward B and later on Ward A. The patients from both wards welcomed the idea and while many offers for help came from them, there were only 14 patients from Ward B and ten from Ward A whose interest survived and who had taken an active part. Both groups working together *organized themselves* into small committees for such duties as decorations, cooking, shopping, serving, and cleaning up. The patients carried on their responsibilities under supervision of staff, but by now were encouraged to initiate ideas and make suggestions. The O. T. personnel helped with the decorations and accompanied the committee to do the shopping. Miss K. helped with the baking and with the setting up of the dining hall for the party. The ideas to hold the party in the larger dining hall, rather than on the wards as in the past, and to invite male patients were among those suggested by patients from Ward A, the less advanced of the two wards.

The party was a "huge success" and not a single untoward incident occurred throughout, despite the fact that almost 200 persons participated.

Later Miss K. called a meeting of both groups. She opened the session with praise for the "good job" they had done and then asked for reactions to the event. Most were very pleased and asked to have another party for Thanksgiving. One patient complained that the men (patients) did not pay attention to her and in general were indifferent to the "girls." When asked if all felt the same, they said yes: most of the men "were sleepy" and did not want to dance, but "at the end they became friendlier." As a result of the discussion the women decided to invite male patients from different wards for the next party. They also suggested that there be more refreshments and more cake. Miss K. here faced the patients with the reality of costs and suggested this matter be discussed at the next meeting.

The next meeting took place five days later. The patients came in with ideas for raising money. Some Ward A patients decided to contribute their "bingo money" (winnings) for two weeks. Miss K. asked if the rest who played in the game wished to contribute their winnings. All said yes. On Ward B the patients came with other ideas. They thought a letter to the office would help and they had such a letter written and sent to the proper authority. He was very pleased with the letter and read it to the staff at the next seminar session.

A discussion of the therapeutic value of such meetings took up most of that session. Practical suggestions as to how to direct such meetings with patients grew out of the deliberation. When Miss K. and the two occupational therapists met with the Supervising Psychiatrist to plan expansion of group discussions, he expressed the view that "group therapy meetings are very dangerous" and disapproved of the idea. Despite this warning, they established weekly small group sessions on both wards after the Thanksgiving party.

In both wards the first topic was how to raise money for future parties and how to get paid jobs in the hospital.

The Ward B group suggested that during the holidays they would make money by selling cigarettes and candy to the twice-a-week visitors and to staff. When asked how they would arrange the selling of these goods, they thought that a table placed in the lobby of the building would serve the purpose. Others thought that a "window display" would be better. The group was not interfered with in discussing and deciding on their ideas. Two patients, whose thinking was not too realistic, argued for window display. Finally a third said, "Forget about the window display. We don't have the time or the money, but we have enough tables." At this point the meeting ended with Miss K. telling the patients how pleased she was with their meeting and promised them to investigate how their plans could be carried out administratively.

On Ward A the group asked if it were possible to get part-time jobs in the community to raise money for their enterprise. When Miss K. asked them what kind of jobs they would like, it became clear that most of the patients had no skills of any kind. Miss K. suggested that they first try the hospital industries. This seemed to disappoint them. None offered to work in the hospital.

The administration vetoed the plan of selling cigarettes and candy as this could compete with the hospital community store (though the latter were anyway obtainable from two vend-ing machines). Instead, the administration offered $50 as pay-ment at the rate of 50 cents an hour to patients who would wrap Christmas gifs for the 3,000 patients in the hospital.

At the next meeting the patients were told that the idea of

selling sweets and cigarettes was turned down because it was competing with the community store business. This proved to be a blow to them. One of them complained that "this is not a permanent job; it is only for Christmas." Miss K. agreed and said that the offer of $50 was better than nothing and that she would see what could be done in the future. Because only two and a half weeks were left before Christmas (1966), preparations for the party and the play kept the patients busy.

A week before Christmas the play-organizing group received the boxes and the items for the gifts. A suitable spacious workroom with large tables in another building was offered to them. When the patients at the ward meeting were asked who would like to make some money for the project, 10 more patients from Ward A and five from Ward B responded. The reason for the small number of the latter was that, unlike in past years, many patients had been on leave to their homes for the holidays and a large number of holders of "honor cards" had been off the wards at various tasks and occupations when the meeting was held.

When the "workers" arrived in the room assigned and were seated around two large tables, Miss K., instead of instructing how to proceed, which was the usual practice by staff, asked them how they would like to arrange their work. One patient who had had experience in factory work said, "We'll make a factory setting; the work goes faster. For example, one girl will give out the boxes, another girl will do the first item, the second another item, and so on, till we get to the last girl, who will tie the ribbons." All agreed to this, and the work started with enthusiasm. In a period of two hours the patients finished one hundred and twenty boxes. Miss K. told them that they accomplished more than she had expected, and asked them to work in the afternoon, though she would not be available. One of the patients said, "Don't worry, Miss Nicky, we'll surprise you."

During the afternoon the patients made up two hundred boxes. The following day was Saturday, Miss K.'s day off, and she asked one of the attendants to work with the patients. On Monday, the patients informed her that they had finished all the

Christmas gifts and asked when they would get paid. She told them that as soon as she got the money she would pass it on to them. The next day she paid them and each signed a receipt as required by the administration. Miss K. concluded her report of this project as follows: "I cannot describe in words how happy the patients felt. They all thanked me *and kissed me*."

When the plays were over in the spring of 1966, Miss Kralides suggested that the groups could be used not only for planning plays but also for discussion of any topic of interest that presented itself on the wards, as well as personal matters. The groups gladly accepted the suggestion and met weekly for an hour each week.

At first the groups from the two wards met separately. At the beginning, the patients on Ward A, because of their backwardness, did not respond as well as those on Ward B. While a goodly number joined up, there were quite a few who absented themselves from the meetings. Miss K. then thought of combining the meetings with Ward B, which participated regularly. The sessions were held in the conference room on Ward A. The Ward B patients were aware of the situation and encouraged their mates on Ward A, telling them that they would try to help them solve whatever problems they had to improve their ward as they had improved theirs.

During the discussions, some members of the groups verbalized their abilities to relate by saying such things as "I can manage and supervise 10 patients to do the beds." Another said, "I'll undertake to do the baking, cooking and such things." These statements were not idle boasts for they actually acted upon these assertions. The discussions definitely brought out leadership abilities in a number of the patients who had gradually become indigenous leaders in the life on their wards. This occurred also on Ward A but for a shorter duration and was much less widespread.

During a certain period, six patients from Ward A joined those of Ward B when Miss K. went on her vacation. Upon her return, the Ward A group indicated their desire to meet on their own, despite the fact that some of the patients on Ward B urged them to continue the combined meetings and pressed them to improve conditions on their ward. They would say, "We will help you improve your ward as we have improved ours." However, the Ward A patients decided to meet separately. One of the topics discussed by the groups of both wards was their preparation for jobs in the community. During this discussion subjects like the importance of personal appearance and definite understanding as to what one wants to gain from a job were considered at the participants' suggestions. Patients asked Miss K. whether they should disclose the fact that they had been in a mental hospital.

One patient in the Ward B group pointed out the importance of having "confidence in one's self in relating to the public." There was evident a certain degree of insecurity and lack of self-esteem on the part of the women, and Miss K. suggested that these topics be discussed. The patients spent three sessions deliberating the problems of having confidence and improving one's self. Miss K. once offered as an example of her own experiences during the war in Greece, how she was able to succeed in her underground work and survive. These personal references and revelations appeared to free the patients to speak about themselves. Many admitted to lacking confidence and they discussed among themselves ways in which they could build it up.

Some said, "God gives us confidence;" another, "You gain confidence, only when you test yourself." Still another declared, "You learn confidence when you are in the hospital." This last assertion set off a lively debate and the patient who had made the statement supported it by describing how she had tested herself in the hospital and had gained more confidence as a result. She then proceeded to describe the fears she had experienced when taking over the baking groups, which had gradually abated. Miss K. explored this matter with the patient and led her to recognize that she was still apprehensive to an extent. Thereafter, when the patient directed the baking groups, she felt much freer and indicated that she had no difficulty in encouraging "the girls" to assist her.

During the third session of the discussions of confidence, a patient read to the group an article on concentration from the *Reader's Digest* which she had brought in, and after finishing the reading, conducted the discussion of her groupmates which resulted in a general agreement that they now felt more at ease and suggested that it was time to start another topic. Miss K. felt that the content of the three-week interchange generated considerable anxiety among most of the group members, which mounted and was reflected in their tense facial expressions and the tone of their voices. The anxiety was relieved in the choice of the topic for the following discussion—planning an entertainment.[9]

As patients improved and went home on leave-status or were transferred to other wards, Miss K. spoke about the groups to the newcomers who asked to be included. She thus filled the vacancies, still determined to hold the numbers in the groups to a minimum. Some of the new patients had known Miss K. from the other building whence they had come and had heard about the group meetings. When she inquired of one of the groups as to what plans the members had, many suggestions came forth for educational as well as other types of activities. Among these were reviewing English, speech improvement, discussions on health problems, visits to museums, and producing more plays and more frequently. Some of the activities suggested were soon put into operation. Among these were the speech improvement class under the direction of Miss K. and a class in English directed by two of the more intact and better educated patients. The health education class utilized literature from the city Department of Health. During the group meetings that were held concurrently, plans were laid for art activities and plays for the ensuing year.

Among a group of newly transferred patients was one who had proved unmanageable on her previous ward and was placed

---

[9] Miss K. grew apprehensive by the evident disturbance of the patients and had consulted the appropriate supervisory staff member who counselled her to "ignore" and to go on. This was contrary to our position that introspection and self-analysis are to be avoided with psychotics due to their ego deficiencies.

on Ward A. She was a young woman who had obviously had good schooling, majoring in psychology. She came from a home of higher financial circumstances and better background than the others. From the very beginning she openly expressed contempt for the group meetings, for the ward and for the hospital. One of her vitriolic comments being, "You like animals here. I cannot live with you." After many repetitions of such derogatory and contemptuous remarks, one of the older patients rose from her chair and in a rage shouted, "If you don't like us, you can leave immediately." A prolonged quarrel ensued between the two. During the hot interchange, the newcomer said, "You make this your home. You like it here because you feel superior among the others. They are inferior, they are stupid, they are idiots." At this the other left the meeting. The offending patient remained sitting, abashed with bowed head, obviously remorseful. At this point Miss K. terminated the meeting.[10]

Neither of the two patients attended the next weekly meeting, after which time the older of the two returned. The group discussed a variety of topics and suggested practical matters for discussion, such as how one can get more appropriate clothes; how to improve one's appearance; how to solicit jobs; why one is respected; places to go shopping, and how to obtain money for necessities.

WORK WITH INDIVIDUALS

The intent of our project did not include intensive work with individual patients. We had hoped that this would be added in the future as some of our patients became accessible and a special staff of psychotherapists was entrusted with this part of the effort at rehabilitation. However, it was inevitable that some of the women would require special attention to bring them into

[10] The gratifying feature of this episode was that the patients did not go beyond verbal recriminations. In the past, such outbreaks always led to hair pulling and face scratching. Of special significance is the fact that the older resident had been among the most irascible, orally abusive and pugnacious on Ward A.

217

the stream of the ward life. Justina (p. 203) was one of these. Another was Miss Harrow, one of the small number who were taken under Miss Kralides' wing and others who received supportive attention from me, among whom was the "poetess" from whose writings we culled at several points in this volume.

Among the score or more of the incendiary patients whose violence was easily and most often spontaneously set off with no apparent reason and who could be reached only through an individual relationship was 44-year-old Miss Harrow. In the chart of her case recorded by the psychiatrist, we find the following entry:

Before initiation of the project, Miss Harrow was one of the most violent patients who would physically attack fellow patients, personnel and even visitors. In her rages she would throw at them any object at hand. It is interesting that during the life of the project, Miss Harrow did not attract our attention with such outbursts. The friendliness of the staff and the relaxed climate of the ward seemed to quiet her down. She no longer attacks people, but still continues her isolative existence. She communicated with no one, had not participated in any of the activities and had never gone out for a walk (before the inauguration of the project).

Miss Harrow was next to the eldest of five siblings. Her background was described as "unusual," having had many girl friends but never "going out with boys." She was very backward, having been in an ungraded class where she had reached the fourth grade and still could not read. When she was 18 years old, her brother helped her get a job in a factory, with which she was "very satisfied," although extremely nervous, irritable and given to stuttering, but talkative and not particularly timid. At first, she always talked about the people she worked with and would go out daily to purchase lunch for one of her workers. A friend had told her that she was foolish to "waste her own lunch hour that way." She discontinued this practice, but felt the co-worker was now angry at her, later claiming that everyone was against her and that "someone pulled her hair." One day she returned home from work earlier than usual and declared that she "could not take it any more" and became uncontrollably hysterical. She was admitted to a mental hospital at the age of 22. Soon after she was transferred to Brooklyn State Hospital. The entry in her chart read: "Patient was totally uncooperative. During the interviews, she mutely stared at the wall, was bodily rigid, withdrawn, perplexed, dull and negativistic. Insight and judgment were absent."

She had been hospitalized for 22 years, residing most of the time on Wards A and B. The patient has received several courses of ECT with temporary improvement. Since 1955, she has been on Thorazine. On September 25, 1962, she was placed on convalescent status in the custody of her father, but on October 14 of that year, was returned as unmanageable.

Miss Harrow resided on Ward B when Miss Kralides joined our project. The patient was isolated and withdrawn, always sitting in the same area of the "sun-room." From the very beginning the patient was suspicious of Miss K. and did not respond to her "good morning" greetings. She watched Miss K. as she played different games with patients but did not herself participate in them. Miss K. made it a point to be kind to her and encouraged her to join in the various activities.

After three months of this, Miss Harrow came to Miss K. voluntarily one morning and asked if she could play bingo with the group. Miss K. pulled a chair over for her and gave her cards to play with. Although she sat with the group every day thereafter, she was unable to concentrate on the game. Most of the time she could be observed talking to herself very softly and appeared totally preoccupied with her thoughts. Because she could never attain "bingo," and because the patients ridiculed her for it, Miss K. decided to sit next to her and help her. At the beginning Miss K. "covered" the patient's bingo numbers and to get her attention called the numbers twice. She would ask her to look at them on her cards. Gradually Miss Harrow concentrated more and more, especially when she appeared to be winning. On these occasions she always thanked Miss Kralides.

Miss Harrow now took to waiting for Miss K.'s arrival each morning and greeted her with a smile. One day when the St. Valentine play was being prepared, she asked Miss K. where she was going, and being told that she was going to the lounge, asked if she could come too as she would like to be in the "singing group." Though she did not sing, she would hold the mimeographed song sheet in front of her during the rehearsals. Since then, Miss Harrow participated in all the activities on the ward.

Whenever Miss K. would come on the ward, Miss Harrow would immediately offer her a chair, and when Miss K. announced a need for some help, such as cleaning tables, and putting things in order, Miss Harrow was always the first to volunteer. Gradually she began to take on responsibilities in which Miss K. was not involved, such as sweeping and mopping up floors and the like. She was particularly interested in working in the kitchen, but worked very diligently in other capacities as well. Miss Harrow remained limited in her ability to freely relate to the other patients, however, but she has become generally more cooperative, friendlier, and, in view of her limited intellect, able and willing to answer simple questions.

The need for and effectiveness of individual relationships and personal attention in the treatment of patients of the type ours were is even more dramatically illustrated in the case of Geraldine, the patient we described as the most violent in the hospital. Geraldine was actually afraid of physical encounter though she was in a perpetual state of rage, with eyes shooting hatred at everyone, especially toward male visitors and personnel. [The precipitating event in her psychotic break was an out-of-wedlock pregnancy and the refusal of the putative father to marry her.] The abridged report on Miss Kralides' relations with this patient follows:

The patient was admitted to the hospital in 1954 with the diagnosis of Schizophrenia, Catatonic type. For one and a half months before hospitalization, she lost interest in everything and sat in one corner. She refused to answer inquiries and ate in silence, except for occasional flare-ups of screaming epithets and curses. After admission to the hospital, she was mute, negativistic and subject to auditory hallucinations. She was always a management problem because of her devastating hostility and extreme aggressiveness. At times she remained withdrawn and occupied herself perfunctorily with O.T. but never produced anything. Her behavior was bizarre and unpredictable.

Geraldine was very hostile toward me from the moment I came on the ward. Instead of responding to my good morning greetings, she would curse me. When I was conducting some activity or conversed with the other patients, she would kick chairs and throw the table games around the room. I was aware that she was seeking my attention by these acts, but when I attempted to give it to her, she would scream and curse me.

For the first three months of our project, Geraldine participated in none of the activities and continued being very violent toward everybody. She spent the afternoons sleeping, always on two chairs in the same corner. It took her all this time before she perceived that I had to share my attention and interest with other patients, for she angrily remarked many times, 'You don't love me. You love them more.' She finally seemed convinced that I was treating all the patients alike and she began participating in some of my activities, but displayed extreme fear of failure.

When we started the second play, Geraldine asked to be included. Since then, she grew friendlier both with me and with the other patients. She now often went shopping and even helped in the domestic work on the ward. Now that she was more tranquil she was allowed to visit her sister's home from which she had been barred for many years, and is in general more cooperative.

About a year after her new personality emerged, she made an unauthorized trip to the home of one of her brothers, where she remained a full week. She seemed agitated when she returned, with her earlier hostile and tense appearance, semi-closed eyes and aggressive and loud threatening voice. However, she calmed down after a day on the ward, and regained comparative tranquility. Unlike her earlier irascibility and flashlike uncontrollable outbursts of rage, she now demonstrated considerable self-control over her impulses. One morning, for example, she was at a point of exploding against another patient, when I gave her a severe look. She immediately curbed herself and abruptly stopped the conflict. After a rare outburst that would upset everyone around, she would come up to me and apologize for it, saying, "Forgive me. I did not mean it. You know that I love you," and would proceed to kiss me.

Having been made aware of the importance of relationships in patients' improvement, individualized approach was resorted to by a few of the attendants as well. One such instance is the following episode between a disturbed patient and a diffident, soft-spoken, kindly, elderly attendant.

The patient attempted to hoard some books that had been sent to the ward and, the attendant noticing it, told her that it was "not the right thing to do," as this would prevent others from using the books. When the attendant turned away, the patient in a rage threw a chair after her, though obviously without intending to strike her with it. After the occurrence, the staff member had made an effort to placate the patient, with the result that a friendship emerged between the two. The attendant then invited the patient to spend a weekend at her apartment where, being recently widowed, she lived alone. The two spent a pleasant two days together, which included a visit to the patient's sister and her family, as well as a movie.

The poetess had spent many months isolated in a corner of the outside porch and endlessly hallucinated. One morning she had broken out into a series of violent acts when she had thrown medication into the face of an attendant, a cup of hot coffee at a female clerk in the community store, struck the nurse and two patients, kicked me and bit the O.T. worker. Because of the new policy emanating from the project, she was neither restrained nor punished. This patient was an ardent Catholic and at times would run off to pray in the neighborhood churches. Some weeks later she came up to me and with a shy smile handed me a poem she had written. After reading and enthusiastically praising it, I suggested that she let me submit it to the monthly mimeographed bulletin published by the patients. The patient's joy as displayed on her face at the suggestion would be difficult to describe and she wondered if I would really do it. When I reassured her, she asked that her name be omitted, only the ward be listed. I assured her that this would be done.

This episode was the beginning of a prolonged friendship which brought her out from the depression, and her joining the typing school. Her improvement was so marked that her sister, who shunned her for years, now welcomed her at her home and even entrusted her young children to the patient's care. This patient was one of many who had no homes to go to and, in the vast majority of our patients, their relatives completely broke off with them.

The poem this patient submitted to me follows:

Faith and the New Year

The New Year sometimes comes in like Spring,
Your heart feels strong and the birds sing,
The air smells fresh all around,
And peace of mind at last is found.

New Year's resolutions are made by all,
Hoping they will last throughout the fall,
As the year rolls by we sometimes weaken,
But if we have strength our faith will deepen,

For God understands that some are weak.
What seems very difficult today
May seem somewhat easy, if we just pray.
So, be like a child, and don't give up,
Though the road of life is sometimes tough.

Another poem reflecting the deep religious feelings of this young woman follows:

Within These Bars

Tension, Headache, everywhere.
We get by on Heavenly Prayer.
From time to time there's Discontent,
Because within us, we are Pent.
But we don't let this get us down,
For up above is a "Heavenly Crown."

Patients who had developed meaningful and close relations with a staff member were apt to make the greatest progress. Because psychotic patients, like children, operate on a primary process level they can move toward secondary elaborations only through "transference" and identification with an intact individual. In a hospital, this individual is a staff member. The few random examples cited above demonstrate this fact.

It must be kept in mind in this connection that, like children, psychotics do not transfer feelings as do nonpsychotic persons where the object is felt *as though* he is a parent. In the case of children and psychotics, the object *becomes* the parent and feelings toward him are not projected as in ordinary persons, but rather displaced. This is why psychotics act out their love and hate toward therapists in individual treatment, and to staff members in a hospital. This also explains the incidence of homicide of therapists by their psychotic patients, that is, displacement of patricidal drives inherent in parent-child relations.

PUNISHMENTS AND RESTRICTIONS

The usual, time-honored and very much overworked procedure of punishment for mild transgressions (the more "serious" misconduct and outbursts brought on confinement in a camisole and/or being locked up in one of the small rooms off the wards) was "restrictions." The psychiatrist would prescribe the nature, extent, and duration of the punishment, which would be tacked on bulletin boards in the ward offices. The attendants and nurses referred to these slips of paper strung up on the board and were guided by them in dealing with patients. The instructions would read:

"——— is not allowed to leave the ward for three weeks."

"——— cannot leave the ward unaccompanied for 10 days."

"——— should not be allowed to go home for three months."

"——— is not allowed to use the telephone for two weeks."

"No home visits for ——— for two months," etc.

Sometimes as many as 18 or 20 such slips would be thumbtacked to the bulletin board, but indirect suggestions by us to the first two psychiatrists of the ineffectualness and inappropriateness of these measures went unheeded. We did not attempt to make an issue of this, thereby disturbing the staff power structure and preventing hostile countermeasures on the part of staff against us and the patients.

As our program had taken root and the patients grew more

224

tractable, and as acting out was incomparably diminished, we were able to persuade the third psychiatrist to eliminate these punitive measures. After a brief period, no episode ever presented itself that required punishment or deprivation; in time, even rebukes became unnecessary. The bulletin boards were devoid of any instructions for infliction of penalties thereafter, and still are.

Extension to Other Services

Considering the inherent limitations of staff and the total hospital climate, it was felt that our program was as well on its way as it would ever be after 15 months of consecutive weekly seminar sessions, reinforced by the supervised activities program, the extensions of both on and off ward occupations. From this point on, it was incumbent upon the staffs attached to the wards to carry on on their own. I continued to oversee the ward life, but reduced the seminar sessions to once a month, placed myself at the disposal of the staff for consultations whenever they felt the need, and added thrice-a-month training sessions for staffs from other wards and services in the hospital. This step was in conformity with the stated aim of the project to retrain attendants. I left the choice of members for this group to the administration who knew the needs of the hospital, and particularly the chief nurse who also acted as chief administrator.

The group included members of several services: two psychiatrists, one supervising nurse, four ward nurses, an instructor from the Nursing School, two psychologists who had attached themselves to our earlier seminars toward the end of the first series, the new (supervising) attendant who had been placed in charge of Ward A, and Miss Kralides who joined the first seminar near its conclusion, and three "rotating" attendants from each of our two wards. Because of the greater sophistication of most members in this group, it was possible to conduct the discussions on a somewhat higher level. However, because we could not draw on actual situations from wards, the content

225

inevitably was more abstract and theoretical, as a consequence of which, the material was bleaker and less pertinent
than was the case in the first series.

As an initial step, we arrived by the discussion method at a
definition of psychoses, identified basic types, the meanings of
their manifestations, listed life needs and therapeutic measures
for patients, reviewed the traditional ward settings and practices
as well as the techniques in vogue for dealing with patients in
ordinary circumstances and in crises, and ways of meeting emergencies. With these as a base, we proceeded to help the participants to consider patients in greater depth by stripping the latter
of the stigma of their illness, analyzing the stereotyped attitudes
toward them, and pointing out the prevalent methods of treating them only as *patients*. Thus we injected the idea of considering patients as *persons* with needs, strivings and potentials.
Members of the group received these ideas variously; some with
skepticism, others cynically. A considerable number, however,
for various personal and tactical reasons, accepted them supportively. The greatest resistance came from a psychiatrist in the
senior category who eventually dropped out of the seminar.

The major handicap in this series was the dearth of pragmatic material from the experiences of the participants to draw
on for our discussions, which was not the case in our first series.
It was necessary for us to draw upon our experiences on Wards
A and B for illustrations as points of departure for the discussions, which were really not typical for other wards where the
patients were much more intact. At different stages we presented films that illustrated some of the content of our deliberations.
The fact that most of the illustrative material was not drawn
from the common experience of the participants weakened the
impact. Nevertheless, the chief nurse (and administrator) reported that nurses had spoken to him of "the broadening of their
perceptions of patients" through the seminar sessions. While
the intellectual level of the members of this seminar was by far
higher than of those in the first, it did not go to the heart of matters we discussed as deeply and did not engage the interest of
the participants as did those in the earlier group who were re-

examining their own actual experiences. "Only experience can be translated into experience."

ROTATING ATTENDANTS

At about the time when the second seminar group began its sessions in October, 1965, the rotating system of training attendants (other than those on Wards A and B) had been introduced at Dr. Beckenstein's behest. The primary intent of the project was retraining attendants in the hospital generally. Wards A and B were chosen as a testing ground. Although the step was in keeping with our commitment, it contained many risks and handicaps for our patients.

The plan as suggested by Dr. B. called for removal of four retrained attendants from each of the two wards (half of the staff) and substituting for them an equal number from the other (traditionally open) wards on the same service (i.e., the same building containing less disturbed female patients) for a period of four months. This procedure was to be repeated in the series at the termination of each training period until all the attendants had been exposed to the new approach. At the same time, the members of the original group of 16, with two years experience, and the others with the shorter course, would hopefully introduce and demonstrate *the attitudes* toward patients and some procedures they had acquired on Wards A and B.

I demurred at this arrangement on several grounds. First was the fact that our highly unstable patients would be deprived thereby of the continuity of relationships and the emotional security they still needed. Some of the patients still referred on occasion to a specific attendant as their "mother," and being deprived of them would shake up the patients to their roots. Such a rotation of staff would have a less disturbing effect upon patients on the other wards who were much healthier, less fearful, less dependent and, therefore, less intensely involved with "mother figures."

My second objection was that a blanket rotation, without choice as to personal suitability of the recruits for the type of relationships and of functions we had attempted to inculcate, would expose our fragile patients to treatment that would erase, or at least weaken, the gains we had achieved. Another objection, to my mind, was that the brevity of the period of retraining envisaged would be inadequate to affect inner changes and the conduct of the short-term trainees. Still another one, which I did not openly verbalize, was that I had little confidence in the judgment of the individual who would be responsible for carrying out this plan as to suitability of this transient personnel.

However, in view of the nature of the project's original commitment, I could not too strenuously oppose the change, and it was put into operation. The subsequent years have proven my skepticism unfounded. Those of the new recruits who have been appropriately chosen took to the new approaches like ducks to water. Partially because the reputation of the project preceded the recruits' coming to the wards, it inclined them to accept the new practices, but, in our opinion, they did so mostly because, to our surprise, they proved to be of an unmistakably higher caliber personally, and seemingly also, educationally. Our impression was confirmed by Miss Kralides and another competent professional staff member with whom we have discussed the situation. This impression, in a sense, validated an earlier one when we stabilized the "relief" personnel drawn from the other wards when extreme shortages occurred on Wards A and B earlier in the life of our project. Another earlier suspicion was also confirmed, that consciously or unconsciously the original group of our attendants were specially selected for their potential capacities to restrain violent patients rather than for sensitivity and empathy.

Having discovered that short-term training recruits were being selected at random, we suggested that they should rather be chosen more discriminately, i.e., women who have the needed empathetic dispositions, adequate intelligence, and flexibility, and in addition, have some standing among their fellow workers so that they can influence them upon their return to their own wards. This development recalls the fallacy of my original demurral against testing our theories with the most disturbed, chronic and hard-to-reach patients, as against the "average" hospital residents who would have been more accessible. However, my assumption here, too, had been wrong, for in the long run, the more regressed patients on Ward A have made greater progress than the "better" patients on Ward B.

WORK WITH EVENING STAFF

The greatest drawback in our program, which was greatly felt by patients, the day-staff and ourselves, was the inconsistency in the treatment patients received at the hands of the day and the evening and night attendants. Because of the time element the latter could not have been included in our morning seminars, and evening sessions had been precluded by a lack of replacements to supervise the wards. The evening staff was of particular importance since they oversaw the patients between the hours of 3:30 P.M. and bedtime, which was in many cases not until midnight, as many patients resisted retiring at any set hour. There were three attendants assigned to each ward, but due to off-days, only two were available at any given time. However, on holidays and due to absenteeism and illness, a substantial amount of time went by with only one or no attendants. In the latter instances, the responsibility for the unmanned ward devolved upon the staff of the other ward. In instances where this ward was also short-handed, the supervising (building, service) nurse would assign an attendant from one of the wards on the lower floors.

All the attendants on duty during the evening and night hours, as well as the relief workers who were pressed into service for our wards, which they greatly resented, were conversant only in the traditional practices and attitudes. The new ideas for life on wards reached them only as vague rumors and they treated our patients in their accustomed manner, with authority and restrictions. The wards were kept locked, camisoles were resorted to, overdrugging practiced, and patients put in isolation for infractions. Perhaps the following incident will make the quality of the evening ward climates tangible.

During one of my two evening visits to Ward B, a patient came up in great distress, with intense fear in her attractive blue eyes, plaintively and breathlessly imploring as she lightly and involuntarily stamped her shoeless feet, "Doctor, I want to die. Give me something that will kill me. I want to die. I want to die." Nearby stood the night nurse (the only staff member who turned up that evening), who whispered to me this startling question: "Should I put her in a camisole?" I gazed at her in surprise and in a low tone said, "No, she needs an injection." No doctor being readily available, the nurse looked up the patient's chart in the office, on which the prescribed medication for this particular patient was indicated. She then administered the sedative. We helped the patient to the top bunk of the double decker in the (medical) isolation room. The nurse proceeded to leave the room, but I reminded her about raising the grate that would prevent the patient's rolling off the bed.

Later, when I returned to the ward from my visit to Ward A, I asked the nurse how the patient was getting on. She walked to the isolation room and flicked the outside electric switch which flooded the room with brilliant light. I quickly flicked it off, but not before another patient, not under sedation, was startled from her sleep—a typical example of the callousness and disregard in treatments they, as nonpersons, usually receive. I am still not clear why a trained nurse would suggest a camisole to a suffering nonviolent patient. An aftermath of this episode highlights the psychotic patient's capacity for keen observation and awareness, not always apparent. During my daytime visit to the ward a few days later, the patient accosted me and with a serious mien softly said, "Doctor, thank you for what you did for me last night. I felt awful." This was the only time she had addressed me in the two years of our acquaintance. She was one of the withdrawn, quiet patients.

In our effort to allay the evening situation on the wards, we asked the chief administrator to inquire from the attendants of each of the wards whether they would take turns staying two hours beyond the 3:30 p.m. end of their working day, two days a week, and make up the time by coming in two hours late in the mornings. At the ward staff meeting he called for this purpose, not one found it possible to do so, the reasons given having to do with the care of children and travel distances at night. However, a subsequent occurrence confirmed the "solidarity" principle by which hospital staffs operate. Some days later I met on the campus one of the attendants on Ward A who volunteered the following: "I feel very guilty, Mr. Slavson, about this business of staying later. I'll be glad to do it. I have a married son in the neighborhood [of the hospital] and I can stay over with him the two nights." However, she did not have the courage to act counter to her fellow workers at the meeting.

The refusal by the attendants to extend the day as suggested, rang the death knell to three plans we had in mind. One was to continue the activities until the evening meal, instead of imposing inactivity and boredom on the patients after the day-staff left. Another was the plan for a one-hour seminar once a week for the evening attendants before they started work. Still another was the failure of introducing a tea-break at bedtime which would occupy patients in the preparation, serving and cleaning up, and the lift they would have gained from it. Upon our request, the administration allotted $450 for the latter project, of which we could not avail ourselves under the circumstances.

AUTOMATIC SPREAD OF THE PROGRAM

Because of the time limitation and the responsibility of concentrating on the wards assigned to us, there was little opportunity to sound out or observe what changes may have taken place in practices at other points in the hospital as an outcome of our project. However, theoretically it is permissible to assume that in the compact culture of a residential institution, rumblings would be set up of any new development, which would reverberate in all its areas. There was ample evidence that the tidings of our project spread on the campus and beyond its confines. Not only did it reach the ears of administration and of all branches of the professional and subprofessional staffs in the hospital, but the maintenance people and those in the other services as well knew of the "changes on the fourth floor of the W. Building." What was even more surprising was that patients from the other wards in other buildings seemed to know details of our patients' improvement.

At first some of the peripheral staff reacted with skepticism and frankly said so. In this group were even the chauffeurs who drove me to and from the hospital. They *knew* "from experience" that "those patients are hopeless" and that the only way to "hold them in line" was to use the old methods; otherwise they would go berserk. Others of the staff were at first cynical and would look at me with embryonic smiles playing on their lips, but later their aspect on seeing me betrayed a mild degree of awe. The upper professional staff were, from the start, by and large, accepting, if not frankly encouraging and a few were genuinely hopeful that it would work.

Evidences of tangible spread of the idea came to our attention, however. Dr. Beckenstein narrated that the psychiatrists on the corresponding disturbed two male wards introduced some of our practices they had heard about, and as a warning to their (male) attendants to cooperate told them, perhaps semihumorously; "You fellows start on this program or the old man [Dr. B.] will send that fellow Slavson up here." He later reported that 24 patients on those locked wards were now free to leave the wards on their own responsibility after "signing themselves out," and that activities were added in the "intensive treatment" ward in another building with machinery in one of the smaller rooms. In the one orientation session I had with the 12 "relief attendants," i.e., personnel who were recruited from other wards in W. Building on days when absenteeism on Wards A and B depleted the staff beyond the point of safety, I asked, "What do you do on your wards the first thing in the morning? Do you do the housekeeping chores, or do you work with patients?" The encouraging rejoinder came, "We used to do the chores first, but since your project, we take care of patients first."

Other developments that may be included in this category was the fact that two members of the psychologic staff asked to join our seminars and attended them regularly; also two male

232

psychologists in training were assigned by the director of psychology to work with activity groups on the wards one morning a week, so that they would become acquainted with the new developments in patient care. As a further development, teaching staff of the school of nursing became regular members of the seminars, and the director of the school, who kept meticulous notes of our discussions throughout, included the basic principles of our program in the new (mimeographed) handbook for nurses and attendants in training.

However, of greater significance than these identifiable phenomena are the subtler, less palpably evident changes in attitudes that had spread throughout the hospital community which Dr. Beckenstein noticed in his peregrinations to the wards and contacts with staff on all levels. He often spoke of these. A new cognition arose among all of the staff—more hopeful and more appreciative of patients as human beings with less bleak futures and possibilities.

We have not attempted to ascertain whether any of the practices that had been initiated at the Brooklyn State Hospital have spread to other institutions via the automatic spread of news, professional "gossip," or through the State and Federal officials who had visited our two wards and seemed very approving of them. We have learned, however, that in 1968 *the New York State Department of Mental Hygiene adopted a policy of enclosing toilet bowls in cubicles at all the institutions under its auspices.* Dr. Beckenstein thought that this step was probably taken as a result of the "fuss" we made on this score which seemed to have pervaded beyond the boundaries of our institution.

7. *Impediments*

As we progressed with our program, innumerable details countered our aims and began to impinge on us. Despite the carefully planned details of the physical setting, a myriad of minutiae began to appear in an unending succession: failure of electric switches, inadequate shower curtains, lack of places for storing of floor mops, loss of pails, broken electrical appliances, dead light bulbs, flooding of shower rooms, overheated wards, missing shoes, lost keys and numberless other such details. No less burdensome was the eternal lack of supplies with no one interested enough to request replenishment: the standard arts and crafts materials, tobacco and paper—both or either one—for making cigarettes, kitchen materials and occasionally even shortage of drugs so essential for our disturbed patients, and many, many others. The perpetual need to re-adjust time schedules plagued us almost beyond endurance. In our effort to prevent rigidity and mechanization, and in seeking flexibility to assure spontaneity and individuation, much judgment was required from staff as to timing and resolution of conflicts, judgment which they unfortunately did not possess. To achieve order without creating confusion (and resentment) was no small enterprise for untrained staff accustomed to functioning impersonally and by rote. There were none among them who were able to ex-

234

ercise discrimination. This gave rise to endless dislocations in the program and periodic regressions back to accustomed traditional routines that activated violent reactions in patients. A few examples of the many innumerable problems will suffice:

On many days the wards seemed dingy, depressing and dim —the lights had not been turned on by the night shift and none of the day staff registered it! For the purpose of sensitizing them to the situation, instead of flicking the switch, we would call this to the attention of an attendant nearby. Nonetheless this occurred repeatedly and often. Only after being asked why the lights were not on, the attendant would flick the nearest one of the three switches, lighting up only part of the room, and remain unaware of the others until this fact was again specifically called to her attention.

Very frequently when patients begged for cigarettes and when directed to roll their own, it would be discovered that the tobacco supply had run out. Inquiry from the O.T. worker, who was responsible for replenishing these supplies, revealed that she had "forgotten" to bring it along, but even then did not have the initiative either to call her office on the telephone for a delivery or to borrow some from the other ward.

One day I observed that Ward B was lacking in O.T. activities and that an unusual number of patients were idle and walking around. An attendant, whose duty it was to help with O.T., was sitting idly at a table near the supply closet. When asked why there were no O.T. activities, she replied that the O.T. worker who had the key to the closet did not come in that morning. When asked if there were no other key available, she volunteered that there was one in the supervisor's office on the first floor, but she had not taken the initiative to fetch, or to telephone for it.

One day no mid-morning coffee was being served on Ward A. Inquiry elicited the fact that the electric urn sprung a small leak. No effort was made, however, to meet the emergency and prevent disappointment for the patients. We then suggested that the urn from Ward B might be borrowed, since the coffee-break was over. Thus an unpleasant situation was averted.

One of the patients from Ward A regularly created a disturbance in the dining hall when there were no second and third helpings of meat, which was her favorite dish. During one of our visits to the dining hall during the mid-day meal, one of the attendants called our attention to this patient, setting forth the difficulty which was imminent since she now sat at the table with her potatoes uneaten, apparently contemplating another trip to the food distribution alcove. We suggested that the attendant go over to her and quietly tell her to finish the potatoes and return the tray and utensils to the kitchen. When told to do so, the patient calmly proceeded to consume her food, and just as deliberately returned her tray; then, without a word she repaired to her ward. Apparently, all the patient needed was the mild direction to divert her from her habitual pattern.

After some of our attendants had been transferred to other wards in the building (as part of the training policy) and when relief attendants were needed (due to absenteeism), former staff people were sent for to fill in. The ward and supervising nurses thought that this was a good plan since the patients knew their former attendants. We pointed out that this practice can be upsetting to the patients whose earlier feelings of attachment or resentment would be reactivated. While administratively their idea was preferable, therapeutically it would be more desirable that strangers be called in to relieve. This plan yielded much better results.

A sample of the numerous matters that needed consideration and action to keep the program at an effective level follows: patients crowding at doors waiting for "line up" for meals; getting permission for patients' use of front elevator (instead of the food lift in the rear of the dining hall); opening door to stairs; evening program; ward meetings; absenteeism of staff; summer program; arrange for psychiatrist's office on same floor as wards (which was never affected); classification of patients; procedures for expediting delivery of materials for the program; equip the "beauty parlors"; arrange for rest period for one of the nurses; discuss plans for baking; discuss dining hall problems; off-ground trips; activity center for sun-room where patients sat

236

idly; discuss prevention of flooding shower rooms; discuss how to prevent vanishing of books and magazines; investigate the episode of defecating in empty dining hall[1]; use of half-way house on campus; how to draw in recovering patients into the larger community; counselling groups for families of patients; individual and group psychotherapy for selected patients; unsupervised showering by patients on Ward B; see social worker re: A—— C——; secure film for seminar; see business manager re: needed cash; discuss heart condition of Mrs. Q——(attendant) with Dr. Beckenstein; discuss with Dr. B. transfer of staff member; discuss with Chief Administrator transfer of attendant; discuss plans and frequency of walks; afternoon program; activities for interval between 11:15 a.m. and noon (lunch); plans for party; arrange for a pool of cigarettes; should there be a male recreation worker on the ward?; procedures for engaging strollers in activities; discuss attendants shouting to each other and to patients across the wards; piano lessons for individual patients; discuss patronizing manner of newly assigned attendants; discuss supervising nurses' taking attendants off the wards to do other chores; Miss Nicki's relation to ward charges; safe storing of materials; get weekly lists of staff absentees; magazines for sun-room (day-room); re: staff coming late; discuss quality of music and advisability of mass dancing; question of physical contact by staff with patients; staggering staff to extend day beyond 3:30 p.m.; work with evening staff; add qualified music therapist to staff; music instruments for wards; re: $50 for recreation materials; arrangements of chairs; indicate occasions when use of restraint is permissible; use of "beauty parlors"; visitors to wards; attendants wearing dark glasses on ward; set-up in sun-room; FM players and records; select out promising patients for intensive rehabilitation and psychotherapy; etc., etc., etc.

Among the sources of frustrating impediments to the progress of our project—beyond the understandable insecurity and

<hr>

[1] We traced this episode to Shirley as an expression of her resentment against the woman in charge of the dining hall. This woman whose contempt for patients has already been reported insisted on locking them out of the dining hall.

resulting resistance on the part of the professional staff, the attendants and the nursing staff—were the many restrictive administrative rules. Rigid regulations were imposed by the State, such as the accountability and safety of patients, rigid staff classifications, inflexible designations of duties and numerous similar legally defined regulations that were completely unsuitable for a therapeutic living process and hampered our work, which demanded flexibility at every turn. Our patients needed a pliable and fluid environment on a background of order that would favor human relations and activate dormant life urges. We viewed these elements as having meanings beyond re-education. They were symbolic of acceptance, of confidence in the patients' powers, of trust in their abilities, of interest and affection from all of us.

Obviously only basic components could have been envisaged and arranged in advance. As the project progressed, the needs for adjustments, readjustments and changes, additions and eliminations became tangibly evident and imperative, but many of these could not be made due to administrative and legal restrictions. No funds were available for the essential structural changes such as the building of the kitchens, for example, nor were we allowed a washing machine or drier for our laundries. Funds for these and for such things as extra trips and other expenses had to be raised by the director of the hospital from a benevolent voluntary organization of men and women in the community attached to the hospital. When we thought we could motivate participation in the creative arts and crafts by selling the patients' products at the regular semiannual public sales and compensating our patients for their work (though these were to be token compensations), we found that this step would counter a state law prohibiting remuneration for such work by patients. When to circumvent the law, a sum of money could have been raised through a charitable organization for this purpose, we discovered to our surprise that the restriction applied even when the source of money was outside the hospital budget.

According to fire regulations, smoking was allowed only in

238

the lavatories, the walls of which were of marble as were the toilets, washing bowls, and the outside porches. The safety of these surrounds was obvious. Nonetheless there was nothing to prevent a patient from setting herself on fire should her irrational impulse so move her. Thus, theoretically, patients could not smoke in the day-hall or "activity room" as they played checkers, chess and other table games, or quietly sat around talking or walking about. A sign in bold red letters was conspicuously displayed announcing this prohibition. The imposition of this rule resulted in much tension and resentment; it occupied the constant attention of attendants and nurses; placed the patients on a level of little children needing disciplining and reminding; added to the strain between patients and staff, and tended to concentrate the patients in the toilet room foyer where they sat around on the floor, since there was room for only a few chairs, while placing the patients away from the arena of creative and group activities.

The matter was thoroughly discussed at one of the seminar sessions and the risks of allowing smoking in that room carefully considered. It became clear after a thorough analysis of all details that there were no hazards at all in the activity room; there were no flammable materials that could be set afire unless one intentionally set a match to the paper used for drawing, and since patients had no matches in their possession, this was not likely nor had it ever occurred. All agreed that there was no realistic basis for the ruling. The outcome was that the ward staff tended to overlook this technical transgression of the rules, though they were not specifically suspended.

It was recognized, however, in the discussion that smoking in the elevator was a possible fire hazard, a fact that had been previously overlooked. The press of people and the air currents set up by the moving vehicle could have constituted a hazard. Smoking in elevators was, therefore, prohibited and rigidly enforced, but not before the matter was discussed with the patients at ward meetings and they understood the advisability of the restriction. To assure conformity a standard sign in bold red letters was placed outside the elevator doors and prospective pas-

sengers were required to snuff out their cigarettes before board-
ing, a fact of which patients invariably reminded each other.
There has never been a willful transgression of this rule, though
on occasion a patient would from habit forget, but upon
being reminded by a staff member or another patient, would
promptly extinguish her cigarette without demurral. Never has
there been any untoward incident in this regard during the years
of the program in any of the areas and rooms on the wards. The
only accidental fire that occurred was in a *permitted* area, the
outside porch.

Perhaps concomitant development revealing the improved self-image of the attendants would be of interest. As a
result of our discussions with the attendants relative to fire hazards, the supervising nurse drew up a rather long set of rules by
which they would be guided. These rules were mimeographed
for distribution without consultation. We felt that this step may
have been construed by them as bureaucratic authoritarianism
and as a lack of confidence. We therefore asked them at a subsequent seminar session whether it would be necessary to have
their decisions typed and distributed. The attendants unanimously decided that this was unnecessary; they would enforce
the safety rules without such an ukase.

The budget for our project was met by a grant from the
National Institute of Mental Health through the New York
State Department of Mental Hygiene. It included a separate
item for materials, along with salaries, fees, equipment and so
forth. The fiscal year for the project began on the first of July.
At the beginning of the second year of our project, the funds
had been forwarded from the National Government to the State
Government. However, there was an unexplained delay in re-
leasing the money to us. Despite repeated telephone calls from
our business office to the State Department, the funds were not
released for about three months. The project employees went
unpaid for that period of time, but what was more serious was
that we were unable to obtain supplies to carry on the program.
The Occupational Therapy Department agreed to lend us the

needed supplies; but none of the materials and equipment such as table games and recreational outfits essential to our work was available. The table games were especially needed, for they helped engage the older women and the "burnt out" schizophrenics, who were not motivated to participate in the more active occupations.

Our wards began to show signs of disorganization as a result. The aimless milling around began to reappear and an ever-increasing feeling of tension was becoming evident. To prevent further deterioration, we made several urgent requests from the fiscal officer for an advance to buy games and other supplies necessary to carry on our work. The consistent reply was that as far as he was concerned, he could not advance funds without proper authorization.

We waited for some weeks helplessly observing our program slowly going to ruin, and still no money forthcoming. In desperation, we bought supplies from private funds directly, rather than through the regular purchasing channels, thereby preventing another delay of two months or more. The climate on the wards markedly improved at once, as the patients could now keep themselves occupied rather than remaining idle. We were informed, however, that this was an illegal act; no private funds should have been used on a State project! After more than three months, the funds had been officially released to us.

Another serious handicap was that all purchases had to be made through the "regular channels." This also involved much delay in bureaucratic paper work and routines when we needed materials at once while patients were still interested in a project or in an individual activity. As a result of such delays, spontaneity remained ungratified and unutilized. It would often take six weeks before we could get things we needed *at the moment*. A note in our diary reads: "Seven months have elapsed and we still do not have the wherewithal for carrying on our work." One of the reasons for this delay, as it was explained to us, was that local department and other stores hesitated to fill orders from the hospital because payment of bills was delayed for months due to the fact that they were being processed and paid through the

State office, which usually is overtaxed with innumerable items from institutions and offices throughout the state.

A major impediment was a rule regarding personnel practices that prevented us from adding to our staff a "coordinator" who would carry on a full-time basis the responsibility for these matters and the total activity program. Our original proposal for the project included a position of a "coordinator" to carry out the various plans and projects determined at the administrative and professional conferences. A salary was provided in the budget for such a person. As our project shaped up we found that the variety of expertise this job involved was not possessed by any of the existing professions at this or any hospital.

The multifarious responsibilities engendered by the job involved many organizational talents and a variety of knowledge and skills, in addition to personal gifts of observation, empathy and capacity for human relations and a high degree of maturity. We concluded that these functions could best be carried out by a *psychiatric group worker*. When we broached this matter to the administration, we were informed that no such classification was listed on the state employees' roster; that we would have to accept a "supervising nurse" for the position. Having become acquainted by this time with the knowledge, scope and appreciation of the active life process and the degree of involvement and dedication of the run-of-the-mill hospital personnel, we delayed making an appointment in the hope that some other solution to our problem would present itself.

Meanwhile we had undertaken to attend to all the minutiae involved, which were carried on a part-time basis for a year, of about eight hours a week, until Miss Kralides joined us and took over the management of some of these matters. Miss Kralides had been associated with the Recreational Therapy Department for seven years and was assigned officially in that capacity to our project, but not as "coordinator," though she partially fulfilled the functions we envisaged.

The oppositional forces working against our project that

had been latent from the very start became apparent in its second year. There were among the staff at all levels those who looked at it askance as a wild idea that would never work; there were also the skeptics with their doubts that our patients with their histories of violence, sloth and hopeless degradation could ever be rescued from their fate; there were the frank opponents to whose power and status the project was a threat as they could no longer function traditionally in their capacities and felt unable to make the transition to the new roles; then there were the more menial workers who, in addition to their inflexibility and rigid habits, feared increased responsibility and more work, on the one hand, and loss of authority over the patients on the other. It was our well-founded feeling that the common underlying motive in these reaction and attitude variations was enormous fear of, resentment, and subtle antagonism against the patients and even contempt for them.

The fact that we got under way and succeeded in achieving the results we have recounted, can be attributed to the unreserved support we have been receiving from the director of the hospital. The charisma of his office and the fear of his power secured for us the overt cooperation from all levels of staff, but the reservations and subtle sabotage could not be eliminated even by this. Sensing the attitude of the staff, especially those of the higher echelon, we made it a point to have the director physically present at as many of our seminar sessions, supervisory staff (luncheon), administrative and small specialist meetings and frequently also on our visits to the wards, as often as his enormous duties and involvements would permit.

It was essential that we at all times emphasize the director's commitment and interest in the project, his unflagging support of it and of its direction. In fact, after the first several seminar sessions at the height of the paniclike reactions of the ward staff and some of the supervisors, I intentionally absented myself from a session in order to give the director an opportunity to present to the staff the potential possibilities of the project, the advantages that would accrue to them from it, and especially my qualifications, past experiences and my standing in the profes-

243

sional community. The latter was necessary, for come what may, I was considered an interloper, ignorant of hospital practices and procedures.

Obviously the time and attention he devoted to the project added greatly to his many hospital, departmental, professional and community duties and it was necessary for him to detach himself from the project after the first year, though still maintaining keen interest in its doings. The director's physical absence emboldened the hard core of a few strategic members of the supervisory staff to unfold their colors and various subtle and not so subtle strategies to defeat it began to make their appearance. However excrescences of these dormant attitudes were noticeable from the outset. As early as January 4, 1965, or about 10 weeks after the initiation of the ward activities and six months of seminar discussions, an entry in my diary reads:

After the seminar, one of the activities supervisors and the [second] psychiatrist requested a conference with me. Apparently they have discussed the matter in advance and now wished to involve me in it.

The topic they brought up was taking groups of patients off the wards for activities at other places in the hospital such as Occupational Therapy. I was somewhat taken aback by this suggestion, since this was contrary to the very basic intent of the program, of which the two women were fully aware. Our plan required that the patients were to engage in work that had meaning to them in terms of interest and free choice in the context of and as an extension of their daily lives. Both had attended the seminars where this point was repeatedly and thoroughly considered. In addition, the supervisor and I discussed this matter in a private conversation in her office about a month earlier when I stated that we would do what they now suggested when the patients were ready for wider reality. But the principle of free choice would still have to prevail rather than the current practice of indenture.

I reiterated that in the groups that were *taken* off wards to special activities, only a few proved interested enough to participate, while the majority sat doing nothing or fell asleep, and that such groups may serve the ends of custodial care, but were not suitable for the therapeutic or re-educational activation of patients.

During the discussion I asked two women what they would do with the groups off the wards. Their response was that they did not know, but would keep consulting me on a weekly basis as to procedures. It was obvious that what they aimed at was subtly to take over the direction of the project, thereby increasing the prestige of the particular department supervisor. We agreed, however, that patients possibly from both wards who displayed special talents in some areas could be formed into groups, and turned over to specialists who would fan their interests in the activity.

From the start, this plan was doomed to failure, for our patients' need at this juncture was tranquility and good relationships. The occupations had value to them insofar as they served as means toward these ends. Efforts at forming interest groups met with complete failure until some years later when a small number of the patients became ready for specialized occupations. When an effort was made, even three years later, of putting such a plan into operation on a wide scale, it had to be abandoned. The small number of patients who responded to the announcement of the formation of off-ward special-interest groups did not actually attend any of them. These events finally convinced the staff of the patients' attitudes toward special interest groups and they no longer attempted to impose them on our patients.

In the second year of the project, word began to circulate that the ward and O. T. staffs were complaining of the monotony of their jobs under the new plan. While none of this had come *directly* to our or the administration's attention, statements to this effect were "inadvertently" dropped by the nurse and supervisor of the department involved. They complained that the staff remained sedentary for too long periods of time, when working with patients at the "tables." It was felt that they should be moving about and doing physical work as in the past. These complaints did not seem to have any foundation, for as the tranquility on the wards set in, we encouraged the attendants to vary the activities at will and introduce whatever interests and occupations would be acceptable to the patients, including spontaneous trips and visits off the wards, special cleaning jobs and other household routines, trips to the gymnasium and the general lounge.

However, the attendants who had never exercised any initiative and for years awaited direction from the nurse in charge, characteristically did not follow through on our suggestions. In view of the fact that the plateau in interest in the project did set in as the wards and patients no longer presented "exciting" problems to be solved, we considered these putative complaints as part of the smoldering resistance to the unaccustomed practices and values. Now that the director was not attending to the project, the fear of insubordination having been eliminated, the subsurface resentments and jealousies tenuously held in restraint could now come to the surface.

There was another development that occurs to us in retrospect that may have contributed to, though by no means could be regarded as the major cause of, the declining interest in the project. After 22 months of uninterrupted weekly seminar sessions and meetings with the attendants and the top-level staff we felt that all the minutiae of our theory and program had received thorough consideration and no longer required further repetition. We have, therefore, inaugurated a seminar for staffs of other wards with a view to imparting to them knowledge of our practices on Wards A and B and of their outcomes.

As already indicated previously, the personnel of this seminar included psychiatrists, psychologists, nurses and the replacement attendants assigned to our wards. This seminar met three times a month, the fourth being given over to the staffs of our own demonstration wards and the top-level staffs as auditors who still remained interested. The top-level staff were excluded from the new training seminar, since its content was largely a rehash of the earlier ones. At the same time, and for the same reason, we terminated the luncheon meetings as well. It was now the task of the various staffs to carry out plans and incorporate them into practice. This decision may have been a serious error.

It seems that the top-level staff, some of whom were involved in carrying on the program, and others in a supervisory capacity who were in the second line of participation, lost contact with the project on the one hand, and on the other felt left out and, perhaps, even rejected. The latter fact was intimated to me quite indirectly much later in a conversation by one of the group who was in a position to know reactions of the staff in the entire hospital. It would appear that our assumption that the top-level professional staff no longer needed the status-tie was faulty and had a negative effect upon the development of our work.

We have alluded a number of times to the disadvantages that were inherent in the limitations on the scope of our authority and the demarcations of our functions. Because of the nature of our place in the scheme of the hospital's organic life, our project continued to be for a long time an accretion to its body rather than becoming integrated into it by the process of what biologists term intussusception. As we have shown, the principles and some of its practices have in time been absorbed to a degree in spite of this, but nonetheless its having been introduced from the outside militated against the project's potentials and presented us with many difficulties. Among these was the arbitrary assignment and shifting of staff by the administration without consultation with us as to the suitability of the new recruits.

The nature of our project and the demands it made upon the ward staff required people of special personality qualities and gifts, which were difficult to come by. As we have already indicated, the staff we inherited were far from being adequate for the task, and we have invested great effort in retraining and reconditioning them. However, when vacancies occurred, they were filled by others usually chosen from other wards *at random*, without taking into account their personal suitability for work in our program. This practice was carried out in relation to attendants as it was to psychiatrists, with resultant endless difficulties for us, a situation that became acute when the system of rotating attendants as a retraining device was introduced. Newcomers to whom our procedures were alien, but who were temperamentally disposed to our orientation could have been more readily absorbed into the project. Those in whom the project countered temperamental dispositions and ideational convictions resentfully attempted to accommodate themselves and participated at best half-heartedly, bringing on a lackluster element to our work.

One can speculate, in the light of the ever-present political machinations in institutions such as a mental hospital, as to the motivations for the attempt to abrogate the very foundations of our project. As events have later revealed, it was a strategy to curb the "authority" of the project's staff by undermining the program's undeniable success.[2] This has especially become evident when, in the course of its development, the need for the active participation on the part of the departmental supervisors had gradually diminished. As the attendants and the specialists became accustomed to their roles in the gestalt of the program, and the major adjustments, expansions and modifications had been accomplished, the need for their participation, beyond occasional consultations, disappeared. As their status was thus diminished, their growing indifference and criticisms can be viewed as unconscious reactions to this loss.

In a closed system such as a hospital is, departmental rivalry and antagonisms among its constituent segments are not uncommon. Each makes a bid for pre-eminence and they often do so by devious means. Such antagonism existed in a particularly virulent form and of long standing between some of the departments on whom our work depended. It was the supervisor of one of these who instigated the suggestion for decimating it by introducing prematurely off-ward special-interest groups to which we have already alluded.

Our project, however, suffered a real setback when we lost by attrition our central activities person on one of the wards and by transfer of an equally effective staff member on the other. The replacements *assigned* to us had been of greatly lesser personality and skill qualifications. One of them was frightened and withdrawn, while the other power-driven, harsh and unfeeling. She was solely activity, rather than therapeutically oriented, and always vociferously attributed the blame to patients for deviant

---

[2] A confirmation of this assumption is supplied by an episode that took place on the very first day when Miss Kralides came to the wards. The two nurses immediately went to the Chief Administrator and asked him to clarify her role for them with an implied complaint that they saw her as making inroads on their authority and usurping some of their functions. When this came to my attention, I asked Miss K. to limit her area of activities, even though that diminished her usefulness to the patients, and to nominally put herself at the direction of the nurses. This incident suggests how much of a threat I must have been, but due to my close relation with the hospital director, reactions remained unexpressed.

conduct and nonparticipation.[3] From closer observation it became clear that what was transpiring was in part, at least, motivated by the long-standing competition and antagonism with another department in the hospital. This later developed into an insuperable dilemma for us.

We obviously could not become embroiled in an internecine struggle without damaging our work or risking impermissible emotional strain. We, therefore, chose to ignore these and other similar developments. However, we apprised the appropriate administrative authorities of the problem and continued to repair fences whenever possible. An unexpected incident, however, brought home the seriousness of the damage that could be wrought by unsuitable personalities on a project such as ours.

Upon my first visit to the wards after my first absence (of a month, due to a subway strike) since the inauguration of the project almost two years before, I was duly shocked by the tension pervading both wards. The tension was particularly noticeable because it had been absent for more than a year and a half. Visibly, the aspect of the wards had not altered, but the subtle, qualitative alterations were indeed startling. Gone were the placid expressions on most faces, and the friendly, smiling greetings of the recent past. Patients sat about with tense, stony faces. Even those who were engaged in the proffered, now meager activities did so in uncomfortable silence. There was no communication, either verbal or nonverbal, among patients and between them and staff. In the past silence was not infrequent, but it was the product of, and denoted, inner tranquility in the majority of the patients. Now one felt a silence of discomfort, of suppressed anger and fear.

An incontrovertible evidence of the tension that now dominated was given by two instances of physical aggression against me that morning. As I was standing near the office a patient passed me and, quite unprovoked, pushed me violently as she

[3] She was the person who reported on the trip with patients which appears on pp. 189-191.

murmured something under her breath. This was one of our strolling patients who had passed me innumerable times before in her peregrinations usually looking at me fixedly and on occasion would even faintly smile. In addition, this patient was not characteristically aggressive, nor unduly agitated. She was more of an isolate. The fact that she was able to bring herself to attack me indicated that the climate of the ward increased her anxiety and tensions.

Later, when I visited the small lounge where Miss Kralides was with a group, a young patient, who was kept in restriction by order of the court because of her sexual promiscuity, came up to me and demanded that I transfer her to another ward. She no longer liked Ward B, she said, she wanted to go down to a lower ward. I explained as I usually did in such instances that ward transfers were the domain of the psychiatrist and that I had no authority to affect such changes. In the past, this young girl had always been extremely friendly toward me, and would engage me in conversation. Although she clearly knew what my functions were, she nonetheless proceeded to use me as the target of her rage, and with eyes shooting fire, insisted that I transfer her "immediately" to another ward. My explanation was rejected with great vehemence and complaints to the effect that she had been given the "run-around." She stepped up toward me menacingly, with a combative stance as she shrieked and appeared to be on the point of attacking me physically.

Because this episode was acted out in the full view of about 25 patients, and given the fact that there was no secluded area where she might have been calmed down (though this possibility seemed quite dubious in the state she was in), I took the only avenue of terminating the unpleasant and surprising scene by turning on my heels and walking out of the room.

There was no doubt in my mind that these two events stemmed from, and were symptomatic of, the general climate on the wards. Another aspect of this situation worthy of note was that both patients were from Ward B. Despite the greater pathology of the patients on Ward A, none displayed hostility to the same degree as did these two. It seems that due to the antagonis-

250

tic climate on Ward B, which stemmed from a member of the top personnel, the patients harbored a greater quantum of covert hostility than did their counterparts on Ward A, where the staff were most friendly toward me.

My observations were brought before the attendants' seminar, as was our wont in all matters, but the few who mustered courage to speak up defensively denied being aware of this regressive complexion of the ward climate. However, I was armed by the corroboration of my impression from several individuals with whom I had spoken, and I was sure of my ground. The ward psychiatrist, after considerable and obvious hesitation to ally himself with "authority" and against the "proletariat," confirmed the correctness of my impression. There was no doubt in my mind that the attendants' benign and tolerant attitudes toward patients were in no way decreased during my month's absence. This was obvious from their manner and conduct, and confirmed by a few staff members who were objective and of high integrity. The cause of this breakdown was indubitably the lack of orderliness in, and smooth running of, the daily life of our highly unstable population during our prolonged absence and unavoidable staff shortage.

The culminating episode of the internecine struggle between the two departments occurred soon after. Subsequent to the first seminar session following my absence, the workers of one of these departments headed by their supervisor approached me with a unique plan: they would transfer their activities to the small conference rooms (which could hold no more than six patients) and leave the others on the wards to their own devices, with perhaps an occasional visit to the activities room. This suggestion, which obviously was inspired by the eminently effective work with groups of 20 to 25 patients by Miss Kralides, was surprising, for it ran counter to the very core and philosophy of our project. Being at a loss as to the best way to deal with this unexpected development, I suggested that we all give the matter further consideration and discuss it at some future time as a group.

A few days later, having thought the matter over, the unsuitability of the plan became quite clear and I called the supervisor on the phone. She agreed that the occupations which were conducted openly on the ward attracted a goodly number of patients and also had a quieting effect upon many others. We again explained, during our rather lengthy conversation, the importance of the specialists as "pace setters" for the attendants and patients. We also speculated as to how the bulk of the patients would be affected by this plan.

When I came to the ward two days later, I found the patients lost and milling about and the tables at the centers of activities bare and unoccupied. On Ward B about ten sheets of drawing paper had been spread out on one table and nothing on all the others. Later when I went to Ward A I found that nothing at all was supplied the patients, who seemed lost milling about *en masse*.

I questioned the nurse on Ward B, who was visibly upset and angry. She angrily replied that a small group was in the conference room. Puzzled by this, I asked why this was so, and she replied truculently that she was told *that I had approved* their working in the little room instead of on the ward. Walking up to the conference room in uncontrolled anger, I saw the worker with six patients quietly at their tasks. I *ordered* her (!) peremptorily to take up her station on the ward as before to which, without a word, she complied instantaneously, with her charges following her. Soon the ward resumed its usual character.

Ward A was the obvious instigator of this plan, with four patients serenely at work while 61 idly milled about. I repeated the order and she, too, with her four adherents trailing after her, returned to the activity room with alacrity, and protesting in a subdued voice, set up the usual activities. Soon after, I visited the supervisor in her office, who self-consciously evaded discussing the situation.

Obviously, I could not become involved in so sordid a business and had to take drastic steps.

252

8. *Progress*

How can one assess with any degree of certitude the improvements that resulted from our efforts? Had we set the stage for a statistical evaluation we may have obtained some data in personality changes and value-realignments which might have been reduced to some form of tabulation, graphs and statistical data. This was not our aim, however. But even if it were, the controls and exposures that would have been necessary for such a study and the *a priori* conditioned setting for it would have blocked, if not altogether prevented, the spontaneous unfolding of the idiosyncratic personalities that had unquestionably occurred in our patients and some of our staff. We may have obtained averages and reliabilities, but only at the cost of neglecting the inner lives of our patients (subjective feelings not being especially susceptible to measurement) and perhaps also at the expense of whatever peace and tranquility we had been able to achieve.

The more suitable recourse left to us was the recording of day-to-day observations of events and evaluations of the ongoing phenomena as they had occurred. To prevent possible bias, we avoided relying on any one person's evaluations. We found reliability in the consensus of spontaneous, most often unsolicited, reactions of persons whose opinions could be adjudged trustworthy because of their uninvolvement. Part of the content of this chapter will, therefore, be devoted to a small number of randomly selected observations, estimates and reactions by patients, their relatives and official and unofficial visitors, in addition to the writer and members of the staff—all of whom had been acquainted for varying periods with the state of the two wards prior to the inauguration of our program.

We can recall that as early as the third day of the quieting occupations, and before even the partitions in the toilets had been constructed and lockers, kitchen, laundry and cosmetics room installed, with the wards still kept under lock and key, we witnessed the striking change in the prevailing climate on the wards. We noted in our diary that "even more remarkable were the friendly smiles on the faces of many patients on the wards and their friendly greetings. On Ward A six or seven patients surrounded me with various requests and questions. They, too, were friendly. There was no trace of the pervasive tension of only a few days before, and with a few exceptions on Ward A, no evidence of truculence or anger among the patients. On this ward, only Hannah strutted back and forth with her customary angry murmurings."

Given the state of our patients, not to mention the conditions under which they were living, and considering their inability to respond to even the most rudimentary human relations and certainly not to any direct therapeutic intervention, we turned our attention to extirpating the circumstances that perpetually brought on tensions and caused disturbances. That the program has eminently succeeded in this was attested to grudgingly by the most skeptical covert and overt opposition. While setbacks inevitably occurred, they were in time comparatively mild and infrequent, as well as short-lived. Even then the basic climate undeniably continued to be one of placidity and comparative friendliness among patients and between patients and staff, and to some degree also between the staffs of the two wards who had been for a long time at odds with each other.

We considered it a triumph when, at one of the small luncheon administrative sessions, the director of the nursing school for several decades who knew the hospital most intimately, remarked that she had observed "much friendlier attitudes among these two formerly warring groups." At the same luncheon (January 4, 1965), Dr. Beckenstein observed "how much better the two nurses (in charge of the wards) appeared as compared with the time before the project was started" and added, "Both also look more relaxed and lively and had color in their faces." [From the taped minutes of that session.]

About a month after the start of ward activities (and four and a half months of seminar sessions), the Chief Administrator who doubled also as Chief of Nursing Services reported at the psychiatrists' meeting as follows:

I think the resistance [on the part of attendants] has lessened. They are much more cooperative. I think they feel they are becoming a part of a program. We've always in the past, talked about, read and heard about team concepts. I think now we are involving them [the staff] in a team concept, because in any contributions they make we try to go along with them [encourage them]. Of course, with any group of people, particularly with the type we have, many of whom had no skills before they came to the institution, and who suddenly are given a role where they are going to contribute, I think as time goes on you will find much more interest and cooperation and understanding. I can already see the difference in the attendants' attitudes.

MR. S.: What's the difference?

CHIEF ADM.: Well I notice their conduct with the patients. They are not hollering. I don't hear that yelling as much. When once in a while without being seen I come in unexpectedly from the back way—I have a few ways of getting into the building—I don't hear that yelling. I don't see the pushing. I don't find any—shall we say—assaultive tendencies on the part of some of the personnel. We've had to deal with that occasionally in the past. I think they're much kinder to the patients and I think several of the people [attendants], who have been problems, are much less troublesome now.

In time, one could observe, in addition to the occupations, patients sitting about in groups of three or four quietly talking; another group busily engaged in the kitchen with the large electric coffee urn, setting out 70 cups and saucers, arranging cookies on trays, which other patients had baked the day before, piling all this on wagons in readiness for serving mid-morning coffee; two patients of their own initiative quietly absorbed in a card game, or groups of six to 10 sitting together with an attendant, quietly conversing, or playing or watching some table game.

As our program progressed and free mobility was made possible by the unlocked doors, patients left the building, in many instances unsupervised, and some even walked off the grounds.[1] Groups of patients went on trips and, as recorded, even on bathing parties at an ocean front. It was now not unusual to see some taking loving care of fellow patients, and in one instance, it was reported that several patients, following the example once set by an attendant, sang to quiet down one of their disturbed mates. In the dining hall, patients could be seen feeding others who were more disturbed or less able to handle the implements, a practice which we discouraged, since it infantilized the latter and prolonged their dependence.

Although from time to time fights did break out among the patients (since assaultive trends die very slowly in those who are so disposed even among "healthy" persons), there was only one instance of assault and that by a new patient in the first two years of the program against a staff member, which had been a common occurrence in the past. The staff member provoked the patient when she ignored the rules we laid down for dealing with disturbed members of our community.

About five and a half months after the inauguration of the activity program, and eight and a half months of indoctrination of the attendants, members of the Board of Visitors, appointed by the Governor of the State of New York, toured the hospital, including Wards A and B. The following is taken from the report of the then secretary (now the president) of that body:

We went through the entire W. building. It was the first time that I had seen Wards A and B in several years. What a change! On Ward B

---

[1] Our insistence that this be permitted met with imperative and concerted opposition from the ward and other staff as a danger of physical injury to the patients. Our position was that because one or two patients might be injured, *all* of them should not suffer deprivation. As we envisaged, there has *never* been a mishap from this source during the five years of the project.

the door was open, the patients were quiet and orderly, sitting around tables and doing occupational therapy, knitting, crocheting and needle work. I also saw a room set up like a kitchen, which the patients were using for making coffee, cookies, etc. Then there was a room with washers and dryers for them to do their own clothes. At the far end of the ward, there was a room set aside as a beauty parlor where patients could primp up. The appearance of the patients was a good indication of how well this facility is used.

On Ward A [the "worst" in the hospital] there has been considerable progress but not as good as on Ward B. The door here is still locked,[2] but the patients here were generally orderly and came running up to us, inquiring as to who I was, making all kinds of requests, such as "When am I going out?" *They did not seem to be so concerned about going home.*

A note in our diary dated January 7, 1966 indicates that we, too, were impressed with this phenomenon. It reads:

In the past, patients on Wards A and B would constantly descend upon the psychiatrists, the director and myself, pleading, but more often demanding, that they be allowed to go home. This tendency has greatly diminished and was on the wane altogether when the new male psychiatrist appeared. More from habit than need, some patients renewed their requests to go home. The psychiatrist, who "caught on" to our basic attitude toward patients and our philosophy of rehabilitation through the seminars and observation of the new climate on the wards, adopted a simple device to stop this type of pleading and demanding. He would simply say to all the patients who requested it that they can go home any time they wish and as soon as they can arrange it with the relatives. This simple permissive device completely stopped within a month all references to going home. The patients accepted the fact and the reality that going home was a matter between them and their relatives.

Three months later the occupational therapy supervisor of the New York State Department of Mental Hygiene, during her annual inspection visit to the hospital, was

. . . very favorably impressed with both wards. She was surprised to learn that the patients were not specially selected for the project, and that these were considered the two most disturbed wards in the institution. She felt that our patients did not seem overtranquilized, and also

[2] These doors, too, had been unlocked soon after.

257

that the attendants handled a particular episode that occurred during her visit extremely well. She visits all of the institutions in the state, she said, and felt that this particular project was the best she had seen and would be well worth emulating in other institutions. [From a report by the supervisor of the occupational therapy department at the hospital].

The New York State Medical Inspector, on his annual inspection of the hospital, stated at our seminar, after the first year of our project, that "these were the best disturbed wards of any hospital in the state. I visited all of them."

About 10 months after the start of the ward program, the consulting psychiatrist, who seldom visited the wards, did so, and his findings follow:

(Re: Ward A). The first and most sustained impression was of the air of quiet activity that predominated. It was not the sort of drugged quiet or noisy, haphazard confusion of prior visits. Apart from several patients sleeping in chairs, *but none on floors*, there was a purposeful air which pervaded. Patients, singly and in groups, were engaged in a variety of activities—housekeeping, coffee-break preparation, some games, a number of occupational devices, reading, arranging for activities off the ward—to mention the most obvious.

The several attendants were busy each at her own task, with administration, occupational, and participation aspects. There was no congregating on the part of attendants. Each seemed to know what she was about and to be attending to it. There was conversation by people in couples or groups. There was never a shout, scream, yell, fight, altercation or disturbances as the morning moved on.

My original purpose was to enter the ward to speak with a number of patients about whom questions had been raised in the conferences (seminar). I thought a more direct evaluation might be helpful. I located the first, Miss F——, and promptly entered into a conversation with her notable for its ease, friendliness, development, and subject matter. Also remarkable was the fact that while several other patients made tentative efforts to speak simultaneously with me, the simple reply I would offer her in turn was sufficient to have each of them draw off and wait. This was in marked contrast to a former experience where what had started as a dialogue became a group affair despite the same suggestion.

I spoke with the Misses F——, N——, and T——. The nature of the conversations varied in content and relation to reality but each was able to maintain some semblance of a real relationship. Specifically,

Miss F——, who spoke of her original fear regarding being killed and then indicated that it was this that made her uneasy. She then apologized for thinking that I was there to kill her, as she had said before. Miss N—— and Miss T—— who have been reported as provoking each other spoke with me about the other's behavior and each spontaneously suggested that perhaps if they stayed away from each other the fights would be less frequent.

One patient, a young woman of a particularly withdrawn appearance and behavior, to whom an empty cup had been given, was simply seated staring into it. I asked whether she cared for some coffee. When she nodded her head I invited her to the table where coffee was dispensed, but rather than having her cup filled for her, she stood in confusion. I conveyed to the attendant the idea that an alternate approach be used. She promptly caught on. Thus another patient poured as our withdrawn patient held out her cup. She then proceeded to add cream and sugar herself, after which she quietly began to drink. In a moment her eyes became less glossy and her gaze actually focused on me.

Mrs. B—— (an attendant) was at the coffee table and by her conduct encouraged a self-help process for the patients. She neither pushed them nor pampered them. I then left with several farewells and a promise to return, and moved on to Ward B.

(Re: Ward B). Essentially the same situation prevailed here. The charge nurse was busily engaged in a variety of activities: medications, advising, and ward duties, as were the attendants. I had time to speak to one patient (Miss G——) in some detail. The conversation again was notable less for its content than the friendliness, and contact with reality which it revealed. Again there was no sustained interruption by other patients. A number remembered me from visits and had welcoming recognition with conversational aspects to their words. Most seemed to be going about their business with a minimum of fuss and bother. I made no attempt in either ward to engage personnel in conversation. Some attempted, but I begged off citing the pressure of my limited time and number of patients to be seen.

In summary I would say that a degree of organization was to be discerned, a quality to be sharply differentiated from regimentation. There was a great degree of individual latitude and a corresponding freedom of activity being shown. The atmosphere was relaxed, purposeful and friendly. I am almost tempted to say that some patients seemed to have an inner-directed aspect to their behavior rather than simply a response to schedule or orders.

Following a visit from a U.S. government official to observe the wards, a member of the administrative staff reported as follows:

Mr. H—— expressed a desire to photograph our most disturbed female wards as he felt that female patients act out their psychosis in a way that is more dramatic pictorially. Dr. Beckenstein and I took him to Wards A and B. He just sat on each of the wards for a while in order to feel the climate. . . .

Mr. H—— carried his camera and flash equipment with him. A number of patients asked him what he was doing there and he simply answered, "I'm going to take pictures." Some patients asked him to take their pictures and this he did. After spending about half an hour on each of the wards, Mr. H—— asked to be taken to the wards where "destructive patients are kept, where patients throw feces around." Dr. Beckenstein and I assured him that he was on our most disturbed wards, and that these were the most regressed female patients in the institution. He then thought that perhaps Dr. Beckenstein's presence had an effect on the patients and that the employees were working with the patients in the manner they did because of his presence. Dr. Beckenstein, thereupon, left the wards.

I remained on the wards with Mr. H—— from about 10:45 A.M. until about 12:15 P.M. We went from ward to ward and he photographed whomever and whatever he thought would be of interest. Two patients had crying spells and he followed the attendants and the patients into the conference room[3] on each occasion.

He noted that there was only one patient lying on the floor and wondered about this. I told him that patients were not only allowed, but encouraged to lie on their beds whenever they wished. He was surprised to learn that the dormitory was not kept locked. I took him into the dormitory on one of the wards. Only three patients were lying on top of their beds. One patient was doing some dusting, and when asked by Mr. H—— why she was doing this, she answered, "Because I live here."

The usual morning activities were going on. Some of the patients were working on Occupational Therapy projects, some were playing games and some went out on walking parties, some did not participate at all.

Just before noon we went into the patients' dining room. Two attendants were in there with three patients and were encouraging and helping them to feed themselves. About noon, patients started to come into the dining room in groups of approximately 15, got on line by themselves, picked up their trays and food, got seated and started to eat. He was particularly impressed by the feeling and kindness that our attendants showed to the three "problem feeders" and was pleasantly

[3] This was one of the smaller rooms which we set aside and furnished for calming disturbed patients, thus preventing group contagion, and for small group meetings of the ward staff.

260

surprised that there was not a large line-up of patients waiting to receive food. There was no din, pushing or shoving and there did not seem to be any personnel overtly directing this activity.

We left the fourth floor at this time and while I was prepared to show him other wards of the hospital he wanted to return to Wards A and B, after lunch. We got back there at about 1:15 P.M. On Ward B, eight patients were in the kitchen baking cup cakes, some were playing games and others were doing Occupational Therapy. On Ward B, pretty much the same activity was going on. Some of the patients were preparing to go to Music Appreciation (conducted by Miss Kralides) and we went over to the small lounge to see this group.

After this period he left very much impressed by the wards, but with possibly some doubt that he had really seen our most disturbed patients.

The feeling of belonging characterized by the phrase "Because I live here" was gradually spreading as revealed in an entry under the date of December 17, 1965.

On Ward A, two patients have, *on their own initiative*, undertaken to clean the windows of the ward [of which there were scores]. I was told that this was the first time this ever occurred. Similarly on Ward B the panes on the doors leading to the outdoor porch had been decorated by patients with colorful drawings on the glass. A series of paintings done by other patients were hung on the walls.

Dr. Beckenstein, who frequently visited the wards as a routine during the relatives' visiting hours, reported their gratification with the changes in the patients. Many volunteered their reactions and verbalized them with happy expressions on their faces. A brother of a patient, the only one in the family who ever visited her, once applied for a temporary transfer to an institution near where her family would spend the summer. He said that she would then be returned to the hospital. This was obviously not possible to arrange. During the conversation the brother was asked by Dr. Beckenstein whether he thought there had been improvements on Ward B, where his sister had been in residence for some years. "Oh yes," he exclaimed, "the ward is moving. Things are much better than they have ever been, much better."

In time the relatives of the patients in these wards, formerly referred to as "Siberia," have become fully accepting of them. In the past there were constant demands and appeals that their kin be transferred to the lower ("better") wards. This was no longer the case now. As early as June 28, 1965, the supervising psychiatrist of the service (building) on whose decision such transfers depended, and to whom complaints were referred, remarked how impressed he was with the fact that "so few requests for ward changes were being made and the number of complaints, compared with the other six ("better") wards on the service, was now negligible." In fact several patients who had improved sufficiently to be transferred to the "better" wards (to make room for new "disturbed" patients) requested that they be put back on Wards A and B. Their plaint was that "there was nothing to do down there." And in at least one instance it was reported that a patient from one of the other wards, who had seen the activities on our wards, said, "I think I'll go down and break something, then they'll send me up there."

The general improvement of self-image and reality testing is reflected in the enterprise of one of many patients who acted in a similar manner, though they did not always abscond as the following one did.

E——, one of the shadowy, withdrawn patients, who seemed to have retreated from life, had broken off all communication with others and refrained in her complete inversion from participating in the ward life. She seemed to have become somewhat enlivened by the new active climate and had thereby attracted Miss Kralides' attention. The latter attempted to draw her into activities with indifferent success, but Miss K. persisted in speaking to her and turned her attention to this patient at every opportunity. To this E—— began to respond.

After about a year of continued attempts by Miss K. at drawing her out, the patient mustered enough courage to run away from the hospital after a weekend at home. She had told Miss K. that she had discussed her difficulties with her husband during her visit. From this point on, she frequently imparted to Miss K. information about her problems and thoughts, a clear indication that she had been made ready for psychotherapy, which we had envisioned for many of our patients, but which we unfortunately were unable to provide.

Improved attitudes of patients toward life on the wards took a vastly more positive turn. For example, during a conversation in July, 1965, two patients volunteered to me that they now enjoyed living in the hospital. One of these was the neat-looking white half of the Siamese twins who then had blanket permission to spend as much time at her home as she wished. This patient confided to me that her mother constantly "nagged" and made life uncomfortable for her. During another conversation, she complained that her brother had, on two occasions, suggested that she "strip to the waist." "Now," she said, "this isn't right, Mr. Slavson, is it? He is not my husband. This is incest!" Obviously, direct psychotherapy with this patient would have been very fruitful.

A symptom of the general relaxed climate on the wards—and in the patients—was marked by the change in their response to the appearance of a psychiatrist or hospital official. As already reported, in the past these events brought a flock of women around the visitor with numerous questions, requests and demands for privileges and emoluments. The most frequent of these were for cigarettes and for going home, with the latter vastly predominating. Other patients would attempt to engage the visitors in a variety of conversations, largely of a delusional nature. These spontaneous congregates completely disappeared in a comparatively brief time as tensions relaxed. Persons who came to the wards in discharge of their duties were no longer so molested. [4] The eagerness generated by the anxiety and insecurity that prevailed drove patients to infantile indiscriminate dependence and mendicancy. As the patients grew more secure in their new environment and in their relations with the ward staff, and as a degree of inner identity emerged, their libido grew less free-floating and their conduct more dignified and mature.

[4] Groups of college students and other curious visitors were now prohibited from these wards as intruders into the *home* of the patients.

No longer did patients "use the dayroom as lavatories" at night, and often during daylight hours, as the Chief Nurse reported, and the unpleasant task for the day-staff of cleaning up no longer oppressed them. Nor has the resistance of attendants to their new roles and to abandoning antiquated attitudes and practices toward patients been as much in evidence, except, of course, in the truculent stony-faced few on Ward B. The situation reported at the psychiatrists' conclave by the Chief Administrator at the early periods of our program was no longer in evidence. At that time he had reported:

I ran into a strong feeling of anxiety this week, because of the changeover in the meal situation. Some of the nurses and some of the employees feel threatened. They don't want a change.... They just don't want to change. Tuesday morning and this morning (Thursday) I was up there. The nurse (on Ward A) did not come in. She feels that she is being overexposed in the (seminar) group. The nurse on Ward B had a schedule arranged.

I was up there (on the wards) about 7:10 this morning. She came in at 7:31 or two and thought (groundlessly) that I was criticizing her for her tardiness and that she didn't get a chance to look at the schedule. We were anxious to get the patients fed. They were dressed. A question came up about clothing. On Tuesday there weren't enough slippers and stockings. These are practical things that we have for the functioning of the wards. So this morning, what happens? There still wasn't enough. This was on Ward B. When the day girls (attendants) come on, one of them goes down and gets stockings and slippers. I had the night supervisor up there every morning since Tuesday: Tuesday, Wednesday and Thursday.

And there had been some sort of a friction between them. The night people are willing to cooperate, but the day people are not on time, including the nurses in charge of the wards. So consequently the patients haven't been getting to the dining room until 7:45. This has created a problem with the activity on the wards. It is important that we get people to assume responsibility for running the ward. Mrs. B— (an attendant put in charge) tried to do it, but I'm not sure that she isn't running into trouble with her peers, because I think they resent her telling them what to do.

We have quite a problem on these two wards. I don't know how we're going to approach it to make them accept the change. I don't know whether the anxiety was created by their being in the group (seminar) here. I don't think they come out with their real feelings when they are in the group. I think there are many things that should be ironed out on the wards through conferences according to who the individuals involved are . . . . They feel that you're trying to do something to them. I don't know. I can't quite put my finger on what it is. I never ran into this type of thing. I can't say it's undercover hostility, but there's something wrong here.

    Mr. S.: Subtle resistance?

    C.N.: But they're trying to be cooperative. They're trying to. I don't think they understand yet.

    Mr. S.: How do you feel the psychiatrists could help in this situation . . . ?"

The above indicates the mood of despair that pervaded the hospital staff at the project's inauguration, against which we had to struggle. While irresponsibility of staff and breakdown of routines occurred, in time they have greatly diminished in frequency and intensity, and we had extended periods of a smooth running community life which ultimately became the permanent pattern.

From time to time, patients and staff would speak to the social worker about the project. Being aware of the heavy burden she was carrying, we timidly asked her to record some of their reactions. The following is a brief memo from her:

One of the patients who has been an active participant in the program, dropped in on December 9th (1964) to talk with the worker. She was now in much better contact than she has been for some time. In reference to the program she said, "the ward is less deserted [sic] now. Now that the attendants don't feel so deserted, they are more kindly to the patients." She said that when she comes in after breakfast in the morning and finds the O.T. materials on the table "stimulating and they take my thoughts off myself and I don't feel the hopelessness I used to, wandering around between meals." She said she has been using a sewing machine, spoke of her interest in this activity and of the jobs she had held in a "sheltered" workshop in the past. She expressed interest in the possibilities for creativity through sewing. Obviously reactivated by the ward program, she said that she had long wanted to do editorial writing, had done good work in typing and other skills in the past, and requested placement in a community mental health service agency where she had been employed before.

A number of other patients have spontaneously talked to the worker about the partitions in the toilets, something patients throughout the service have been longing for ever since the worker was assigned to the hospital in 1951. The lack of privacy in toilet facilities has always been very traumatic for patients. One of the reasons many patients reluctantly go to very disturbed homes on visits and for longer periods on probation is because of the privacy afforded them when there in bathing and toileting. As one patient said of the partitions, although the swinging half-doors had as yet not been in place at the time, "they may be able to see my front now, but I have privacy in the rear."

Worker has many records of comments of patients on convalescent status about their nightmare memories of having to undress and shower in the presence of other people. One of the patients, who had been an office worker, but remained completely inactive on the ward, now expressed a desire to be allowed to use a typewriter for practice at the O.T. office, obviously as a result of the stimulation she had received on the ward.

After the discussion at the ward meetings about having a stove installed, several of the patients spoke to the worker of how they looked forward to doing cooking of the kind they liked.

When the lockers arrived and were placed at the head of each patients' bed, a patient who was telling me how much she liked her ward now, said with much pleasure, "This is the first time I had a closet of my own."

Most important to me are the happier faces, the more alert conduct and the reduced hopelessness and apathy on these two wards.

The social worker also cited the case of a patient who in an interview with her said that from the age of two on she had been shunted to and from numerous institutions and foster homes until she came to the W. Building, after a short stay in another ward and building. (She was extremely pugnacious and being unsuitable for a free ward was transferred to the disturbed ward A in W. Building.) Though educationally retarded, she was placed in a typing class after being exposed to the new program and the warm treatment by attendants who had now been retrained. She commented during her interview that "You, in the W. Building, take an interest in me. I have never known kindness. I always had to fight." Because this patient had no home to go to, she continues to live in the hospital, but is during the day employed in the community.

The social worker remarked that a considerable number of other patients expressed similar sentiments in their interviews with her and that an increasing number of patients are being returned to their homes, others who had been transferred as uncontrollable from other wards to wards A and B are returning to their regular wards. One patient, in her 30's, who was transferred to ward A as uncontrollable, was now doing voluntary work in a nonprofit community agency, returning to the hospital for the night as she, too, has no home.

A sampling of others with similar records of improvement was reported retrospectively by the social worker at the end of the fourth year of the project on a small number of patients. They are:

T.S. who was deeply depressed, completely uncommunicative and at times catatonic, refused to eat for prolonged periods and required tube feeding. She has been in the hospital for 15 years, most of them on one or the other of the disturbed wards. During the second year of the project, she returned to the community to a furnished room with housekeeping privileges and had lived on her savings from her former employment before hospitalization. This sum was supplemented by Social Security and disability allowance. After two years, she returned to the hospital and was placed on ward A, after which time she had improved sufficiently to return to the community again. The hospital is keeping continued contact with her, and according to the Social Worker, T.S. is doing well.

E.S. was hospitalized directly from high school, where she was an A student. She was on ward B for 18 years, where she was described as hopeless. Just prior to the inauguration of the project, she had started a program of volunteer service and went back to her very pathological home, but was returned within a few months in such a state that all she was capable of was lying on the floor of ward B. Even the persistent efforts of a specially assigned social worker failed to arouse her. With the introduction of the project, E.S. began to move, responding to the ward activities and to the kindness from the staff, a kindness she has never in her life known. After two years, she returned to the community —and is attending business school, without any relapse.

A.H. was hospitalized in 1955 and directly placed on ward A, because of the seriousness of her disturbance. When she was brought to the hospital, she was completely detached from reality; her eyes protruded from the sockets, exposing the whites, and she did not respond to any efforts at communication. She behaved as an automaton, requiring to be led as she was unable to walk by herself. The problem of this patient was that her only relative (with whom she had lived) was an extremely disturbed and probably a very psychotic person who would activate A.H.'s symptoms and maximized them through her treatment of A.H. A.H. responded to the environment, after some time, on the ward, though never actually participating in any of its activities. She, nonetheless, improved sufficiently to be placed on an open ward and in a typing school. However, her relative surreptitiously took her home when the patient was on the hospital grounds. After a brief period she had a relapse and was returned to the hospital.

This was repeated a number of times before the project was started. As a result of effects of the project, this patient greatly improved, and when the relative again "sneaked" her out, she remained away much longer than ever before, and continuing so well adjusted, despite the pressures by the relative, that discharge from the hospital was warranted. Nevertheless the pathogenic situation in the home was too much for her and she was returned to the building where the best adjusted patients reside. In the opinion of the social worker, the fact that there was no need for her to be placed in the formerly disturbed wards indicates some significant improvement in her ego integration and improved controls, which the social worker attributes to the effect the project had upon this patient.

S.F. was one of two twins. Both girls were committed to the hospital; one of them however in a less disturbed, agitated state. The other girl was placed on ward A. She has been completely disorganized, extremely depressed and frequently disoriented. She remained in the hospital for 16 years.

Social Service Department found that she was too irrational to be referred to any rehabilitation program available. As the project got under way, she asked to see the social worker and began to visit her regularly to discuss the possibility of her being released from the hospital. She showed progressive improvement and pressed the point. However, the Supervising Psychiatrist did not concur with her request and she took leave on her own from the hospital.

B.B., a young attractive blonde women, whose marriage had broken up, seemed extremely confused although she did talk. Some of her conversation was somewhat rational, but beyond a certain point she would digress tangentially and become irrational. She had serious problems in relationships with family and friends, as well as on the wards with patients and the staff. The violent temper tantrums, to which she was given, required restraint. She was admitted in November 20, 1958, and in the second year of the project, improved sufficiently to be allowed to return to the family on convalescent status. Her conduct warranted discharge from the hospital. Two years later she was employed and apparently getting along well.

N.M., a teenager, had been in difficulties in an institution for wayward girls and as a result was committed by the court for observation in a psychiatric hospital, instead of being sent to a Detention Home. She was involved in many incidents of shop-lifting and was sexually promiscuous, largely because of her parents' own misbehavior in that area, of which the girl was aware. The committing judge ordered that N.M. be strictly supervised and thus prevented from getting into further difficulties by absconding. Therefore, she was placed on ward A and her movements greatly restricted. Thereupon she threatened to break the windows of the ward unless she was allowed to have her own way. When denied, she smashed several windows. As a result the girl was transferred to ward B where she remained during the project. After two years she had improved sufficiently to be able to go out into the community and live by herself. She drops in to see the social worker and other staff members every so often and expresses deep gratitude to them, glowing with happiness. She is earning a living doing a variety of temporary jobs such as clerical work, waiting on tables, etc. She attempted to enter a nursing school, but because of her inadequate qualifications and background, was rejected. At this writing she has been out two years without any untoward incident. She has a small apartment and lives alone.

R.W. was admitted to the hospital in October, 1957. She came in as a teenager, parentless and living with disturbed relatives. The girl appeared almost normal; she related well to people but acted out in the community. She had a transilient personality, flitting from one thing to another, was unfocussed and unable to mobilize toward any goal. R.W. would start things and quickly drop them and take up other interests. She did not commit any act that is usually classified as delinquent, and was rather adjudged psychotic. Because of seeming normality when she came to the hospital, she was placed in the typing class and after a period of psychotherapy was returned to the community. She took up with and lived with a comparatively young married man, whose level of intelligence was considerably lower than her own.

After a brief period of life under these circumstances, she reverted to her original behavior and had to be hospitalized again, this time being placed on Ward A. She was now much more inwardly disturbed. Two years after the project started, in which she actively participated in a manner that was adjudged normal at the case conference, it was decided that she be treated again in the community. Accordingly she was returned to her husband, who had visited her regularly while she was at the hospital.

She lived with her husband in a small apartment, but after a year he drifted away. She now lives alone and it was reported to the hospital's Social Service Department that she maintained good relations with her neighbors, was liked, and getting along well.

Because of this adjustment, she was discharged from the hospital.

J.S., who was homeless and without any relatives, presented many difficulties to the staff for many years. Having an unstable and an epileptic personality she was given to temper tantrums and, though helpful to her ward-mates, interfered in their lives. She was disliked by some of the ward staff because of her meddling and stubbornness. J.S. had been in the hospital for many years and passed through many crises. After one of these, of a rather severe nature, when she was sequestered for a time and returned to her ward (A), she had decided to establish herself in "business." At this writing she sells coffee, pastry, candy, ice cream and cigarettes, and cosmetic products, instead of running errands and obtruding herself in the lives of other patients as she did in the past. She usually arrives on the wards, lustily announcing her wares, which are purchased by those who have some funds. This enterprise was conceived and initiated by herself and she operates on a salaried basis. She obtained a concession from the Community Store and continues to help and protect patients who are physically or psychically disabled thereby needing such help. The importance of this development is that she is still living out her own masochistic behavior but on a more mature and more realistic level. She once justified her conduct in an argument with her former psychiatrist on the biblical basis that "one must love and help his neighbors." She confided to one of the staff that she now had "a boy-friend" on the grounds and inquired from this staff member whether she could work for the Epilepsy Foundation. It is not known to us whether her epileptoid state was made known to her or whether it was an intuitive reaction.

All the improvements reported above occurred in the first two years of the project. A considerable number of patients, who had no families or homes to return to, as well as some who were not ready for life in the general community, had been placed in the half-way house that was opened on the grounds as part of the hospital, as they no longer needed the protective situation of a hospital ward.

The attitudes of many attendants, as well, grew more benign. Early in December, 1964, as I walked into the office of Ward A, I came upon two attendants engaged in conversation. On seeing me, one turned and said, "We were just talking about you." The other, an older woman said, "We were just saying how much you have done for our ward; how much better things are now. Before it was constant pressure with work—trays of food had to be carried in and out of the ward" (referring to the slow and problem eaters who were fed on the ward separately; by now all took their meals in the dining hall with the other patients). She continued: "We had to clean up [excreta] after patients all the time and there was always some kind of crisis situation. When there was a party, we had to do all the work. We did the serving, the cleaning up and everything else. Now the patients are doing all this work." She then confessed that, "At first we did not believe that things would work out the way you told us they would, but they did," and added with intense feeling, "You did a lot for this ward, and we want to thank you."

The other, a much younger woman, interrupted the recital from time to time to emphasize some points somewhat melodramatically, and when the first had finished, she said, "You are President Kennedy, model 1964. Kennedy was my president and what he did for the country, you did for us. I was always hoping for a savior and you are the savior I was hoping for. I used to be so exhausted after a day's work that even after a long sleep I could hardly get up in the morning to go back to work. Now I am not so tired any more. As a matter of fact, I planned to quit this job and do anything, even housework, anything to get out of this. Now I like it and I want to stay. You have done wonders for us and we thank you."

Toward the end of this recital, the most perceptive and dedicated of the attendants, to whom we had already referred, walked in and as the others finished, I turned to her and said, "These ladies are telling me what they think about the new program. What do you think about it?" She: "Well, before the program the situation was so tense that I used to lose control of myself and people here used to tell me that I was sometimes worse than the patients themselves. I was so unhappy and so tense that I had forgotten how to smile. I was so upset all the time. I got a bad reputation in the hospital because of the way I acted. Now I can smile again. We never felt that what we did was of any importance. We were just nobodies and most of the time we didn't know what we were doing. Now we understand what we are doing. We understand the patients better and *we feel important; we are somebodies*, and now I can smile again."

In a conversation with the attendant in charge on Ward A, which one morning early in January, 1965, was in a somewhat more disturbed state (this being Monday, after an extensive holiday of the New Year and weekend, a day after family visits, as well as the fact that there were only three attendants present, instead of the five or six that should have been there) she stated among other things, "We could not run the ward with the staff I have here today without the program," and then referred to the fact that a number of the patients were occupied with various activities and, therefore, the usual large number of strollers and the resulting milling about were reduced, thus minimizing tension.

It so happened that the R.T. worker was also absent that day and only the one O.T. worker was on the ward. At one point, not a single attendant was present. The charge attendant was in the office, another was occupied in one of the smaller rooms, and the third had left for her coffee break. Despite the absence of supervision, the patients had settled down on their own and nothing of an untoward nature occurred. Even Hannah who usually screamed did not cause any disturbance.

At another point the attendant in charge said, "In the past, we used to be afraid to remain alone with a patient in a room. There was [sic] always two of us to make sure that a patient did not attack. We don't have to do this any longer." Later in the conversation she said, "When we came in in the morning, we often used to find a mess on the floors, feces and everything. This we don't find any more."

Such appreciative attitudes were never verbalized or otherwise conveyed on the other ward, except for one elderly attendant who was about to retire because of age and was happy to see the changes. She would occasionally remark, "how much easier things are." She was reported to have said to someone that she was happy to have lived long enough to see "such improvement in the hospital." This general coolness to the new project undoubtedly emanated from the person in charge.

Improvements, however, were not limited to the attendants alone. One of the chauffeurs, a comparatively new appointee, who drove me home from the hospital, once said to me, "Mr. Slavson, they are saying some nice things about your work." I asked him just what was being said and who was saying it. Somewhat self-consciously he proceeded to tell me the following: "I once saw two women patients sitting by themselves in the community store lunch room. I didn't remember ever seeing them and I asked them if they were new. 'No,' they said, 'we wasn't down here a long time. We used to come down here often before, but now our ward is so interesting that we didn't come down here for some time.'"

Early in January, 1965, i.e., about 10 weeks of the ward program, Dr. Beckenstein recounted that he had gone up one Sunday to the dining hall where the visitors and patients now met.[5] He asked about 10 relatives of patients individually whether they had observed any difference in the wards. All said that the wards were now quieter, nicer, and they all seemed pleased with the change. In one instance, a relative of a patient came up voluntarily to Dr. B. to say that the wards seemed quieter and the patients much happier. He wanted to know what had happened to cause this change.

The policy of grouping patients indiscriminately for activities and "life groups" which we found on the wards seemed to us unsuitable for our very confused and unstable patients, ex-

[5] We shifted relatives' visitations from the wards to the large dining hall where each family could occupy a separate table and thus have privacy, instead of being crowded with patients standing about, listening and interfering on the wards. This, and the improved state of the patients, greatly increased the number and frequency of visits.

273

cept, of course, for their value in maintaining personal care and grooming. By our ignoring the existence of such groups we affected their demise. It was our belief that patients, even as regressed as ours were, would under favorable conditions ultimately be impelled by instinctive *social hunger* to spontaneously establish some relationships with one another, self-selectively. This expectation was fulfilled as reflected in an entry in our diary, dated August 5, 1965 (about 10 months of the ward program). It reads:

For some weeks now homogeneous groupings made their appearance. On Ward A, today, several patients, who had for some time been preparing the mid-morning coffee, sat together quietly conversing in the kitchen after their chores were done. (These were the chronologically younger girls, who had undertaken this responsibility voluntarily, not by assignment or rotation.) Yesterday, as I was passing the open kitchen door, one of the patients called out to me inviting me to join them . . . . Three older patients sat at a table quietly conversing. It was a common, almost daily sight to find as many as eight or ten patients crowded around a table with an attendant absorbed in conversation. Sometimes, while a few played some table games, others would stand around and kibbitz interestedly.

Progress in this direction was further noted on January 7, 1966: Spontaneous small groups of three and four patients continue to spring up. It seems that past mutual antagonisms have given birth to mutual acceptance and friendliness. For months now one could see these small groups playing various table games, sitting or standing around talking or working together. Occasionally two patients on their own would toss a medicine ball to each other. More enduring were the groups at table games and those who sat quietly near each other at a table apparently deriving satisfaction simply from proximity.

Of late, during the last month or so, these homogeneous or "friendship" groups took to going together for walks on the grounds and to the community store. Small groups, two, three and four could be seen leaving the wards unsupervised on their self-chosen excursions. The patients were required *to sign themselves out by entering their names into a book* lying open on the desk in the ward office, as they went out. This procedure was instituted by the ward staff themselves. No patient had ever absconded during this period. It is not impossible that the staff will grow secure enough in the future to allow the patients to go out without the ritual of even signing out. [In this connection our difficulty was the three young alcoholic patients, who would, at every opportunity, abscond and return in a state of intoxication, which made it necessary for us to keep the door to the stairs locked.]

On January 2, 1966, a visiting day, Dr. Beckenstein went up to Wards A and B and found only a few oldest and most deteriorated patients on the wards. About a quarter of the patients were in the dining hall with relatives, the others having taken advantage of a beautiful warm and sunny day to enjoy the freedom of the outdoors.

A note in the diary dated January 3, 1965, about 11 weeks in the duration of the program, reads:

During the party as I was standing on the ward and talking with Mrs. T—— [an attendant], a patient whose name was not known to me came up to her and voluntarily surrendered two books of matches which had been given her when she purchased cigarettes, in conformity with the rule that patients were not to have matches in their possession.

On the same day, I found Ward B in excellent condition. Nearly all of the patients were quietly occupied. There were hardly any strollers and none lay on the floors. At around eleven o'clock I noticed that the pianist and flutist of the "strolling players" were going into the ward. I suggested that they first play for Ward A, which seemed to be in a less organized state. As soon as the musicians began to play, almost as a miracle, all the patients who were not seated at once quieted down and settled in chairs to listen to the music. A number of them sang along. General spontaneous singing, however, arose when the musicians struck up the lilting, familiar tune of "Let Me Call You Sweetheart." As the song was played and sung, a pleasant smile of reminiscence brightened the face of a middle-aged woman who was not singing but continued with her knitting. A few of the patients broke into silent nostalgic tears. "When Irish Eyes Are Smiling" and "Moonlight" brought hefty response from all as they joined in. The musicians began by playing very loudly and in a fast tempo. We asked them to reduce the volume and to slow down to an appropriate pace, which they did, with favorable response from the patients.

The harassment under which the attendants labored in the past had abated. There was no longer the perpetual scurrying about with tensed faces to get "things done" which they thought was required of them. Tranquility and relaxation were the rule now, upon the continuing of which we constantly concentrated. We emphasized at our seminars the theme that no worthwhile activity program or salutary human relationships can exist in a hurried, tense atmosphere. The attendants ceased grumbling about shortage of staff as the patients were now occupied, didn't mill about in large numbers and didn't get in each other's way. No longer being bored, they no longer got into fights with each other. The gentler treatment on the part of the staff was paramount to this change.

Very significant was a discussion at one of our seminar sessions during which some of the more alert and more involved attendants openly verbalized resentment against the psychiatrists who, they said, treated the patients "off-handedly so that whenever a problem came up they gave little or superficial attention to the patients." Such open flaunting of authority would have been inconceivable before the project was introduced, and as far as we could ascertain has never occurred in a regimented hospital caste system. These staff personnel, lowest on the professional rung, who had been accustomed to abject subservience, were able to raise their heads in disapproval and rebellion, now that they felt an identity and a new sense of involvement. At one session an attendant bluntly said to Dr. Beckenstein after he had made a statement, "I disagree with you Dr. Beckenstein," and proceeded to make her point, and when a new psychiatrist sought to limit the freedom of patients unless they worked on O.T. projects, the attendants on Ward A openly rebelled against him. His response to this was withdrawing from active participation on the ward, limiting himself to emergencies only. The effect of involvement was demonstrated by another very striking development.

When I first came to the hospital I was warned that it is not unusual for staff, as well as patients, to steal various articles and supplies and remove them from the premises. We brought this matter to the attention of a staff luncheon session when the introduction of arts and crafts, culinary and cosmetic supplies and other materials was discussed. The opinion was uniformly supported by the assembly. However, despite the fact that the day attendants had the keys and free access to the O.T. cupboards, the kitchen with its costly equipment and such staples as sugar,

276

PROGRESS

eggs, cake mixes, flour, as well as table utensils, and the beautician equipment, nothing was ever removed. It seemed that the sense of inner dignity engendered in the personnel through the changed image and responsible involvement inhibited them from any indiscretions along these lines. Such changes in attitudes and values on the part of staff could not but communicate themselves to the patients.

277

9. *Decline and Residues*

What human perversity could not fully achieve was to some degree accomplished by time and circumstance. The corrosive effects of personnel difficulties as a result of the attrition; limited staff reserves and the quality of replacements available; the inevitable cooling off of enthusiasm in the staff and administration as the "newness" and "excitement" over the dramatic changes in the patients and the wards had worn off, all began to slowly make themselves felt in numerous subtle and covert ways. One of these, of course, was the surprising declaration that the quieting activities had begun to irk the staff. Quite suddenly they yearned for more physical and motoric action rather than meeting the needs of patients. The onset of monotony in repetitive occupations is entirely understandable, but healers and educators cannot escape them; they are inherent in the nature of their occupations, as they are also in many other trades and professions.

After the preliminary steps in obtaining tranquility in patients and the wards, we have repeatedly encouraged staff to introduce variety in their work, as already indicated. In fact, at several meetings with the O.T. workers we suggested additional materials and projects beyond the limited traditional occupations as outlets for creativity and originality in staff and in pa-

278

tients. None of these, however, were followed up. The traditional and familiar seemed to require less effort and was preferred: none of the staff had the slightest suspicion of their own lack of resources and inventiveness, qualities which would have undoubtedly widened their operational fields and added stimuli and variety to their own and to their patients' lives.

The plan of rotating attendants for training purposes—as necessary as it was for raising hospital standards—was far from having a salutary effect on our program. The security patients derived from continuing relationships and the identification they have established with the attendants were vitally important both to their recovery and to the orderly day-to-day living on the wards. Removing them could not but increase fears and anxieties which in turn affected the stability of ward life. At the beginning the patients were disturbed as one of them said to the social worker, "They took away the attendants who knew us and we knew them. The new ones don't know us." However, these losses were amply compensated for by the vastly higher personal and cultural levels of the new trainees as compared with our former staff. In time, the patients, now on the whole more integrated and emotionally stronger, accommodated themselves to the changes better than we had envisaged, since their needs for acceptance and respect continued to be met.

Long before Miss K.'s departure after the third year of the project and the curtailment of the activities on the wards, we were faced with a serious problem in the fact that, finding the wards no longer yielding satisfactions, the "honor card patients," (i.e., the lesser disturbed patients who were free to come and go without being accounted for or supervised), took to leaving the wards *en masse* early every morning and staying away all day, returning only for meals. Each had now found and pursued interests outside the wards which also removed the most constructive members of the community and the salutary influence they had had on its life. Visible deterioration began to set in some areas, especially where the daily chores were concerned. Also, the community was deprived of the examples it had been setting for emotional placidity. The resulting unneutralized concentration of pathology by the absence of the healthier patients added to the staff's burdens, though the conditions on the wards never reached the nadir in which we found them at the start.

We had from the outset disapproved of the "honor card" system. It set up castes among the patients: those with privileges which had been denied the vast majority. As in the case with all humans, our patients, too, seemed to accommodate themselves to these inequities without overt demurral but, in our opinion, they must have harbored resentment to being thus discriminated against.[1]

During the brief period when, at our insistence, honor cards had been eliminated, *all* patients who so wished could leave the wards, the building and the grounds without restrictions by simply entering their name in the register as already described. However, this practice seemed to have created a great deal of anticipatory anxiety among the staff, who had visions of patients being run over on the streets, becoming victims of a variety of mishaps, or getting into other difficulties. While these doubts were not borne out during the brief period of unrestricted movement, and despite our urging at the seminar discussions that the practice be continued, the staff, who felt directly responsible for the safety of patients, seemed too timid to do so, and when the restrictions were reintroduced, we did not feel justified in pressing the point.

As already indicated, we were compelled to eliminate recreational activities on the wards, because they generated noise that distracted patients at work. We also noted the unsuitability

[1] The grounds for awarding these cards were intended to encourage and remunerate "good behavior." It was intended also to motivate others to earn this advancement, an obviously spurious gesture for hospitalized psychotic patients generally, and especially for those on our wards who were far from being able to generate strivings by such measures or to mobilize ego strengths for the effort required. The task of the mental hospital is rather to affect inner integration by chemical, milieu, relationship and psychotherapeutic means, before patients could make such steps.

of the replacements of the occupational therapy staff for the particular needs of our patients. The rotating trainees, though by and large of a better personality caliber than were most of the original group of attendants, were all at the beginning bewildered by the unorthodox and unaccustomed life patterns on Wards A and B. Though they heard laudatory rumors and most were well disposed to the changes, meeting up with them face to face, however, generated insecurity and discomfort. It must be said, however, that once the ice was broken, their conduct was, in most instances, laudatory. Their errors were at least on the side of omission; and this was better than it would have been in the area of commission, i.e., being aggressive and dominating. The fact that hesitancy and the sense of "lostness" reappeared periodically with each batch of new recruits reawakened the patients' insecurities, and the interruption in transferential relations established by patients with each succeeding group of attendants did not serve constructive ends in the therapeutic process. The full blow of its effects, however, was partially mitigated by the four original attendants who had remained as trainers of the newcomers.

In about the third year of the project, and after the resignation of the frightened and withdrawn O.T. worker which coincided with the transfer of her counterpart on the other ward, we were informed by the supervisor of that department that only one worker would be available for both wards. She would be available, we were told, on alternate half-days on each of the wards. However, in the afternoons, she would also conduct O.T. activities in the dining hall for patients of both wards. On the first several afternoons three or four patients out of the 130 turned up, after which none availed themselves of this preferred opportunity and it was accordingly discontinued. Obviously, the interest on the part of our patients was not sufficiently sustained to follow it to the new locale. This development validated our original contention that *creative activities would have to flow from visual stimulation and that the setting for them be part and parcel of the living environment on the wards.*

A rather different reaction by patients to a somewhat similar situation puzzled us and we could not find an adequate explanation for it. When the wards were being repainted in the early period of our program, the O.T. activities had been at our suggestion relocated in the dining hall to allow the four or five staff painters to do their work. This setting proved salutary in inciting interest in the activities. The smaller tables could accommodate only six persons. This dispersion of workers seemed to please them and an unprecedented number took up projects and worked concentratedly. The rather large room presented a bevy of occupations, quiet and orderly. The response to the materials by far exceeded that on the wards.

Our project suffered a serious setback after the third year when Miss Kralides resigned for a position of better opportunities and greater professional security. Following our suggestion, she carefully prepared the patients for this eventuality promising that she would continue to come to see them. On the day of her departure a party, arranged by the patients on their own initiative and carried out solely by them, was held and she was presented with a scroll that read, "We are sorry to lose you. We will never say good by, but so long." The scroll was signed by 96 patients. True to her promise, Miss K. spent one evening a week on the wards on a voluntary basis for a year; she refused offers of financial remuneration. Instead of engaging in activities, the patients asked her to conduct the discussions she had initiated more than a year before.

The activity program had now come to a partial halt. Only the one O.T. worker remained active on the curtailed schedule, i.e. alternate half-days on each ward. The number of participants as a result diminished. Off-ward activities have been expanded with the attendants taking on responsibilities for them. As we shall see presently, despite these deprivations, the tranquil and more decorous aspect of the wards survived, as did the more relaxed and felicitous appearance of the patients and the benign attitudes of the staff toward patients. However, there was agreement among some of the most involved staff members that the decline in the vitality of the program was the removal of the persistent and meticulous supervision and the change in the direction and content of the seminar sessions with the attendants which again met weekly. The relaxation in the follow-up on details and on the insistence that staff discharge their duties fully and expeditiously, led to the neglect of details which form the texture of a benevolent and therapeutic climate where patients can feel secure and accepted.

Our withdrawal from directing the minutiae of the ward life and activities in the tentative belief that the training of staff had penetrated the individuals involved, and that it was incorporated into pragmatic behavior, was obviously unfounded. However, despite the automatic lowering of standards and personal cooling off on the part of most of the participants, there was no diminution of the basic humane attitudes toward, and the treatment of, patients. These survived, and it is our conviction that the old patterns in dealing with patients will never reappear.

The removal from the wards of most of the attendants who had been exposed to the very intensive supervision and training during the first two years greatly crippled the activities program. And Miss Kralides' departure deprived the patients of the expansion and richness of life she had provided. It is noteworthy that the improvement in patients taken at random, and reported on by the social worker, occurred during the first two years of the project, and mostly during the second year.

RESIDUES

During the life of the project, yearly evaluation conferences were held at the end of each fiscal year. Participating in these sessions, in addition to the members of supervisory and other top staff who had been variously involved, were outside consultants in psychiatry, medical sociology and psychiatric nursing. The agenda was a flexible one, usually consisting of a report by the active participants in the work on the wards, supplemented by the reactions and observations of the other staff members of the hospitals. The reports were followed by free discussions by all those present. The deliberations were not limited to our program alone, however, but were allowed by the chairman, Dr. Beckenstein, to flow over into theoretic and philosophical channels that served to broaden the scope of the project and the vision of the participants.

After a recess during which the assembled lunched together in the doctors' dining rooms, the three special consultants reacted to and evaluated the earlier reports, making suggestions for the future of the project.

As far as the general climate on the ward was concerned, a visitor would find their external aspects not very much changed. It was still predominantly tranquil and comparatively serene, but the altered covert quality would not escape the intuitive, perceptive observer. The doors remained unlocked, patients were still free to move about; in and off-ward interests and occupations had not been discouraged. A modicum of O.T. activities were provided on both wards by the one worker who had the double responsibility for them. What one failed to see were the open, smiling faces, the free and friendly interactions among patients, and the absorption in work and creative common interests that were strikingly apparent during the height of the program.

The most advantageous ramifications were to be observed in the behavior of the attendants toward patients—the humanitarian quality had been retained. The patients were treated with respect which had been implanted during the life of the project, and the attendants' conduct was devoid of the crude shouting and harshness of which the Chief of Nursing Services complained at the psychiatrists' conference.

A statement on January 4, 1968, by Dr. Abbot Lippman, the medical consultant to the project, who had taken over the conduct of the seminar in the middle of 1966, reflects well the state of the wards.

I visited Wards A and B during the holidays and was impressed with the quiet of the wards. Patients didn't seem to be too agitated because of the holidays, and only two were in the dormitory doing household duties. There was no excitement on the patients' part because of the presence of a new person, my daughter-in-law, who is a physician.

She was very much impressed with the state of the patients. The patients acted casually toward her and conversed with her on a person-to-person basis. There was no begging or complaints.

Even H—— H—— was quietly playing dominoes. She didn't ask for cigarettes or try to hug me as she used to. Mrs. K—— who was slightly agitated, followed me around for a while. She wasn't as agitated as she usually is and was not acting out. The original mob spirit was now completely absent. I spoke to the patients about the holiday decorations and their visits home. They responded normally as people in the community do. . . .

A beautiful stereo supplied to the patients on Ward A about two years ago was not in use, and patient I—— S—— asked why they could not use it. Other patients pointed out that the key for it is in the possession of someone outside of W. Building. There were no records to play, even if the key were there. This was mentioned in the past, but it seems to solution was found. I found also a shortage of cups for the coffee breaks on the wards. . . .

The survival of the attitude of staff is well demonstrated in the report to the seminar session dated October 17, 1968, by the Remotivation Nurse:

. . . the ten patients of Ward B decided on a trip to the Statue of Liberty. At a planning session each *was given* a responsibility: one patient *was made* responsible for the money to be used for fares on the bus; another for subway fares; still another for the money for food.[2] The patients decided they would have their lunches at the Statue of Liberty cafeteria. They hinted in a roundabout way that they would prefer that I wear street clothing instead of a nurse's uniform, which I did. The patients on their own dressed in their best and were quite presentable.

At the cafeteria they suggested that I go first so that they could see what I chose for my lunch because they thought that the food might be expensive. I reassured them that we had enough money and they could choose whatever they liked. Before we left, all the patients signed the "Visitor's Register," each giving her home address, and they bought cards to be sent to the Chief Administrator.

Before we boarded the boat for our return trip, I noticed that the patients were eyeing the jelly apples nearby and suggested that we could each have one. We ate them on the boat on the way home.

A significant alteration in behavior, at least, if not in inner attitude was displayed by one of the most callous staff members

2 Here again the adults are treated like little children.

285

who could have been rightfully characterized as a "slave driver" because of her worship of *work* as an index of the road to health. She was stern, unsmiling, a temperamental disciplinarian and an "authoritarian personality" who characteristically spoke in a cryptic manner and with a dictatorial tone of voice. Once when a patient grabbed her sunglasses, obviously to provoke her, instead of turning it into an issue with disciplinary aftermath, or at least rebuking the patient as she would have done in the past, she said in her even, cold voice, "Why don't you go up to the mirror and see how they fit you?" Another, more obvious attack on this staff member by a patient occurred on another occasion. In this instance, a patient grabbed her from behind in a strong, tight grip and held her immobilized. Instead of losing her temper and displaying irritation or struggling, the staff member now calmly said, "Gee, you're strong. See if you can lift me." With this, the patient let go of her.

The stories of the two episodes went the rounds among the staff even beyond our wards. The overt transformation of the woman surprised all who knew her. Nonetheless, she still held fast to the conviction that work, no matter how forced, was the golden panacea for the patients.

Thus, in summary, it can be said that while the activity content of our program had been diminished to a point of almost extinction for lack of adequate leadership, we did succeed in setting afoot a more humane hospital culture, not only for our group but also for the mass of patients in the institution. Reports have been coming in for some time that as a result of the palpable improvement in the most notoriously unmanageable patients on our "Siberian" wards, the former suspicion and punitiveness had greatly diminished on many other wards. There were now very rare instances of restraint by camisoles, which was resorted to only in extreme cases or when a patient in a state of anxiety requested them; they were also removed at the patients' request. A significant development attesting to the influence of the project upon the practices in the hospital was that in the fourth year of its existence, O. T. activities were introduced on five of the eight wards in W. Building.

As to our own patients, freedom of movement continues to be maintained and, as shown, an unexpected number left the hospital. A larger number are being maintained on protracted leave status in their homes. With adequate staff to follow them up, the number of those could be greatly enhanced and conditions approaching recovery affected.

Perhaps observations made on random visits to the wards during a period preceding the fourth evaluation conference, three-and-one-half years after the start of the ward program, would make conditions graphically tangible.

Both wards were found to be quiet with some patients concentrated on desultory occupations and table games, with a few engaged in individual projects. There was no milling around, though several of the habitual strollers, especially on Ward B, were at their self-imposed tasks. Others sat in groups around tables, with or without an attendant, playing table games, knitting or drawing. A goodly number, mostly from Ward A, were out at various off-ward activities or on walks. Only one patient, a perpetual stroller, was sleeping on the floor in the foyer near he dining hall door.

However, what was most impressive, as compared with the scenes presented at our initial visits three-and-a-half years before, was the physical appearance of the patients and their facial expressions. They were more comely and wore better fitting and more appropriate dresses. None was barefooted or in stocking feet. The faces without exception were devoid of severe anxiety, rage or fear, though they lacked the animation and almost eagerness of a year ago. There were no staring eyes and obvious detachment from surroundings. Many new faces were among the residents who also appeared to be placid. There were friendly, smiling greetings from the older residents and inquiries as to our health and well-being. The mid-morning coffee break continued to be a gala occasion, managed exclusively by the patients, though patients on Ward A complained that this small repast was being omitted on many occasions. Ward A was still directed by an attendant since the transfer of the nurse three years before, but this time by a newcomer who did not impress one with either her alertness or dedication. She was in the office with the door locked against the patients.

Ward B was placed in the charge of a new nurse who had not been exposed to the retraining and reconditioning provided by the project. On both wards the new approaches to patients were perpetuated mostly by the few old attendants who still remained on the wards and to varying degrees supplied continuity in the new practices.

Perhaps observations on our most difficult cases would more faithfully reflect the effects of the sanguine life on the wards. Sadie's perambulations had become less shuffling. It now approached normal walking, though she walked slightly sideways. When spoken to, she looked penetratingly at one as though trying to understand, a contrast from her inverted expression of the past and the tendency to look beyond the person who addressed her. The nurse reported that her incontinence occurred seldom and sporadically

Hannah still walked about with a detached, somewhat distraught expression on her face, but she no longer emitted the periodic screeching which was her original stock in trade. Upon seeing me, she walked over and smilingly made some unintelligible statement, and proceeded with her stroll. Justina no longer stood swaying from one foot to the other against the west wall fingering her rectum and genitals. She now sat on a chair near a large group of patients who, with an attendant, encircled one of the centers of activity engaged in a table game. There was no other staff member in sight. Justina's face, though still inscrutable, did not have the vacuous, withdrawn quality.

As I started toward her, she stretched out her right hand and shook mine with no change in countenance, but looking straight at me. Jeanne, the foetal patient, was nowhere to be seen. She apparently went out for a walk, as the number on the ward was small. In fact, Justina was sitting in a chair which occupied the very spot that had been Julia's domain for years.

One of the reports at the fourth evaluation conference was given by the oldest and one of the most dedicated attendants from Ward A. She said, among other things (taped):

. . . Sometimes there's one or two staff on the ward since this project started. And before this project started, Ward A couldn't be run smooth with less than five or six staff on the ward at all times. Now we can run that ward, I have been up there, Miss G—— can tell you, all alone. I said to the patients, "you have to take over," that's how much our patients have improved since this project started. "You have to take over. You're going to take care of me today." And they work along with you, with teamwork; teamwork means a lot. They work along with you and take over, they do all the activities, the morning activities. They take over the activities if I have to send some patient to Building Ten.

The better patients will take those who are not able to walk or go alone. In fact we don't, we do not have the patients up there now that cannot get off of the ward; that do not go off of the ward. Before this project, we couldn't run the wards smoothly unless five or six employees was there . . . I didn't think it could be done [to] open up these doors. When this project started, and no mistake . . when they said they were going to open up the doors, I even told Mr. Slavson it couldn't be done because the employees on the wards were a little frightened sometime to walk down the ward alone. And now the doors are open at all times.

And I remember we had these meetings about working, about the doctors working along with this project . . . We had about 10 or 15 patients eat on the ward every day. And we had to feed them. So, by attending these meetings, we would discuss round the table, Mr. Slavson and the doctors and Dr. Lippman, that they [patients] are not animals, just have patience, and working with them patiently, they'll learn to eat for their own self. Well we didn't believe it. We do not have a patient that eats on the ward. We do not have a patient that we have to feed. Some of those same patients are there. Some of those patients have gone home since this project started, and before the project we had one room just for jackets for restraint. There are no more jackets on the ward. We don't use jackets [camisoles].

But before we had plenty jackets on the ward. And by the employees attending these meetings, getting ideas, it couldn't be done if we didn't have these meetings, and everything, every Thursday. I don't think we could have done this by ourself . . . . We get our ideas and . . . I remember Dr. Lippman saying just a few minutes ago, well we're at the point now where we would like to get some ideas from you where to motivate our patients higher. 'Cause they are ready to go higher now. Our doors are open. They go out and come [back]. Before we had to pick up patients, go out and pick 'em up by 'em running away. We do not have a patient to run away. I remember discussing around these tables, that you give them a privilege and don't keep 'em locked in or anything they'll stop running away. Very seldom do we have patients who run away.

VISITING CONSULTANT: Simultaneously with this program, which I see as a remotivation program, do you have to use medications and so on? Tranquilizing drugs?

ATT: We have [to] use medications [for] some of our patients. And some we do not. The doctors tell us to use our own ideas [judgment]. If we think a patient is doing wonderful, we'll discuss it with the doctor, we will not take a step [re-medication] unless'n we do discuss it with the doctor . . . .

Another staff member from Ward B stated that:

The program has helped an awful lot. And, the patients, they seem to take more of an interest. We have a program going on today where they [patients] are making a party for Miss T—— [a long-term attendant promoted to take charge of another ward]. When I came back Sunday they told me that they took up a little collection and were going to have a party. They asked me what did I think they should get to eat. They were talking about tuna fish sandwiches, and one of the patients went out and done the shopping and *I told* her to look in the ads and get, you know, something a little cheaper that had the sales. So she did and cut out coupons for mayonnaise, and in fact she asked me if I had the [news] paper, if I'd bring the coupon and I did. It was 10¢ off on the coupon. And they went up and they bought the celery and things and today they are having a party. They got flowers, and they had the gift all wrapped up. They were inviting, I guess about 80 people. And she was going to get a card. And this patient's a very good drawer so *I told her* to make a nice card and paint it herself and put all the names on it. She thought that was a good idea. She done that last night. I didn't see it yet.[3]

---

[3] The supervisor of Recreation stated that the patients had arranged, on their own initiative five large affairs during the winter for which they did the shopping by themselves in the neighborhood stores. Arrangement of parties seems to have become part of the cultures of the two wards. [No other wards on the service have had parties, instead, the patients attended community affairs arranged by the Recreation Department.]

10. Reflections and Recommendations

REFLECTIONS

Developments justified our assumptions that at the start our regressed patients were psychologically on the level of children. This assumption led, as the project progressed, to the facts that (a) we begin with them as such; (b) that we would have to implant in all concerned—staff as well as patients—an attitude of hopefulness that they, the patients (as well as the staff) can and will grow under favorable conditions toward greater maturity and to some degree of reality testing; (c) that to achieve this, our approach would have to be basically an educational one, in the widest sense of the term (as differentiated from schooling); (d) that we may expect differential gains in the great variety of individuals that constituted our population, according to their native potentials, length of chronicity, and the depth of regression, i.e., the intensity of the original traumata and corresponding compelling needs for the psychotic defense; and (e) the importance of classifying the patients and evolving differential procedures suitable to the different conditions—psychologic and/or constitutional. This we were not able to achieve.

As already indicated, we were struck by the childishness of the patients on our first visit to the wards. Their immaturity was clear from their clustering around the director and myself, with a jumble of supplications, demands, and blatant mendicancy;

the childlike direct and uninhibited approach to a stranger on the part of many of them with questions as to who I was and why I was there, and from the even more striking *attitudes* of dependence and naked lack of self-respect.

In reflecting upon the effect upon us of that brief visit and our *a priori* intention of providing so-called creative activities as well as an expanding environment (reality) for the patients, it became clear that our (unconscious) assumption that such procedures would lead them out of their confusion, was faulty at many points. These educational contrivances do stimulate responses *ab novo* in the case of children and engage neuromuscular and intellectual activity which in turn set off neuronic conditionings leading to perception and later to understanding. This is the path of orderly growth of the *total* human personality. In the case of our adult patients, this process has already occurred, though in many instances inadequately and segmentally. It seemed to us that what was necessary was to reverse the regressive pattern which the patients had defensively assumed later in life due to their ego debilities in dealing with, or bearing up under, life's pressures. What was obviously needed was a way of helping them *to return to the maturational level they had attained* before their psychic break, and then expose them to experiences that would favor progressive development and ego-integration beyond that fixation point.

In a sense, this process, too, is dynamically one of regression, or better still, *retrogression*, for as they have regressed to infantilism under stress, they were now to *retrogress* (return) to their healthier selves of the past which they had abandoned under overwhelming stress. It was this dawn of a new understanding of our patients' states that altered the content of our original so-called "activity program" which we first had planned. The typical and familiar objects and occupations we introduced instead, such as a kitchen, a laundry, sewing machines, knitting, sewing, crocheting, table games and the interpersonal and group transactions replicated what the patients had experienced to varying degrees during their childhood and youth, while serving at this time to reactivate the already existing imprints and synaptic tracts (engrams) which they had abandoned in their retreat from reality. However, it was most important that we avoid duplicating the harsh treatment to which the patients had been exposed in the past. It was also obvious that patients could not make this retrogressive transition toward health without the support from the staff and the security derived from it. Hence the orientation, re-educational and behavior-reconditioning work with the staff.

Only a continuous buttressing of the Vita-Erg (Life-Work) program by a favorable human environment and warm human relations could have made it effective. Lacking such a climate, the activities program would have been lifeless and as devoid of significance as were earlier desultory and short-lived efforts. Because in the past, activities and the living process in all its aspects had been imposed, programmed and supervised, they lacked vital significance and thus failed to awaken in the participants possibilities for self-realization.

It required only a brief observation of the wards and the few traditional activities carried on by traditional methods to make it clear that they had failed to stimulate or to involve patients. The comparatively few who had not withdrawn from the *required* activities either by staunch refusal to join, immobility, or sleep, and who did submit to routines, seemed to go through the motions robotlike, without inner responsiveness, involvement or aim. What was obviously necessary as a first step was to reawaken the life-urge that had been deadened in the predominant majority, was dormant in others and flickered in the few younger, comparatively more recent arrivals. It was equally apparent that the road to this resurgence did not lie in exposing the patients to new, unfamiliar stimuli. Expanding content and interests are effective in the education and development of the intact personality, and they had become suitable and even necessary to us as well, as our patients improved. But to help each to first return to her point of departure from health into the safety of psychosis required a new *modus operandi*, which tangibly demonstrates a two-pronged approach: to "entice" the patient to return to reality on the one hand, and to begin to tread, with caution if not painful slowness, the road toward human relations, on the other. This, briefly, was the basic plan of our project.

Both staff and patients have complained from time to time that many other programs had been attempted through the years, but as the staff members, usually psychiatric interns and residents, left the hospital, the projects, too, had disappeared. On occasion some of the staff would end these complaints with a remark that our project, as well, would go the way of the others. We were somewhat saddened by this prospect and dwelled upon it at length. Being temperamentally economical in all areas of life—material, emotional, physical, etc.—it seemed like a pity to spend so much thought and exertion upon anything as ephemeral as those projects and programs had been.

In one of the sanguine moments of confidence during a conversation, I conveyed my misgivings to our most resistant nurse who had often reiterated the fact that other projects had come and gone during her long association with the hospital. She very perceptively admitted that although the *activities* we had introduced would not survive, the *attitudes* and the manner of dealing with patients would become a permanent pattern of the life on the wards. This statement set us to a lengthy period of reflection and in time we came to realize the soundness of her prognostication. As the reader will recall, this is what actually occurred; not only did the change in *attitude* persist on our wards, but it significantly spread to other parts of the hospital.

It became clear to us that the reason for the demise of the previous efforts, which did not occur in our case to the same degree, was that they stressed programs and activities exclusively. They employed a behavioristic, pragmatic approach, neglecting *inner* motivations and inner needs. In our project, activities were secondary. Our program was essentially an existential one and the pragmatic aspect was subordinated. The activities and occupations actually were tangible parts of the existential approach, for they demonstrated to the patients the staff's interest in them by conveying to them the feeling that they had confidence in their, the patients', abilities and helped them only when help was needed. The activities also brought staff and patients together in active, meaningful, realistic relations that dissolved patients' fear of human contacts. It was these elements that survived, for they had been internalized equally by staff and by patients.

As one reviews the project *in toto*, one becomes cognizant of serious impediments which arose, that interfered with the full realization of our plans and intents. As already indicated, the major difficulty lay in the staff's attitudes, lack of pertinent training, and inadequate personal and professional qualifications for the type of job we sought. Their unsuitability by way of personality and past life experiences and conditioning for the highly sensitive and complex task could not have been overcome by mere conceptual teaching which, as the reader will recall, we found to be the case after the first three months when the project was limited only to seminar discussions as first intended. The humane feelings, attitudes, and hopefulness that were essential in daily discharge of functions, as well as in dealing with the admittedly annoying, frightening, assaultive and irrational conduct of the patients could not be didactically taught.

Tolerance and involvement must come from within and a degree of spirituality in which material considerations and personal ambitions can play no part. These only too human trends must be subordinated to inner satisfactions that accrue from helping people and in allaying suffering. In this connection, however, one has to be vigilant against falling prey to tawdry sentimentality, to which a few of our attendants were given. In many instances, we had to protect patients against them, for it led to overinfantilizing and overstressing dependence.

Another impediment we found was the traditional rigidly set status of the various staff categories with their ascending power, prestige and authority. This created a dominance-submission relation among the staff and a culture that had the effect of stifling creative spontaneity and wholesome patient-staff relations. The militaristic rigidities to which staff had to submit were automatically, and quite naturally, passed on to the patients. This was inevitable. The caste system had to be replaced

295

by egalitarian and democratic practices—and attitudes. Our success in this direction inevitably had to be of a very limited degree. The personal, cultural and educational conditioning of our effective staff were such that they could not easily change their strongly entrenched images, nor could we depend on their free, spontaneous reactions. As we have already recorded, these were always negative: denying, conditional, or authoritarian.

The presence of constitutional defectives has proven a considerable disadvantage to the growth and working of our project. Their continuous uncontrollable screams, invariably bizarre conduct, interferences with the work of others, interrupting discussions, and similar annoyances and fear-arousing acts, required continuous attention from staff. The climate of tension and resentment they created were of great disadvantage. Some of these patients were completely unable to take part in any of the activities; they set infectious examples to the more regressed psychotic fellow patients, and monopolized much of the attention of both staff and coresidents. In nearly all cases, the constitutionally defectives could not speak, nor understand when spoken to, and nearly all of them were also deaf or were unable to comprehend when addressed. Actually, if these patients were to be at all reached, they would have to be dealt with on an intensive individual basis to arouse in them some degree of psychophysical responsiveness. This would require special skills, which our staff did not possess, and would have consumed most, if not all of their time to the neglect of the more promising patients.

The activity program left these patients cold, as it were; a few would respond, but only under special individual guidance by a staff member. They did gain, however, from the new climate of comparative human warmth and the more tranquil atmosphere. Their animal-like fears and anxieties seemed to have been greatly mitigated and they grew much less intransigent most of the time and disturbed the wards to a lesser degree than at the beginning. Nonetheless, the practice of placing such defectives with the most disturbed patients in a therapeutic setting, is deleterious to themselves and to others. In fact, consideration should be given to relegating them to institutions whose specialty is working with mental defectives.

To vitalize ward life for patients in mental hospitals along the lines implied in Vita-Erg therapy, drastic revisions in the staff structure would be required as well as in the physical setting. This would involve redefining the roles of existing staff categories and the addition of others. Also—and this is probably most essential—there must be revision of qualification standards for staff personnel.

In line with the assumption that mental hospital treatment of patients is basically bifocal, namely, *medicopsychiatric* and *milieu-relational*, the staff must be constituted in accordance with these requirements. It cannot be assumed, as it is in currently prevailing practices, for example, that psychiatric or nursing training—necessarily specialized and important as they are—qualifies the members of these professions to conduct the *living* and *homemaking* aspects of ward life. As we have already indicated, this area is replete with myriad minutiae that are vastly multiplied in congregate mass living, such as exists on a ward, and especially with the mental and mentally defective patients.

We saw how details such as blown-out electric bulbs, defective switches, overheated rooms, lack of materials, ill-fitting clothes, littered floors often containing fecal matter and urine, and innumerable other details that militate against decent and dignified living had been consistently tolerated or overlooked. Such matters require continuous alertness from a person whose sole responsibility would be the managerial details of the ward. These matters cannot be left to occasional correction or the brief, perfunctory rounds made by a psychiatrist, even if his attention were arrested by such minutiae (which in our experience had not been the case). The small, and what may seem to be insignificant, matters do not ordinarily attract the attention of staff who do not have a sense of dedication, or are pressed with other responsibilities, especially when these matters do not happen to be within their professional purview.

Physical cleanliness of the wards compelled much of the attention of the attendants, for failure here was easily detectable by the supervisory and administrative personnel who insisted on near-perfection in this area; supervision of showering is also a considerable and time-consuming task; numerous crises that constantly arise on traditionally managed "disturbed" wards not only consume time but also drain much physical and emotional energy; preparing and administering medication is a task requiring painstaking attention and care that takes up much time; supervision of daily making, as in our case, of 65 beds and sending and receiving masses of linens and clothes to and from the laundry; obtaining and distributing underwear and dresses; helping the physically and mentally handicapped with dressing and personal care; quieting by speech or restraining patients who explode into screaming and violence; settling physical fights, scratching and hairpulling among patients; supplying cigarettes to patients at their demand, which are of necessity kept under lock and key in an office; answering innumerable and often irrelevant and irrational questions that arise through boredom; working at communication so as to counteract fear and loneliness; accompanying groups on walks and taking individual patients to the "community store" or to doctors and dentists, and so on and so on. These and innumerable more demands irrevocably and endlessly occur. Other minor matters are even more numerous, each of which may not require much time, but overload the physical and emotional resources of staff.

Obviously, minor matters in the environment and peripheral supplies—that is, supplies not directly serving the basic and essential routines on the wards—cannot but fall by the wayside, remain unnoticed and neglected in the turmoil and pressures that inevitably prevail on all wards and especially on a "disturbed ward." We have seen that even the ancillary staff, the specialists who operated through distinct tools and materials, neglected and actually forgot to replenish supplies. Their *laissez-faire* attitude was more difficult for us to understand, for they were not under the pressures that the attendants and the nurses had to contend with. It seemed as though they, like the attendants, also had been traditionally conditioned through their schooling and professional practice to await instructions and direction from above. Those who had worked on our wards—and we assume that they were a fair sampling (in fact our understanding was that they were chosen for their higher qualifications)—were devoid of initiative, adaptability or originality.

The Psychiatric Group Worker

The logical staff member upon whose shoulders the ward structure, the activities, the supplies and the minor (as well as the major) details should fall would be the person in charge of the ward. Traditionally, this would be the nurse. But the training of nurses for mental hospitals is mostly medical, supplemented only by a comparatively brief theoretic course in the elements of psychiatric management of patients. A very large segment of this schooling deals with the legal intricacies and responsibilities coded by the State Departments under which the mental hospitals operate. These consist of definitions of the rights of patients and legal procedures in dealing with them, accountability, content and procedures of recording all events and occurrences, crises and accidents that may be required as evidence in cases of emergencies or legal action by relatives, details of dispensing medication, and numerous specialized matters.

Unlike the training of medical nurses where actual care of patients is a major part, the psychiatric segment of postgraduate education is purely classroom tutorial. Visits to wards *are* arranged from time to time and ward procedures *are* explained by instructors and staff psychiatrists. Upon graduation, however, they immediately take charge of wards without antecedent empirical inservice experience. Thus, both tutorially and experientially, they are not prepared to visualize the total picture of valid ward life, nor are they made aware of the importance of minutiae in creating a satisfying, let alone a therapeutic, life setting, which is the primary inroad into the mental patient's psyche. If one is allowed to say it, they are too young for the innumerable tasks which present themselves.

In our teaching of parents, teachers, psychotherapists and hospital staff, we have perennially compared the life of man with a painting. Just as imperceptible brush strokes which when put together in a specific relation by the artist form an integrated work of art, so does the life of man. It, too, is constituted predominantly of small matters (interspersed now and then with large and important problems and events) that spin out the pattern of life. It is the small matters that are of true consequence in the life of humans, and even more so for mental hospital residents; in this case, the staff members are the artists.

The creation and supervision of a vital ward life requires extensive knowledge of the nature and processes of, and supplies for, appropriate life activities, games and crafts according to sex, age and cultural levels of patients. Only such intimate and first-hand knowledge equips one to supervise the work of others. Persons in this position must have creative imagination and flexibility of the real expert. No one to whom this aspect of ward life is of only peripheral concern and who carries other pressing responsibilities, such as a psychiatrist or a nurse in charge, can be expected to adequately carry these multifarious burdens.

One in charge of a ward also needs to have a working judgment of the simple, mechanical details that are unavoidably involved. Examples for this may be drawn from our experience at the hospital. During a staff discussion of placing electric pressing irons, which of necessity could not be used on the ward itself where the activities were held and much movement prevailed, the suggestion was made and adopted that they be placed in the small conference rooms and the beauty parlors which were set apart and where no gross movement was going on. We raised the question of electric outlets in these rooms and were assured by the nurse that they were available in those locations. When the irons arrived weeks later, it was discovered that there were no outlets in these small rooms. To install them in the ancient brick walls proved a difficult and protracted project, which could have been avoided had the nurse, who served on the same ward many years, been observant of, and interested in such matters.

The occupational therapy department, upon whom we had to rely for most of our equipment, supplied us with very cheap, second-hand sewing machines which constantly went out of order, causing much frustration to our disturbed and easily distractable patients. The most frequent frustrating occurrence was the slipping off of the belts in these old pedal-operated machines. There was no one on the wards who, try as he may, could replace the belts, which were slightly too large. As a result of these annoyances, both the staff and the patients, after a while, almost completely abandoned this activity. When we requested that the machines be replaced by new sewing machines, the departmental authorities remonstrated at the high cost of such equipment and we never received replacements.

During the discussion of pressing irons, the question was raised as to whether they should be steam or coil-heated. Naturally, the former were more suitable, since the possibility of a fire through misjudgment or neglect would thus be greatly reduced. There was no one among the 40-odd persons, mostly women, present who could enlighten us as to what is involved in the operation of a steam-heated iron.

As it became clear from preceding pages, attention was required to inaugurate the activities each morning; otherwise other interests, such as housekeeping and cleaning chores, higher in priority in the minds of the attendants, would engage them. Another problem was absence and almost habitual lateness of the ancillary therapists. The nurse, who was the logical person to follow up on this, and should have summoned them by phone, was invariably either engaged in other details that preoccupied her, did not notice the intransigence, or was herself absent. In addition, these steps were considered intrusions upon the sovereignty of the particular department and were strongly resented and viewed as complaints. Such intrusions led to interpersonal and interdepartmental tensions, and even hostility.

Nurses, by virtue of their training and their pathology-orientations, know little of the limitless manual and recreational possibilities and appropriateness of specific activities for particular patients. They must rely on the judgment of specialists who are themselves activity-oriented; both are seldom imaginative or enterprising and their work as well as their contributions, are stereotyped and uninspiring. These attributes would have to come through a fully trained person in all of these varied activities, who also has the abilities necessary for creating an orderly, smoothly flowing life for the patients and staff without generating tensions or threatening either of them.

Recommendations

Psychiatric Social Worker

We are, therefore, suggesting the creation of a new staff category which may be labelled as "Psychiatric Group Worker" or "Social Therapist." In him or her we envisage a professionally trained psychiatric social worker whose specialty is group work on an informal educational and recreational basis with added understanding of the nature of psychoses and specific needs of such patients in terms of the assumptions in this volume; namely, the kind of total milieu and relationship therapies that would activate patients to re-establish contact with material reality and relationships with other human beings.

Upon such a person would devolve all the duties and responsibilities for arranging and maintaining a living environment which, while not constituting psychotherapy *per se*, would be therapeutic in the sense we have set forth at a number of points in preceding pages. These specialists may later become known as "Vita-Erg Therapists" and one should be assigned to every pair of nearby or contiguous wards.

A New Type of Psychiatric Nurse

The training of psychiatric nurses for hospital wards, as well, sorely needs revision in the light of newer trends and objectives in the treatment of mental patients. As already indicated, the major schooling and training for psychiatric nurses consists of medical nursing and, only to a minor degree, psychiatric care. It seems to us that this order should be reversed. Concentration in training should be on the latter. Emphasis should be laid on the understanding of the nature of psychoses and techniques of dealing with patients in specific states and moods, which are in constant flux. Psychiatric nurses need to be psychotherapeutically oriented. In fact, they should have the educational and personality assets that would qualify them to do direct, intrusive and interruption therapy. Because of the practice

302

in American state hospitals of including mental defectives and even senile persons on wards with psychotic patients, nurses' training curricula should include studies *and inservice practice* (internship) that would enlighten them on the nature of these various types of maladies and procedures for dealing with them therapeutically or helpfully, as required.

In our scheme, knowledge of the human organism, its structure and function, and the spectrum for potential emotional and mental disturbances must be part of the psychiatric nurse's equipment. It should also include basic understanding of diagnostic categories, their symptoms and characteristic manifestations, as well as the most appropriate approaches in dealing with the variety of patients on different levels. Principles of chemotherapy now already available and in wide use would be taught as they are today, as well as the legal aspects involved. The psychiatric nurse ought to be trained in the various ancillary therapies—such as occupational, recreational, tutorial, music and other therapies—so that she becomes automatically inclined toward, and develops a feeling for, integrating these therapies into the total therapeutic gestalt of the ward. This would make them accepting of Vita-Erg Therapy as conducted by the psychiatric group worker and the new type of attendant.

By their nature, mental patients require more medical attention than persons in the general population. Being organically imbalanced, psychologically regressed, dependent, and largely hypochondriacal, their need for medical attention is extensive. The ministrations of medical nurses is, therefore, essential. Medical nurses may be located at strategic points in proximity to wards, such as treatment rooms, special or physicians' offices, or they may be stationed on a ward itself, so that they can be on call when needed in any of the wards nearby.

We envisage a six-year course for psychiatric nurses after high school graduation, which would lead to a dual academic degree of R.N. and M.A., or a four-year post-Bachelor's degree, in which the curriculum would include the basic courses of anatomy and physiology, chemistry, pathology and other subjects that form the basis of nursing training. In the four years following the undergraduate degree, stress would be laid on the psychological, psychopathological, and therapeutic aspects of the profession as already indicated. The selection, training and education of nurses as outlined would hopefully equip them to impart to their immediate subordinates, i.e., attendants, the requisite therapeutic attitudes and skills.

Training of Attendants

Attention to revising educational, training and personality qualifications of attendants is of the essence. The type and quality of attendants varies in different state hospitals, depending upon availability of recruits in the area in which they are located. In rural areas and small towns where life is more serene, human relations friendlier, and employment opportunities limited, or sometimes nonexistent, a more sophisticated type of men, and especially women, are available. In large towns and metropolitan cities, available recruits are, with rare exceptions, uniformly of lower educational, cultural and personal attainments, which militate against putting into operation techniques that require a high degree of empathy and understanding, flexible, humane attitudes and sensibilities, and reliable spontaneity in relationships. Perhaps it should be mentioned in this connection that the salary levels attract the lesser employable group to the hospital nonprofessional corps and the failure to provide incentives for excellence and advancement act as deterrents to motivation.

In effect, attendants or aides, who are in most prolonged, direct and intimate contact with patients, should have the capacity and the understanding necessary for helping their charges through the myriad simple human interactions that occur in daily group living. They should be capable of empathetically understanding the affect of their patients, as well as their need for corrective human relationships, while maintaining appropriate firmness and self-controls. As was already pointed out, these attributes or capacities are results of breeding and background. Obviously, persons with these qualities and of such caliber are in a position to acquire greater financial reward than the salaries mental hospitals are generally geared to provide. The fiduciary limitations of state treasuries are the limiting factors in these matters; increase in financial emoluments would strain or disrupt their fiscal stability. It is our conviction that this reasoning is basically false.

Appropriate staffing would not increase the cost of hospital maintenance in the long run, and may even decrease it. Adequately qualified staffing would sharply cut the length of hospital stay; significantly larger numbers of patients would be rehabilitated and returned to the community in less time than is now the case. Of course, this cannot be effected by improved attendant care alone. If nurses, psychotherapists, and psychiatrists were properly selected on the basis of personality, and not only on academic training, and if greatly increased social and counselling services were provided to patients and to their families, it is conceivable that mental hospitals could become either extended half-way homes or, for the vast majority of patients, day or night-care clinics. There would, of course, always be a goodly number who would require extended full-time hospitalization and some who could not be rehabilitated at all, given the present state of knowledge concerning the biologic nature of psychoses and of chemotherapy.

Beyond the question of selection, there is the matter of training necessary to equip the comparatively unschooled men and women who serve as attendants or aides. The fact must be noted that in some European mental hospitals psychiatric aides (attendants) are recruited from the better educated segment of the country's population and their salaries are proportionately higher than in the United States in relation to the national averages. It is incumbent upon hospitals in the United States, as well, to supply comparable educational backgrounds for adequate functioning in the demanding tasks to be performed. This preparation is becoming even more crucial as the hospitals attempt to make the transition from custodial to therapeutic modes of operation.

Our project amply demonstrated the value of knowledge as

an instrument in evoking both cerebration and compassion. As the attendants became more knowledgeable about the theoretic bases of the psychotic process and gained insight into the inner plight of their charges, they became more readily disposed to altering their attitudes and their conduct toward them. Had those persons directly in charge of the attendants reinforced their efforts with kindliness, the changes would have been more telling, and even more dramatic.

It is without justification to assume that people, no matter how lofty their schooling and intent, can reach excellence in the type of responsibilities attendants discharge by fiat, fear, or discipline. Humane and compassionate relations must flow from inner spontaneity and not, as one nurse once said to us, "You tell us what to do, Mr. Slavson, and we'll do it." The regimentation that produces this attitude is deadening to everything that therapeutic care of patients requires, or any other true human relation, for that matter. Rote and blind routines in dealing with patients may be in place when custodial care is the aim, but is deadly in the new and emerging role of a hospital seeking to rehabilitate patients and returning them to the community as useful participants in society, each within his potentials. To help patients in this requires more than mere routine services and disciplining as though they were children.

The criteria for selection of attendants would have to include personal endowment and disposition favoring therapeutic relations. These we consider as the essential foundations upon which preservice and inservice training can be effective; without them, all efforts will fall on barren soil. Our project has also demonstrated—only to a limited extent, however, and this, too, due to the unsympathetic attitudes of supervisory and nursing staffs—that, if properly motivated, the housekeeping and cleaning routines that are borne almost exclusively by attendants in hospitals, can be assumed by patients with favorable therapeutic effects. Carrying these responsibilities is essential in the rehabilitation of the psychotic (as well as other types of socially maladjusted) patients. In this role, the attendants would become an integral and very important part of the therapeutic team.

They would thus serve as "psychiatric aides" or "psychiatric technicians," with the accompanying rise in status and salaries, rather than as servants and baby-nurses.

To recruit persons for the job that is now designated as "attendants" (which stamps it even semantically) and to extend their education and development, would unquestionably involve greater financial outlay than is currently the case. But as already indicated, the resulting efficiency and rate of improvement and discharge of patients would set-off this increase.

Another fruitful source of revenue for making funds available with which to raise the level of staff and supply equipment and materials that a Vita-Erg program would require can come from savings on the fantastic outlay in building construction and equipment. The overemphasis on physical appearance and shining marble walls and floors is characteristic of the materialistic values of our society. What is necessary are cleanliness and a moderate degree of aesthetics, but these can be achieved by less ostentatious and less expensive construction and furnishings.

In fact, splendor and grandiosity are counterindicated in the setting of a *residential* treatment facility for economically and socially less advantaged persons. When contrasted with their homes, neighborhood environments and personal habits, the new environment proves frightening and makes them uncomfortable. This is as true of children and adolescents in treatment residences as it is of mental hospitals. (We would not apply this principle to general hospitals, or the sick bays in mental hospitals, where an aseptic environment is of the essence. But it does hold for the living and working quarters in re-education and in therapy.)

Social Services

In our case, it was ironical that patients had to turn to the solitary social worker available for the entire service involving more than 500 patients. One might expect that the patients would have shared reactions with ward staff, psychiatrists, nurses and especially attendants. Beyond the occasional fleeting word of appreciation to me of the improvements in the life on the ward, the patients have discussed these, as far as we were able to ascertain, with only two attendants on Ward A. The matter was never broached even at the ward meetings. Although nearly all of the discussions had been quite correctly directed toward matters of daily living and planning for it, the patients had not been encouraged to reflect upon the changes wrought and to engage in evaluation. None of the leaders of these discussions recognized the value this may have had in activating awareness of reality and engendering discrimination, an intellectual process that is a road to understanding and reality testing so woefully lacking in our patients.

The social worker reported at the seminar sessions, more or less regularly, the growing discriminative faculty among patients relative to the changes in the environment and in their own reactions and feelings. As they moved toward health, they sought her out also to request training for trades, placement in jobs and return to school. Even one of the mentally defective patients (an imbecile) asked that she receive schooling; she wanted to learn how to read and write, she claimed. Of course, the matter of going home and relationships with families constituted the bulk of the consultations and requests. As already noted, very little could have been done for them due to the immensity of the worker's caseload. Very few matters got beyond the first recital.

It seemed to us that social service was the step-child among the professions serving our patients. We were told that at one time this service had been treated more munificently, but a change in departmental regime and budgetary problems caused its curtailment. This is understandable, for the necessity for it is less obvious and less pressing than in the case of other efforts. The results of this lack is less apparent than are those of the other services in custodial care. In a therapeutically oriented hospital, however, and especially one operating on Vita-Erg principles, individual guidance is of utmost importance in helping to fan the psychic sparks in patients for returning to the world of reality, and in preparing their families and the community to fit the rehabilitated patient into the streams of community life.

Suitable social services can do so by utilizing appropriate psychological moments when patients become aware of needs. Even when a social worker's efforts fail, which is only too often the case, the fact that he had responded and thus displayed interest, is an indication to the patient of his being accepted and loved. Even when in another mood the patient abandons his intent, or forgets it, the fact that attention had been given him brings him emotionally closer to the worker and thus another strut is added in the bridge between the patient and humanity. Only too frequently, patients had made plans for themselves for which they were not ready. In such instances, the social worker can work through the matter with them, always holding out hope, and thus another step toward reality is taken.

Ideally, mental hospitals should have two types of psychiatric social workers: *life-adjustment* and *industrial*. In the first category are the workers who would give services needed in supporting patients in accord with individual ego strengths, fragile defenses, talents and abilities during their hospital stay and after discharge. This process may require a protracted period of counselling for the patient and his family and, in some instances, also educational guidance. Preliminary steps in these directions should ideally be taken while patients are still at the hospital and continued for varying periods after their discharge. To assure suitable treatment on the basis of understanding the patient's personality and needs by family members, they, too, require protracted periods of counselling or guidance.

Life-adjustment social workers may employ individual or group guidance and counselling procedures according to indicated suitability for individuals.[1] They would inevitably have to extend their efforts into the community to guide and help

---

[1] Slavson, S.R. (1963), "Steps in Sensitizing Parents (Couples) in Groups Toward Their Schizophrenic Children," *International J. of Group Psychotherapy*, XIII, 176-186. For the basic principles governing this work, see *idem, Child-Centered Group Guidance of Parents*, New York, International Universities Press, 1958.

patients, especially in the initial stages of readaptation to the now less proteced setting than the hospital had been, and be available to deal with difficult or crisis situations that arise. In some communities, social service resources are available that can be enlisted for this post-hospitalization care and guidance.

The function of the *industrial social* worker would be to guide the discharged patient in his probably most difficult and most sensitive area of social readaptation—the job. This would require a meticulous assessment as to the most suitable occupation for each, provide training and preparation for it (in many instances this may be returning to prehospitalization occupations) and, according to his readiness, helping the patient to locate a job or do so for him. After such placement, the responsibility of the industrial social worker would be to continue to help him in adjusting to the work-setting and guide him over crises, mostly in interpersonal relations. In this effort considerable work with employers and also fellow employees may be necessary. For this, special skills and great perseverance is required.

On the surface it would seem that job adjustment should be integrated into the functions of the life-adjustment social worker. This would be the more desirable arrangement. However, the knowledge and skills involved in mediating employer-employee relations are not ordinarily the stock-in-trade of the community or clinical social worker. A special know-how is required. In addition, the painstaking and continuous nature of this effort would absorb so much time and attention on the part of the life-adjustment worker that little would be left for any other services. Obviously, continuous coordination between the two workers would be essential in order to integrate their efforts. In some communities "sheltered workshops," which are sensitive to the needs of emotionally and mentally handicapped persons, are available. In those cases, their staffs can take over the functions of the industrial social worker.

"Ancillary Therapists"

The concept of "ancillary therapists" (occupational, recreational, music, art, dancing, etc.) is questionable in the light of Vita-Erg Therapy. Insofar as its central theme is therapy through the total life situation and the living process, *all* persons who in any way have any kind of impact on patients are equally involved. They all must have the personalities, knowledge, and dispositions that enter into the attitude toward patients. It was this principle that motivated the inclusion in our seminar discussions of the so-called "ancillary therapists" and supervisory and administrative staffs. We also pointed out to the administration the importance of having a male maintenance staff, who at times did repairs and installations on the wards, who have friendly dispositions (which, by the way, they always seemed to have, treating patients with kindness). We have, on occasion, attempted to include the kitchen staff, as well, in our seminars.

In order to carry through consistently the therapeutic approach to patients, the so-called ancillary therapists must have the same understanding of the nature and the variety of manifestations of psychoses and their meanings, as do other staff members, rather than focussing interest on quality and productivity and being critical of patients' works. Their college training in the area of their specialty should not impair their understanding of patients and their place in the therapeutic team. If the higher aims of the therapeutic, as opposed to custodial, are to be achieved, it will be necessary to revise the orientation of these staffs at the source; namely, the professional schools and colleges.

Another change in the staff structure of mental hospitals would seem to be imperative. This is the dual identity of the members of the "ancillary staff." Their designations, and duplication of assignments, status, supervision and job evaluation under the prevailing arrangement are not centered in the area of their function. Officially, they are assigned to the departments specific to their profession, are responsible to the supervisors (or directors) of their departments, and are evaluated by them. This creates a duality of loyalties with, naturally, the bias being from whence salary increments and job promotions stem. Since the theoretic and philosophic orientations of the psychiatric group worker in charge of the ward activities on the one hand, and the departmental directors rooted in traditional attitudes on the other, their interests and opinions would seldom, if ever, coalesce. The resulting conflict cannot but be reflected in the values and functions of the staff with unavoidable endless political pull, strain and confusion, paralyzing the orderly progress of the patients who would be exposed to differing modes of treatment and expectations.

This dual pull had actually occurred during the life of our project. The reader will recall the *tour de force* of the occupational therapists who abandoned the main body of the patients for the small "isolated" groups and the tensions between departments that led up to it. During a visit to one of the other wards on the service, after the idea had spread in the hospital to introduce O.T. directly on the wards, I found the O.T. worker occupied with three patients in the small sun-room. When asked why she did not work on the ward, her reply was, "I like to work with a few patients."

A telling example of a possible source of conflict once arose during our early planning luncheon-discussions with the supervisory personnel. When, at our recommendation, the decision was made to introduce regular walks and trips on and off grounds for the patients of Wards A and B, the supervisor, whose staff would have to take charge of the trips, suddenly asserted, "But you will have to get permission from the psychiatrist for each patient before you can take them out." (Apparently, in the past, such permission was required before patients could be taken off the wards, a rule that did not apply to the residents of the open wards.) Not being cognizant of such a rule, and seeking to avoid a conflict, we did not take up cudgels in favor of the decision and passed the remark unnoticed, though our surprise at the failure of the professionally trained staff member to grasp the basic intent of our project could not have passed unnoticed by anyone present.

Another example was the career of a noncivil-service worker who had his own approach to his work, which we considered adequate. He had been officially assigned to one of the departments, since otherwise he would have been a "floating member of the staff, not accountable to anyone." The supervisor of the department to which he was assigned did not approve of his free approach and hampered his activity, insofar as she still did not have the authority to discharge him or otherwise bring the staff member to task. It took him several years and much effort and machinations to be officially disassociated from the department and to work on his own.

The person in charge of the ward program, the psychiatric group worker or social therapist, should be free to choose his staff from those available in various specialties with whom he feels he can work harmoniously, and when such are not available, to engage his own staff. His evaluations and recommendations should be final and valid for whatever promotions and monetary rewards they may bring. This practice would obviate the many difficulties and disruptions that dual direction cannot fail to bring about.

Functions of the Psychiatrist

The functions of the psychiatrist on the ward were delineated in Chapter 4. Omission of administrative duties among them was not fortuitous, it was intended. Our observation of the role a psychiatrist plays in the management of the total life of the patients on the wards convinced us that fundamental revisions in this area appear to us absolutely necessary. It would be even more so if his therapeutic duties were expanded as outlined in the above-mentioned chapter in the light of the Vita-Erg plan. His training qualifies him best for direct psychotherapy and for supervising and training the clinical staff—the psychologists, the caseworkers and (the new type of) nurses—and also for serving in a consultive role at the weekly staff seminars for attendants and specialists.

The management of orderly living routines, the creation of a therapeutic climate and conducting the activity programs on the wards, all lie within the province of the psychiatric group worker as outlined, and the psychiatric nurse—each functioning within his own realm, but meticulously coordinated. The psychiatrist should not be burdened with the minutiae that the duties of these persons and the attendants entail. Both his time and attention should not be cluttered with them if he is to contribute fully from his specialty to the life of patients and to their improvement. Under the present plan, the final responsibility and accountability for the wards lay with the psychiatrists, but their participation in the management of wards is, of necessity, minimal. The mass of "paper work," reading of charts, dealing with crises, seeing patients (even scantily), attending meetings, conferring with administrative and subordinate staffs that fall to his lot leave little time, energy and concentration to attend to the innumerable physical and administrative details involved in ward management. At present, these details are not available due to the shortages, or when they are absent, these duties are left to an attendant; an eventuality that occurs only too frequently. What is suggested here is that such responsibilities be assigned to the psychiatric group worker and nurse. The latter assignment, being already common practice, the only change would, therefore, be in making it official and thus establishing responsibility where it belongs.

The usual rapid and perfunctory "rounds of wards" made daily by the supervising psychiatrist, in charge of eight wards, accompanied by an "adjutant" in the person of the supervising nurse were, at least in our case, very disturbing to the patients. In the early days of our program, these rounds, which consisted largely of walking through the full length of the ward (entering it at one end and exiting at the other) always caused a stir among the patients who, becoming aware of the "higher" authority, belabored him with requests and complaints, mostly the latter.

Not being cognizant of the circumstances of the complaints from the numerous patients in the service, and the implications of the requests, the supervising psychiatrist would, of necessity, deal with them perfunctorily and evasively. He either referred the supplicants and complainers to another staff member, or ordered the nurse, who always had a pad and pencil in hand, to remind him to "look into the matter," or asked her to attend to it herself. These fleeting conversations were held and settled as the psychiatrist would momentarily stop, surrounded by the nurse and the supplicants, but not infrequently the conversations were held as he slowly moved toward the exit door with the group at his heels. The need for rounds of medical wards is entirely understandable. The personnel surrounding the attending physician are a nurse and other doctors, some of whom treat the patients or are in training, and, therefore, benefit from the senior's opinions and suggestions. The situation on a mental hospital ward is completely different in every regard, but the practice seems to have arbitrarily transferred to mental hospitals.

Ward-Staff Organization

We have attempted to show how the needs of Vita-Erg Ward Therapy require basic modifications in the ward structure and its administration. The following flow diagram is an attempt to indicate these changes in graphic form.

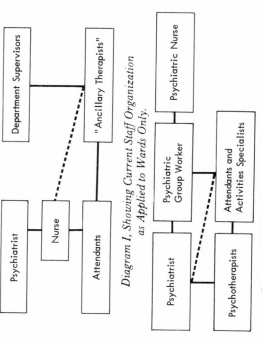

Diagram I, Showing Current Staff Organization as Applied to Wards Only.

Diagram II, Showing Vita-Erg Staff Organization as Applied to Wards Only.

Note: Broken line indicates partial professional relationships, as may be required.

315

The contrast in the graphic representation of the two schema make palpable two important points: (a) simplification of staff organization, hence also simplification in interrelationships and greater efficiency naturally arising from cooperation and synergy; and (b) the team approach among the psychiatrist, group worker, and nurse. Team coordination has come under consideration in some of the more progressive hospitals only recently, though it has been practiced in child guidance and community clinics for some decades. The problems involved in this new development, which are many and vexing, have as yet not been identified and properly worked through. The complexities inherent in the management of mental hospitals are very great indeed, and at times perplexing. Much cautious, flexible experimentation will be required to unravel them. But when the problems will have been solved, the gain to patients will be immeasurable.

It is clear from the foregoing of the functions of the various staff categories—psychiatrists, psychotherapists, psychiatric group workers, nurses, activities specialists, and attendants—that while their efforts are directed toward reaching the mass of patients, they cannot overlook, in this scheme, the idiosyncratic nature of individuals and their specific therapeutic needs. Thus, the attention of staff would have to be divided between groups and individuals, for Vita-Erg Ward Therapy is both group- and individual-centered, and perhaps weighted in favor of the latter. Obviously frequent and continuous interchange between psychiatrist, psychiatric group worker, nurse, and social worker is of the essence if the program is to work.

Limitations of Vita-Erg Therapy

It would be a grievous error and detrimental to future generations of patients to assume that Vita-Erg Therapy is a cure-all for hospitalized psychotic persons. It was introduced and experimented with on wards of seriously deteriorated, long-term, chronic and hitherto "hopeless" cases, but this was only fortuitous. The dominant approaches described in this volume would undoubtedly be more widely effective with the average, more intact patients for whom ego-support through warm human relations, active participation in planning and in the life on the ward are of therapeutic essence.

The fact that an impressive number have gained sufficient strength from our ward life to return to their old habitats and some could hold volunteer and even paid jobs, as reported by our social worker, was surprising to us. That a larger number improved sufficiently to join the "open wards" and made a good adjustment in the hospital microculture was indeed gratifying. But Vita-Erg therapy extended to the total hospital community, if there were staff in sufficient numbers qualified to carry it on, would solve many vexing problems in this field of mental health.

The improvement in our group of patients was commented upon by many persons, only a few of whom were quoted in the body of this volume. Visiting relatives were delighted with the changes in their kin and former staff members who dropped in on their former haunts expressed delight and surprise. The fact that some of the rotating trainees asked to be assigned permanently to the two formerly most difficult wards that had been shunned in the past, and that some patients who had been transferred to "better" wards requested to be returned to Wards A and B, attest to the appeal that the Vita-Erg process, when properly applied, has for staff and patients. But one would still be seriously misled were one to claim that basic structural changes were affected in full-blown, chronic psychotics so that they could hold up against the demands and pressures of an unfriendly world entirely without help. The improvements must be considered as *functional* only.

Vita-Erg Therapy would be much more effective with patients whose egos are more intact than the patients we were dealing with. The normalization of the environment, its stimulation and responsiveness, the human relatedness, arousal of security and self-worth characteristics of Vita-Erg Therapy would prove more effective, and more rapidly so, in those cases where the psychic soil was more fertile. What we accomplished has been to succeed in rendering many of our "inaccessible" members *receptive* to the kind of relationships that form the basis of true psychotherapy.

We have been able to remove much of the moroseness and intransigence of and we have increased the predictability in our patients, thus rendering them better subjects for direct therapeutic intervention. In view of these accomplishments, we must consider these techniques largely as preliminary steps toward direct individual and group psychotherapy, by gifted and well trained therapists, and appropriate chemotherapy, yet to be evolved. Whatever the therapeutic effects of Vita-Erg Therapy may be, its major value, in our view, lies in the fact that it gives content and dignity to the lives of the most psychologically disadvantaged sector of a community's population and is thus an essential part of the democratic ideal.

It would be impossible to convey the travail of the soul-rending disappointments, the exhausting tensions, and the trying patience that a breakthrough into the iron-clad, entrenched conventional values and attitudes that a project such as this entails. Only the late Dr. Beckenstein's unwavering faith and steadfast support made it possible to see it through.

Appendix I: Transcript of Seminar Session

The following is a transcription of the fifth session of the attendants' seminar:

MR. S.: Is there anything special you would like to talk about this morning? (Prolonged silence.) No questions at all? I heard some rumors that you were having some meetings. I don't know the details. Who would like to tell us what went on at those meetings?

NURSE: We were agreeing and disagreeing. There is a feeling (among the attendants) that when one makes a statement that is not believed by another, we feel that we shouldn't have made it. I think there is a reluctance to talk here. They feel that it might not be agreed with and statements may be taken as a criticism.

MR. S.: As defiance of authority?

ATT. (1):[1] Not exactly of authority, but that statements may be laughed at or scoffed at, and the person will be embarrassed. They feel that if what they say is not correct, they might be embarrassed, and that regardless of what statement we make, it *is* what we feel and what we think. This is my concept: even if we are wrong, let's make the statement. No one in the world is perfect and no one can be always right. There is such a word as genius and it's only a word. Nobody is infallible and nobody is a genius—that they know it all. We can learn from each

[1] This is the attendant to whom we have referred previously as the most sensitive and involved with the patients, to a point of detriment. In time, her impetuosity and sentimentalism had greatly abated as a result of our seminars to the extent that she became conscious of her overidentification and was able to verbalize her improvement.

other. And if we make a statement that the others do not agree upon, it's debatable. Sometimes we will never agree with one another. That's what makes the world go around. Even if we don't agree, it's brought out in the open. Let's say it anyway, even if we're wrong.

I remember I made a statement before about singing to a patient. I want to bring out that just because I sang to that particular patient, that doesn't mean that we are just supposed to sit down and sing a solo. What I meant was I had tried many things with that particular patient and just happened upon the singing—and singing happened to work with this particular patient. You just keep trying. You don't leave a patient alone. When she won't eat, you say to yourself, "This patient is in my care, I am responsible for her!" You can't say that the nurse is responsible for her. She is not there. She has left me in charge of this particular patient and it is up to me.

DR. C—— [supervising psychiatrist] called me once and I couldn't come to him because I was feeding a patient. I got into trouble about it. And he remembered and talked to me about it later and I explained to him. But this is my contention: we are responsible for that particular patient at that particular time. As you said before, at that moment we are the mother. The mother does not mean that we give birth to that child or we are supposed to feel the same as we feel toward our own. Mothering of that child means a warm interest, a wanting to do for, caring about that person. You don't have to love a person to care. I think we should carry the word care in big letters in our minds. *I care.* We care about what happens to another human being. I mean *really* care. We really care and we try everything we can. Not just what *we know* is right. We may have people laugh at us; we may have people make fun of us; we may have people call us down. But still, if you think you are right on that particular thing, do it. Talk to somebody about it later, try to find out where you are wrong and make them see where you are right. But I think all of us have something inside of us which is a warmth. . .

MR. S. (interrupting): You say at the moment you are responsible for the patient, therefore you wouldn't leave her. And the second thing is that you made a very valid distinction between the difference of "loving" and "caring." How many of you understood us to say that you must *love* your patients? Would you raise your hands please? Nobody. What is the difference between caring and loving? Mrs. A—— made this very important distinction and I think we should all attempt to understand it.

ATT. (2): There is a difference between loving your child and how you would love a patient. It's blood-love for a child. There is a difference between that. Like Mrs. A—— said, you *care* for that patient. But you can be *like* a mother to a patient.

MR. S.: Substitute mother.

APPENDIX I

ATT. (2): That's right. You can care for that patient, just like you would care for a child. But there is a difference between blood-love and love for a patient. But you can be a mother—in a way—for that patient by caring.

MR. S.: Is that clear? Is there any question here? What is the difference between blood-love and caring-love?

ATT. (2): You have a different feeling of love for blood-love. You may do just as much for that patient as you would for your child, but there is a difference in the love. But you would do just as much. And you can really get close to these patients so that you really love them. [2]

MR. S.: Do we have to be involved as much with patients as we are with our children? Do we have to be involved emotionally?

ATT. (3): I think we don't have to be so, emotionally. You can love a person the first time you meet him; you see something in that person you love. You can see some good in him, especially so in a person you are trying to love, such as a patient. They are here to be helped.

MR. S.: For example, a good pastor, a good teacher has love for the parishioner or the pupil. That is different from the love the teacher or minister gives to his own children, but he still has affection for pupils or parishioners. The difference is that the parent feels responsible for the growth of the child. We are not responsible for what happened to a patient. But we are responsible for what happens to our children. We mold the children, but we didn't mold the patients. Therefore, we are not involved as much. We don't feel that we will be blamed for what the patient had become, but we do feel that the world would blame us, and we would blame ourselves, for what becomes of our children. There is the feeling of self-blame that comes if we don't bring up the child properly. What I am trying to say is that the parent feels guilty about his child but we don't feel guilty about our patients because we didn't make them the way they are. In the parent there is an element of guilt and involvement as a result of that. We don't want the child to grow up bad. We create the child, not only physically but also spiritually. With patients we can become involved like an artist becomes involved in his painting or a musician in his music. So when we speak of loving patients we actually mean, what Mrs. A—— said, that is, we care for them.

There is sexual love, there is parental love, there is love that comes from general feelings of tenderness, and there is oceanic love, the love for animals, mankind and nature. All the great prophets, the founders of religions, loved mankind as a whole and tried to save all of mankind. So there are different types of love. If we love a person we do what is best for that person, even at a cost to ourselves. Many people are in

321

2 At a later session the term "compassion" was arrived at for this feeling. It was suggested by Att. (1), who was our most perceptive and most disturbed member.

love with love. They "spoil" their children because they are in love with love, not with the child. To love the child is also to deny him and punish him when it is for his own good. It may look cruel sometimes, but if it is best for his development, it is not cruel. So we do a lot of things which often hurt us because we love the child more than ourselves. Loving means to do—to be willing to do—what is best for a person even at the cost to ourselves.

I don't believe we are called upon to do this with patients as we are with our children, or to such a great extent. For many reasons, therefore, teachers can do more for some children in many respects than can parents, because their love is healthier. Parents' love can become very unhealthy because of guilt and insecurity and wanting peace of mind rather than what is best for the child, they overlook a lot. They "love" the child and, therefore, do not want to "hurt" him when he should be disciplined for his own good. They don't want to restrain or punish because they think this is not love. So we have to differentiate. And I think the word *caring* is a very good correction; it expresses exactly what we wanted to convey. I am afraid I used a term that was not quite suitable. Any question about that now?

MR. S.: What has she been doing?

ATT. (4): There was some dispute [during the post-seminar discussion) when I spoke about the patient [who refused to join the ward meeting]. What I wanted to explain is that I *helped* her but I didn't cure her. I think there was a little misinterpreting. It was told me [by other attendants], "Don't worry she will come back and do the same thing," and so on. I'm sure I didn't cure her, but I know that I did help her a great deal from the different things that she has been doing since then.[3]

MR. S.: What did you say to her?

ATT. (4): I said, "What's the matter, L——?" She was hallucinating, mentioning names. Not anyone from the hospital.

MR. S.: What did you say?

ATT. (4): I said, "Okay, L——, get up. Come with me. Come with me, I'll help you."

MR. S.: In that [strident] tone of voice? [No.] Give the exact tone of voice, please.

3 The post-seminar discussions led by the nurse of one of the wards were discontinued because of such misunderstandings and the possibility of the nurse's points of view differing with our own would confuse the staff at this juncture.

ATT. (4) [repeats in a soothing tone of voice, then continues]: Sometimes if you have a firm voice, they listen. I don't have to be very firm with her, though. With some of the patients, I do. I found out that was why the last time she had given me trouble, because I was firm with her when I said, "Come on, get up! Get in the chair!" It was like a command. There are some patients you have to be firm with, but I don't have to be firm with L——.

MR. S.: This is most important. You cannot deal with all people —in or out of the hospital—in exactly the same way. We have to use judgment. It is essential that we are firm even in kindness with our patients, however. Firmness is what our patients need, because they don't have enough strength to mobilize their own powers as yet. When we are firm with patients, they build up strength. With some patients we can talk one way, but with others it must be different. We have to distinguish differences in patients, and also the mood they are in.

ATT. (4): I noticed that she had been sick. I said, "Oh, that's terrible, does it hurt? Come on in and I'll put something on it and then I'll *let you* lie down." [Note the term "let you."] I put something on it and *let her* lie down. I asked her if she wanted to lie down in the other room and she said yes. As I was *getting her* [sic] on the bed she fell down and dragged the mattress with her. It slid and she was falling down. And I said "Oh my God! You'll be hurt," and took her by the hand. These are the words she said, "Never mind, don't worry about me so much. It's too late for me anyhow." I didn't get a chance to talk to Dr. R—— about this. She mentioned some people's names which are probably those from her home. But she was very gentle [submissive]. As hostile as she was with the patients a few minutes earlier, she was now very, very soft and in a despairing way said, "Oh, I don't care what happens; it's too late; don't worry about me so much." That was it. As I said, "I didn't get a chance to talk to Dr. R——." I left her lying down.

MR. S.: Were there other patients in the room?

ATT. (4): No, she was alone. Then she was given an I.M. and that was it. I went in a few times to give her water, but left her there when I went home.

MR. S.: Have you any questions, suggestions?

ATT. (4): There was a reason I wanted to specify that I didn't cure her. It was told to me [obviously critically by other attendants] that now she is cured. I am a therapist, they said. So I said *I will keep my mouth shut from now on.* I didn't mean that I cured her. To do that would be a miracle for me. But I like to know that I helped her. Dr. R—— has helped me a great deal to understand her and work with her and we worked together on her.

MR. S.: I would like somebody else to tell me in what way Mrs. V——helped her.

Att. (5): She was kind to her; she used a nice tone of voice when it was needed and she was on the spot.

Mr. S.: What happened to the patient?

Att. (5): She softened up.

Att. (1): She felt she had somebody who cared what happened to her. And when she was bad, someone cared enough to know she wanted to lie down till she calmed down; they cared enough to notice the fact that although she had started a fight, she, too, had been injured. She showed caring, and that's important.

Mr. S.: This is a girl who was terribly rejected by her parents. What are the two types of problem that patients suffer from? One is—

Att.: Fear.

Mr. S.: The other is what? [No response] Fear and hostility. Murderous hostility against people. Which one of these was she helped with?

Att. 4: She was hostile at first.

Mr. S.: What did we say we had to do with psychotics to help them recover sociability? [No response] We had to build a bridge between people and the patient. Was this a way of building a bridge?

Att.: I think it was.

Mr. S.: [Smiling to a silent att.]: What about you? We haven't heard your voice yet.

Att.: I would say it was.

Mr. S.: Are you positive?

Att.: No, I'm not positive.

Mr. S [to another attendant]: What about you? Do you think this is a way of building a bridge?

Att.: Yes, I think so.

Mr. S.: Of course it is. If this happens many times, how do you think the patient will start feeling about other people?

Att.: Better.

Mr.S.: Much better. So if she gets this kind of treatment from everybody—not just the one person who is in charge—but from everybody on the ward and in the hospital, gradually she will overcome her what?

Atts.: Fear.

Mr. S.: She will become convinced that people are not going to hurt her. Her psychotic mother didn't want anything to do with her and treated her badly. Her fear will be overcome and will help the patient to do what?

Att.: To get better.

Mr. S.: She will be able to relate to people. Now she is afraid to

4 Participants whose voices were not recognizable are listed merely as "att."

relate because to be involved with a person is to be hurt. Where did she learn that?

SEVERAL ATTS.: At home.

MR. S.: This doesn't mean that we cannot be firm when necessary. As a matter of fact, you will find patients like Miss T—— who cannot accept kindness or affection.

SEVERAL ATTS.: Sometimes she will.

MR. S.: When she wants it. But when you offer it to her, she will blow up.

ATT.: One day when she had blown up with [attacked] Dr. C—— [supervising psychiatrist] and we took her off him [by force] she wasn't very hostile with us, maybe because there was more than one of us.

MR. S.: She couldn't have been hostile to you because you saved her from her own hostility and she was grateful to you. Even in her state, she vaguely knew she shouldn't have attacked the doctor. But suppose you went over and put your arm around her and said something very nice to her, instead of restraining her, I imagine she would react differently. There are people by the millions, even in the community, who cannot accept love. If you love them, they become anxious or suspicious or frightened because—why?

ATT.: Maybe they have been hurt before.

MR. S.: By whom?

ATT.: Family.

MR. S.: Especially the mother. It is the mother who is supposed to give love. And to the child, the mother gives love when she feeds and washes her, takes her for a walk and so on. All of these mean to the child that the mother loves her. But if the mother is cruel at the same time, her love becomes what?

ATT.: Hate.

MR. S.: Yes, and cruelty. That is the way the child's mind works. People come for therapy with these feelings. They are confused between love and hate. Many marriages are broken up by the fact that one or both of the partners cannot feel comfortable being loved or giving love. Studies have been made on how to give love to ordinary patients, not psychotics. The problem of giving love to patients is a very delicate one. Some patients have to be treated directly because to them this is the way to be loved. That is the way their mothers trained them in love.

ATT. (1): Do you think the majority of parents don't even know they are mistreating children or being cruel?

MR. S.: Of course they don't.

ATT. (1): Because this same patient comes from a family, and I knew this family years ago as a young woman myself. She comes from a home that when you walk in, everything is spoless, everything is shining. It gives you a feeling you must straighten things up before you leave. She grew up in this environment. How in the world could she even play. There's a difference between being clean and overclean.

MR. S.: We know that the mother is psychotic. The mother had to be that way. If she didn't have these defenses she would have been in a mental hospital. That [obsessional compulsion] was her protection. However, the child fell by the wayside. Now then, if you repeat this over and over again [building bridges] and she gradually learns that she can love and accept love and not be hurt, she will change and you are the people who can do it, nobody else. We will show you a film of what caring really means. In that film a child becomes unmanageable and we know he won't stop by himself. Sometimes we do know when a child will stop, but when he becomes unmanageable we tell him he must go home and insist on this. When he comes in the following week, we act as though nothing had happened. This way he learns that he can go just so far, but the love and affection and caring isn't taken away from him. He also discovers that he can obtain affection and love by acting and being more "normal." This can also be done with patients. On the other hand, some (paranoid) patients will scratch your eyes out as soon as you touch them because to be touched is to be killed. Because they are so afraid, they get enraged and it may take two or three people to hold them down.

ATT.: On Wards A and B you spend a fortune on some patients trying to be nice; sometimes trying to quiet them down. Buy them cigarettes. The majority of the patients smoke. They come to us for cigarettes. We buy them out of our pocket.

ATT. (3): When you give them cigarettes you can get what you want accomplished—washing, ironing, sewing their clothes—in half the time. As long as you give them cigarettes they go right ahead and do it. They will do anything you ask them.

MR. S.: What is the first question to ask yourself on the ward or in your personal life when you meet up with a problem like this?

ATT.: You ask yourself how you can solve the problem.

MR. S.: No.

ATT.: Can you afford doling out?

MR. S.: No. Say you have all the money you need.

ATT. (3): It depends on the patient. Will the patient get upset if you don't give him the cigarettes? There are different types of patients. Some of them will smoke their own and then come begging, or steal somebody else's. But some of them may get very upset if you don't give them cigarettes. Those are the ones we give cigarettes to.

MR. S.: What do you say when you don't give them cigarettes?

ATT. (3): In my group I do have a few who get cigarettes from the parents. I know they are there (in the hospital) because they are sick, but

APPENDIX I

they know better and they won't work, they won't do anything, they won't even make their own beds.

Mr. S.: Because they have no cigarettes?

Att. (3): No. Some of them are regressed, but they are not regressed to the point where they can't do anything. Even if they get the cigarettes they won't do anything. But if they want the cigarette bad enough, then they will offer to do something for you if you give them a cigarette.

Mr. S.: This is the established culture of the ward. Every group of people living together create a culture. Every family had its own culture and rituals. The wards have a culture which is passed on from year to year. It is very important that we change this. However, coming back to the original question, what should you ask yourself when you are faced with any situation with people?

Att.: Why are they doing it? Why are they asking for this cigarette?

Mr. S.: Yes. Why does she want so many cigarettes? Once we have answered this question, we may not have solved the problem, but at least we are on the way to solving it. Why do they want cigarettes? Why food from home, candy, why? You know, because we discussed this.

Several Atts.: Oral.

Mr. S.: Yes, because they are on the oral level.[5] This is one of the characteristics of psychotics—they remain on the oral and anal levels and have not reached the "genital" level, which is maturity. They are on the level of the little child. This is not the answer to our problem, but it is a way of understanding it.

Att.: What you are saying to me. Maybe you are not. Maybe I have the wrong conception. Is it that every time they ask me for a cigarette I go in my pocket and give them a cigarette to satisfy their oral needs?

Mr. S.: When you give a patient a cigarette, at what level do you keep her?

Att.: Oral.

Mr. S.: That is, you keep them where they are. The point is to move them on further. They are all like little children, and children are always wanting—"momma, I want a drink," etc. Therefore, we have to do a number of things. I don't know if we can do anything at the moment. Not having seen enough of the wards, I don't know the situation or your patients, how you go about it or how you are functioning. And

[5] The three phases of development—oral, anal and "genital"—were formulated at a preceding session (on the regressive stages of the psychotic patient).

327

this is a very, very ticklish subject, because you are now dealing with the core of the patients' personalities, and we, therefore, have to be very careful. But there are ways we can use when we have the whole program set up. How will our program of activities of being busy all the time help this?.

Att. (3): They will be so busy they won't have time to think about smoking.

Mr. S.: That's right. Keeping them busy and occupied so that the oral craving, the comfort which they derived through the lining of the mouth, will not come to mind. They will be busy; they will be occupied. That is one way. Is there another way? [No response.] We are going to have ways of baking and cooking things so that they can satisfy their oral craving in this way and by whatever else you ladies will work out for the patients to do. [One of them was supplying materials by the O.T. department for the patients to make their own cigarettes.] The third way, and this is what we do with child patients, had to do with the fact that our patients came from very poor neighborhoods, and would ask the therapists for loans of money. These were not psychotics, they were just disturbed kids. We dis- covered that feeding was a very important factor in our relations with them. . . .

We started to do this with younger children, but later we did it with mothers of disturbed children, by leaving cigarettes and hard can- dies lying around, and by serving coffee. This was our first approach, but we did not keep them at that level, for we were able to eliminate the food when the boys became more relaxed and secure in their relation- ship with the therapist. At first we told the therapists to give the chil- dren money when they asked, but later the therapists would go to the session with no more than their carfare in their pockets. And when a boy would ask him for money, they would extract the coins and say that was all they had—just their carfare.

Att. (1): I tried that with a patient once and she said, "I'll go with you to your locker. I know you've got something there."

Mr. S.: Patients cannot be fooled. There may be other ways to handle this and other situations which we will develop as we go along and work together.

Att.: I have often spoken to the mother of one of our patients of her needs for clothing and other things, but the mother says, "Well, she'll have to do with what she has," and she would then avoid me on her visits.

Mr. S.: It seems to me that this is an administrative problem. One who runs the ward should understand not only the patients, but also the family. She or he ought to know which of the visitors disturb the pa- tients and arrange visits for these particular parents away from the ward, and ask social service to work with the parents and see whether or not they cannot be helped to deal with the patients appropriately.

ATT. (1): Some of them you want to pick up and pitch right out of the door. We don't do it, but we would like to. What they do to their own children when they come here!

ATT.: I have a dormitory assignment with 60 beds. In the morning some patients will come over and I will say, "Are you going to make your bed now?" "Are you going to give me a cigarette?" is the answer. I say, "Well nobody paid me for making my bed before I came here. Do you think I should have to pay you for making the bed you slept in last night?" Sometimes they say "yes," sometimes they say "no," sometimes they'll just walk off or go ahead and make it. That's the way I handle it.

ATT.: Sometimes they say, "You *work* here, I don't."

MR. S.: What about the parents who are a problem? What do you think is Mrs. E——'s reasoning when she runs to greet the other patients and ignores her own daughter? What is she doing? [Mrs. E—— was presented as an example of a difficult mother during a discussion.]

ATT. (1): I think she's guilty about something, but if she's so guilty, she ought to do something for her own, first. We have patients who have no visitors and Mrs E—— will go over to speak to them. Sometimes she gives food to patients who we don't want to have it [the food]—a patient who is overfat and doesn't need any extra feeding. We tell her, don't feed her. "It's all right, it's all right," she says. And then her daughter comes up to her and says, "Mom, come over here, talk to me." Mrs. E——will say, "Oh, never mind, I'll see you later." If I had the right, I would keep her out. When she leaves, the poor patient starts screaming and we have her on our hands. She just screams. She opens her mouth and screams. You can hear her scream a block away. It's pitiful. The mother must be awful guilty.

MR. S.: That is a mother who should see her daughter away from the ward. Her behavior looks like guilt, but I don't think it is. What she is doing is being cruel to her daughter. Instead of beating her with her hands as she did when the daughter was little, she is now doing it in this way and in effect says, "To hell with you. I don't care about you and I'll show you that I don't care about you." This mother should never be allowed to come to the ward, or she may be prohibited from visiting until the psychiatrist or social service work this out with her.

ATT. (1) [with deep feeling]: The poor patient waits for the mother.

MR. S.: This is the way to deal with this situation—on an individual basis. We cannot deal with all mothers this way. There are certain mothers and fathers who can be helpful, but what is important is that we have to work with the parents, not only with the patients.

ATT.: Some patients are all right until visitors day. Then they become upset and some stay upset until the next visiting day.

Mr. S.: We had similar experiences in a school with children from exclusively wealthy homes. They would become placid and constructive during the week, but would return on Monday in an awful state and we had to start all over again. You have the same problem with patients and their parents here. What we did there was to involve the mothers in psychoanalysis. We were talking about cigarettes as compensation for doing personal chores. Don't some patients ask for cigarettes in a kidding way; some test you; some really want a cigarette or else? The majority are in the third category, right?

Att.: You have to find out who is kidding and who really wants.

Att.: I am a relief person and don't have a group. We have 60 patients in the dormitory and I have to relieve in the office also.

Mr. S.: Maybe we will have to change this arrangement. In the setting in which you are working as a relief person, you cannot develop permanent relationships. As a relief person you are more a person of authority. You come in for a specific job at a specific time.

Att.: But I'm in the ward most of the time.

Mr. S.: Then why don't you have a group?

Att.: When they started the new groups (assigned to each att., which we eliminated) I was out on sick leave. Some patients refuse to make their bed, but when I offer to help them they will sometimes make two or three beds *with my help.*

Mr. S.: What does this mean?

Att.: They are more interested.

Mr. S.: Couldn't it be a feeling of togetherness? The patient is no longer alone and isolated. This is another bridge, about which we have talked. It is very important. A good way to build an interpersonal bridge is to work with patients and after awhile you can wean them away and do something else alongside with them. You can then also say, "Would you like Janet to help you?" and so get two patients to work together and establish a relationship.

Att.: I've done that too.

Mr. S.: I would try to cut down on giving patients cigarettes.

Att.: I do. Actually I can't afford it. If I had enough money to give them cigarettes I wouldn't have to be working here. Sometimes I have a group in addition to the dormitory, and they want cigarettes. It is a problem, it's a conflict. Some patients you'll give cigarettes to, because they'll work for you and another patient will come over at the same time and say, "Well, let me have a cigarette, too." You actually can't afford to give a cigarette to everyone who asks for it. I try to get the patients who work for me off by themselves and give them cigarettes, instead of doing it in front of other patients.

Dr. Beckenstein: Would you say that some patients have cigarettes when they ask you for some?

ATT.: Oh yes. One has a whole carton, but asks for more all the time and she doesn't smoke them. She collects them. I give them to her because she is a good worker and she sells them to other patients.

MR. S.: Are they allowed to sell cigarettes?

ATT.: We don't know when it is done, but we know that it is done. One patient, on going home for a visit had more money than we did. She sold cigarettes, coffee, steak sandwiches.

MR. S.: Would you say this patient could be described as being on the oral or anal level?

SEVERAL ATTS.: Anal!

MR. S.: Yes. She is at a higher level. Something might be done with her on the matter of cigarettes.

ATT.: She also sometimes gets to the stage where she becomes violent. She didn't want anybody in the dormitory but herself. She wanted to clean it and make the beds and didn't want anybody around "bothering" her. If you went to the door (of the dormitory) and looked like you were going to walk in, you had a bed thrown at you.

MR. S.: I bet she did a very good job of cleaning.

ATT.: A very good job, yes.

ATT.: This same patient, also, as I said, works in the dormitory every day. I usually give her three cigarettes. I have offered her more and she has refused them.

MR. S.: Sounds like a very interesting patient. They are called anal aggressives and retainers. In other words, they are aggressive and also retain, hold on, like in constipation. This is what children do. Some children who are angry with their mothers won't move their bowels for days. This is where it starts, anal retention, like people who have a drive to be rich, to have big houses, big bank accounts, lots of clothes, always hoarding.

ATT.: I have another one like that. She comes in, but not to make beds. She will come in after she has been in the [clothing] store room and stolen a pair of shoes, a coat, dresses, and puts them under her arm or under her dress and wants to hide them under her mattress. She will take sweaters and coats. On the hottest day she will have on two or three sweaters and a coat. We have to tear them off her.

MR. S.: There are people who walk around the streets of New York wearing six layers of clothing, in temperatures of 100 degrees. They are, of course, psychotic. No normal person does this kind of thing. Then there are the men and women who walk around with three or four bags filled with trash.

ATT.: One patient was sitting across from me, facing me, with her coat on her lap. Another patient walked up behind her and tried to slide the coat off her lap without the first patient being aware of it.

MR. S.: These are not kleptomaniacs, for they do it openly. I often see a couple in my neighborhood, both well dressed, middle class people who go around picking out of waste baskets in the streets. They look like normal, healthy people. This activity is different from kleptomania. Kleptomania is the excitement of putting something over on somebody who does not know—the excitement of doing something that is wrong. It has a sexual meaning. These are anal people. Our patient has apparently moved up a notch; she doesn't collect cigarettes to smoke. She gets them to hoard and sell. . . .

Dr. Beckenstein asked the staff to note things that arose during the month of August, list various problems, etc. He announced that there would be no meetings held during August (when he and Mr. Slavson were to be out of the country). He ended up by saying:

During August make notes of problems that may arise. You have now gotten an idea of how to record things that arise and puzzle you in your everyday experiences. You are beginning to learn the meaning of many things. You people know a lot more than you give yourselves credit for, and you shouldn't be afraid to bring your ideas in here, whether you are right or wrong—that makes no difference. It is more important that you are going to learn. And very often you learn more from bringing in something that you are wrong in. So don't be afraid. The sky is the limit. Bring in your material. How many things have gone on here so far that you were given the answer to? Mr. Slavson has helped you to verbalize them. Many of you have found out through your own experience what you now have to present to the rest of the group. You all learn from each other. We are here only to help you learn.

Mr. S.: When the therapists don't make mistakes at first, they never make good therapists later on. When it comes to them too naturally in some situations, the next time they may do something else as naturally which will not be right because they do not understand the situation. By making mistakes we learn reasons and meanings so that they become a part of our equipment. I never had great hope for people who did not make mistakes. You have to make mistakes in order to learn. I learned a few things this morning that I didn't know: One is that the concept of love is confusing, and that rather "caring" is more appropriate. The other is that I thought patients wouldn't attack staff, which was something I misjudged. But I learned. I made my mistakes. I hope you learned something, too.

DISCUSSION

The intolerance of differences of opinions among staff and the aura of disloyalty to the group attached to an individual's communication as criticism are made apparent in this session. They reflect the mechanical subservience of attendants to the existing practices and regime which stripped them of originality and assertiveness. This attitude, diminished in time, persisted to a lesser degree throughout the life of our project.

The ridicule with which Attendant (1)'s more humane treatment of her patient was met from her fellow workers is significant. It exposed their discomfort at seeing one of their number follow some of the suggestions made at the preceding seminars. It also revealed their guilt in having treated patients less kindly in the past and the resulting anxiety. The mounting anxiety that our approach, so antithetical to their practices, generated in the early period of our work, of which all the supervisory staff and the psychiatrists were aware, formed the topic of our discussions at the luncheon meetings on a number of occasions.

The discussion on "love" gave us one of the many opportunities later to expand the intellectual horizons of our attendants and to stimulate their thinking generally. These, we hoped, would affect their attitudes toward, give meaning to, and satisfaction in, their work, with resulting gains for the patients.

Attendant(4)'s narration of the episode with Patient L——— clearly reflects the authoritarian and the clumsy, custodial attitude of the staff members, even when she tried to bring herself in line with our ideas. This was one of our four or five most "feelingful," understanding, and cooperative women, who later learned to deal with patients much more empathically. At this stage, however, though intellectually grasping the intent of our program, she repeated the traditional *modus operandi* in manner and voice. Our focussing on the use of the voice is one example of the innumerable such efforts in the course of our project to impress the attendants with the importance of *quality* of feeling and expression and respect for the patients in dealing with them.

Another illustration of this effort was the pointing up of the importance of considering differences in individual patients and in using judgment, rather than giving blanket responses. We grasped the opportunity presented to us by Attendant (4) to explore the psychodynamics inherent in her interchange with the patient as a psycho-educational opportunity. The persistent questioning was employed both to assure clarity of understanding and to involve the participants in the discussion. The attendants were even in the early session able to recognize that empathy and kindness (even though clumsily applied) were better means to reach a patient than was authority. We also utilized the opportunity to bring into relief the roads by which the psychotic can find his way to reality—i.e., overcoming fear and relating to another person.

The episode presented also gave us the opportunity to bring out the genesis, the inevitability, and the dynamics of the psychotic phenomenon by relating it to the mother, the family and the treatment the patient had received as a child. This material not only enhanced intellectual understanding, but also engendered sympathy and led to a more benign attitude toward and treatment of patients.

When the matter of cigarettes was raised, it was appropriate to repeat the refrain that *one must first understand* the intent of each patient before responding. Attendant (4) again displayed her perspicacity when she pointed out the need to differentiate among patients as to their needs and possible responses, although she did not apply it in her treatment of patients.

The attendants' ability to differentiate between oral and anal phases in patients was somewhat surprising at such an early stage in our work. In our explanation in a previous session of the psychotic syndrome, we had traced the developmental sequence of the human individual, pointing out that the psychotic had not reached the genital phase. The fact that these women with limited schooling remembered the symptomatology of each phase after only one presentation, and were able to properly identify them, was very gratifying.

There may be some question raised as to the necessity, and

even appropriateness, of imparting such information to attendants. It was my conviction, however, that if we expected them to treat patients with judgment and respect, it would be essential that we regard them similarly. People can respect others only if they respect themselves. For ages hospital personnel in their category have been receiving very little respect and it was essential that we treat them as we hoped they would treat their patients. We have, therefore, exercised no reservations in our teaching, and sought in other ways to demonstrate our confidence in them.

We have, for example, supplied bound notebooks for each to make entries of ideas and information of interest. We also arranged for coffee and cookies to be served at a midpoint of our proceedings. As already noted, usually members of the supervisory staff, who were not actively involved in the discussion, would serve from the urn brought down by members of the kitchen staff. Also we have never identified at the seminars a person whose acts on the ward required correction and only on a few occasions, in emergencies, did we directly correct conduct of a staff member on the wards, and even then in privacy.

The discussion of cigarettes also presented us with the chance to make palpable how growth beyond the oral stage occurs through dealing with the manifestations of that level of development, thereby enhancing understanding of patients and the staff's role in elevating patients' psychic development.

It was obvious that many of the complaints, such as refusal by patients to participate in domestic chores and the problem of bribing with cigarettes could have been solved by group discussions and patient committee action (in which we later succeeded only partially because of the failure of top ward personnel to sustain them with consistency), but it would have been inappropriate at this stage to suggest it.

We have found the practice of drawing parallels between children and our patients and relations of children and parents a very effective device for concretizing and making palpable the abstruse ideas we sought to convey. This device was needed only at the beginning of our re-education of the attendants.

When the basic concepts had been firmly understood and incorporated, we no longer had to fall back on such simplifications.

Throughout, our emphasis has been less on informational learning and more on *sensitizing* the staff to the patients as human beings with feelings, with pride and with strivings that had to be respected and nurtured. But we painstakingly eschewed sermonizing, sentimentalizing and generalizing. Of special value in the discussion was the attendants' centering on the patients as persons, their backgrounds, feelings and needs, instead of centering upon their usual preoccupations with work, chores and deviant behavior exclusively as was the case before.

All the staff participants in the discussions were members of Ward A. Those from Ward B, where the resistance was nurtured by a member of the supervising staff, remained silent throughout.

The following is a procedural example of engaging staff in thinking through a problem of dealing with a patient, which we consistently employed in our sessions. In opening one of the early sessions (actually before the activity program on the wards had been initiated), I asked: "Did anything happen during the week you would like to discuss? [No response.] Any situation with a patient?"

ATT.: We tried what we discussed last week with K——.

MR. S.: Did she act up?

ATT.: Well, I guess so.

MR. S.: Did you find out what it was that upset her?

ATT.: I feel that as long as things go her way she's all right. But they have to go her way at all times.

MR. S.: What did she do this time?

ATT.: Well, when we came in (in the morning) she was hollering and screaming and, you know. I guess somebody must have said something to her on the night-shift to get her upset. After we started work she quieted down.

ATT. (1): I happened to be in early, fortunately, and this is what happened. The employees have their own dressing room and when they are dressing they ask that the patients stay out of the room, simply because there are keys that have to be changed from pocket to pocket-book, and there have been times when keys have been snatched when an employee's back is turned, or a dress is going over her head.[6] So they request that patients don't come in while employees are changing their clothing. But K—— did come in, and when she does it the other patients feel that they should be allowed to go in, too. So when she went in, other patients went in and the employees asked her that she and the rest of them leave until the employees were dressed. She resented this and said that she was not like the others; she was not going to steal anything. The employees tried to explain to her that she didn't think that she was going to steal anything, but if she let her stay she'd have to let all the others come in, too. K—— just didn't take this into consideration. It took quite a bit for me to get her adjusted. I took her with me and I told her that I needed her and that she could come in with me later and we need her to go down for clothes and, please, forget about it and that the employees did not mean anything against her. She finally subsided. She got control of herself. She's all right now. But that's what started it.

Mr. S.: Did it take a long time?

Att. (1): No. I would say about 15 minutes. It's not a long time when you're working with a patient. Time is not always to be considered with a thing like this as long as you accomplish what you need. Well, we accomplished what we set out to do. We diminished her distress, because right away she began to fear that she was linked with others into taking a key and that we had to get this out of her mind, and we did. So she became quiet after that. But that's her style, you see, because there are some things that if we allow the patient to do this there are instances where they may pick up, they do try, and on this particular ward (Ward A) there are patients who want to get away, naturally. I know I'd want to get away, too. But the institution is accountable for the patients and we can't let them get away when they want to. We are responsible for them until they can look out for themselves. And if they come in and take a key or snatch a pocketbook we have to struggle to get it back. If one patient takes a pair of keys and you can't find them, you have to search other patients, which is an insult to a person.

Mr. S.: You are entirely right in your arguments. The question is how can we prevent this?

Att. (1): I think explaining to K—— on the side. Taking her off, as we did, and explaining to her why she can't come into the room while the dressing is going on. I mean we did that although K—— is a patient that will forget about what you explain to her quite often and then go right back again into the same situation. We have tried it and we didn't just try this with K——.

[6] As the patients' insecurity had diminished and their affect hunger abated, patients ceased to crowd around attendants when they arrived and no longer demanded entry to the employees dressing room.

Mr. S.: Therefore we have to try something else, right?

Att. (1): Yes.

Mr. S.: If one method doesn't work, then we have to try another. The question, therefore, is what other method could we use to prevent the repetition of this sort of situation? Can it occur again tomorrow or next week?

Att. (1): It might.

Mr. S.: The point, therefore, is how we can work out an approach, a system, a way of doing this, to protect the keys, to protect the workers, the staff, and still not create a situation in which, if not she, it will be somebody else? We have to start thinking how we can prevent this.

Att.: Having a dressing area off the ward?

Mr. S.: That's one method. Where is the dressing area now?

Att.: It's on the ward.

Mr. S.: Is there a door between the ward and the dressing area?

Att.: Yes, and it has to be kept locked.

Mr. S.: Why was this outburst?

Att. (2): She has been treated as an equal. We discussed her before last week and we tried your method and it was working fine. Then all of a sudden. . . .

Mr. S.: But in this case you didn't work my method.

Att. (2): In this case the night shift hadn't been to your meetings. So they are still going on as before.

Mr. S.: Now suppose this happened to you. Suppose you were on that shift. Let's assume that. What would you have done?

Att. (2): I would have given her something to do for me which would have taken her away from the area.

Mr. S.: Let's take you. You were changing your clothes, and K——— came in with four or five other patients following her, because as you know, they are like little children, they just follow along. I don't want to nail you down. I'm just asking the whole group now. What would you have done here? Let's recreate the situation. Let's say I'm one of the staff and I'm there changing my clothes. This is the ward and there's the door and K——— and five or six other patients came in. Now what should I have done?

Att. (2): Well, there's one thing you could have done. The fact that there's more than one, you could say, "Please excuse me, I'm dressing now. Do you mind if I ask you to leave?"

Mr. S.: Okay, that's one way. What's another way?

Att. (2): You should lock the door, which is not always good.

Mr. S.: Now here is another example. They are in the room now. What should I do? You remember last time we talked about the patient who either slept or pretended to sleep through lunch. It was you who suggested that the staff should go along with her. Right?

ATT. (2): Right.

MR. S.: In order to prove to her that we are interested in her and want to help her and that we are good people and good mothers. Now, in order to continue the idea of good motherhood, what should I have said or done to this patient? Anybody? [No response.] You know you'll never be right unless you start being wrong. People who never are wrong never learn to be right. So don't be afraid of being wrong.

ATT. (2): Let's consider that there was more than K——— in the room. That's what was happening today. The room was full of patients.

MR. S.: That doesn't matter, six, seven or eight. What should I have done or said?

ATT. (2): Well, I would do just like I do sometimes. I speak to them very lightly.

MR. S.: Like what? Now tell me what I should say?

ATT. (2): "Would you, please, K———, go out until I get dressed?" Now this morning when she was upset, I walked up to her and said, "K———, would you go down and get the laundry for me, please?" And I was taking my key off the ring at the same time. And she said, "All right, Miss B———." And she had calmed down.

MR. S.: You got away from the question. Here I am in the room changing my clothes. Patients walked in, the door was open. What should I have said to them to carry out the idea of a good mother, of an understanding person, a kindly individual, a person with respect for them. What should I have said?

ATT. (2): Would you say, "Can I do something for you?"

ATT. (3): Well, I don't know. But I will tell you what I would say. I run in and when they follow me, I say, "All right, will you please leave us until I change my uniform?" If they don't go I throw my pocketbook into the locker, grab my uniform, put it on, run outside the door and I say, "All right, let's go to breakfast now."

MR. S.: That's another way.

ATT. (3): That's what I do.

MR. S.: What I would have said is, "Hello, girls. Good morning."

ATT. (2): We've already said that. We shake hands and we put arms around shoulders and we say, if they have no shoes on, "Oh, I'll help you look for your shoes." All kinds of greetings and salutations have taken place. But they still want to come into that room.

MR. S.: I would then have said, "Nice morning, this morning, isn't it?" And carry on. You don't strip, do you? You just take off your outside clothes. Therefore, just accept them there, still realizing that they shouldn't be there. We have to find an indirect way of stopping their intrusion. You see, when people come in to see you, it's because they like you. Or maybe they hate you. It doesn't matter. The fact that you say, "Go out," already puts them in what particular situation?

ATT. (1): You reject them.

MR. S.: Yes, you reject them. You don't want them. Now, you're right in preventing their intrusion. But the point is how to get it done. When you say to them, "Go out. . . ," I would also get angry. As a matter of fact if I did it to you, you would get angry, too.

ATT. (2): Mr. Slavson, don't you think the other (night) employees ought to have some of these meetings? I explained to them some of your ideas. . .

MR. S.: We'll come to that. But the point is that *we* must understand what to do. *We* must know what to do. We will work with them later. That's another problem. You cannot reject patients and not expect an explosion from some one of them right away, or they'll take it out on you later.

ATT. (2): That's one reason I said you should have a meeting with them [night attendants]. Because they had them [patients] with the explosion, we had to calm that explosion down. We were left with what had happened. I mean, she [K——] was stirred up and we were left with this.

MR. S.: You're taking us away from what we must learn. We must understand that once you told the patients, "Go out," you're going to have trouble, if not immediately, later on. A few of them will turn and walk out with the maddest feeling inside which they are afraid to express right then, but they will express it later in some other way, either by disobedience, by not putting on shoes, refusing to go to lunch, or not making the bed. This is what we call passive resistance. You already started trouble for yourself by saying; "Go out." Start talking with patients about anything at all; about what they have been doing; you know, woman-talk. And as you talk, keep changing your clothes. We don't really want to insult the patients. Another suggestion is changing clothes off the ward. Still another one is going in and locking the door, which is not good, either. But it is still better than chasing them out. That's no good at all. And then again—I don't see why attendants should wear uniforms. But that, too, is another subject that we may discuss some other time. Because I think the very fact of the uniform makes establishing easy relations more difficult—like a policeman's uniform. Saying, "Go out" changes your image of being a good person, an accepting person. We must look for ways to prevent situations instead of meeting them head-on with, with patients, it tends to create difficulties. Outbursts and destructiveness may not appear immediately, and when they do, we cannot always recognize that they are a result of something we had said or done some time before.

ATT. (1): I recognize it, because I feel that way myself. I have many emotions and nobody knows what's going on inside. I have my own explosions.

340

Mr. S.: We want to learn how to consistently carry on a feeling of acceptance in patients so that they can love and respect us. When they love us, they will automatically love other people. We cannot tell them to go out. We have to figure out a way of changing into uniforms which will not create these situations. That is the practical problem which on a once a week basis I cannot solve for you. You'll have to solve it by holding a meeting with the entire patient and staff personnel involved—attendants, nurses and the psychiatrists. It has to be a group decision with votes. When the patients will have been involved, you can then tell them, "Remember that the decision was made by all of you, that we should change our clothes in privacy?" Now you have an out. We hope to have discussions in the future with the patients regularly where they will vote on many things in which they should participate and for which they will be responsible. We cannot be bosses over the patients and expect them to assume responsibilities. The only way they will develop responsibility is to let them take part in making decisions.

Supervisory Psychiatrist: Mr. Slavson, could we go into this more deeply, maybe? From the point of view of the actual experience of the attendants in this situation of changing clothes, could each of the attendants say that she simply wants to change her clothes in privacy and that if a patient comes right in after them, to prepare the situation in such a way as to evoke the kind of response that you get even from a patient or from an attendant. For instance, comparing it with the situation where in the house (home) the mother wants to get dressed privately, you know, and the small child comes in while the mother is dressing. I doubt whether it is that simple.

Mr. S.: You're right. It's not that simple.

Supervisory Psychiatrist: Apparently the patient has something on her mind that she wants to let off her chest. She is going in there not as simple childish curiosity, but for some other reason.

Att. (2): Sometimes they know we have their cigarettes (for safe-keeping) you know. So when you hit the door in the morning, they'll say, "Well, can I have my cigarettes now?" And you haven't even gotten in. "Can I have this now or the other things?" See, so this is why they always enter because maybe you have their cigarettes or maybe you have a dollar of theirs and they want it right then and there.

Att. (1): That will be cured, I think, when the lockers come in. They'll be able to keep their own cigarettes and personal belongings in their lockers. And that may avoid some of it.

Mr. S.: Yes, but the theory. At this moment we're not concerned so much with the administration of how things are being done. We are rather concerned with understanding what is involved. Now Dr. C—— is quite right. We know why K—— went into the room. She seeks status above and superior to the other patients. And her being permitted to enter the room with the attendants is a status position for her. She wants to find an image, an identity in herself through identifying or being equal to the attendants. When I met her and talked to her, the thing she talked about was, "I can do things for people up here which I can't do downstairs" (where patients are not as helpless). In other words, this is just a continuation of the same thing. She can come into the room. She is the privileged person, different from the others. Her motive is to become important to herself as well as to the others. The others followed because she did it. From what I saw of those patients, I think it's just a kind of a sheep following the leader phenomenon. Some of them may resent the fact that she came in. But it's more of a mass reaction of follow the leader, and they all came in. No, I don't quite see what you had in mind in drawing a parallel between the mother and child.

SUPERVISORY PSYCHIATRIST: I thought perhaps that your approach in dealing with this kind of problem was sort of a take-off on that of a mother and child.

MR. S.: No, it's not the same.

SUPERVISORY PSYCHIATRIST: You see, there are two aspects to it. One is the mother coming in from the outside, she was shopping—"What you got for me, Mom?" The other is where they have something on their minds that they want to talk about. What would be your reaction when a patient comes in like that? The matter of privacy of the attendant as far as the patient is concerned can be discussed sometimes in an informal way with the patients as to their own privacy. Here we are building partitions (in the toilet) to give them privacy. So how can we relate the fact that they want privacy to the privacy that we want?

MR. S.: Well, this can be done only through group discussions. . . . We're going to have a meeting with the staff and patients in about three weeks, in which we will ask them what they would like to do on the ward. We'll see what we get out of that. We can tell the patients at one of these discussions what Dr. Beckenstein had suggested: "You enjoy your privacy now and therefore maybe the attendants also like privacy." Now, to what extent the psychotic mind can understand this, I don't know, because this may mean nothing to a psychotic. But we will attempt it and see what happens. Our entire project is an experiment, as I had told you before. It is possible that the healthier patients will try to control the less healthy patients. It will be a kind of interpatient therapy. One will say to another, "You know what we were talking about. You mustn't go into the room when the attendants change their clothes. You know that." If this comes to pass, it should prove very effective; much more than if we tell it to them. Please do not tell the patients that we are planning such meetings. Three weeks is a long time for our patients to wait. Maybe we'll tell them the week before, or on a Monday or Tuesday of that week when the Thursday meeting will be held.

DISCUSSION

The fact that the attendant invited the disturbed patient to repair to the "conference room" to quiet her down, instead of reacting on the spot in the usual dominant or threatening manner would be an impressive development, except that this was done by our most sensitive and perceptive attendant who responded with enthusiasm for our plans due to temperamental disposition and her own personality problems to which she herself referred. Even in her case, she had remembered to deploy this strategy because the episode took place a few days after we had outlined the procedure at which we also cautioned the staff not to attempt to stop patients from screaming, but let the screaming die down through the quiet and the comfort of receiving the exclusive attention of a sympathetic staff member. We said, "The patient has to scream until her fears dissipate through the security and support we give her." None of the other staff members would have employed this method at this stage and even she did seldom resort to it with the passing of time until the matter was again brought up at the seminar.

A significant outcome wrought by the relaxed ward climate, the feeling of security, the improved self-image and sanguine human relations, as they became part of the patients' lives, was the disappearance of the avidity for attention when the day-staff appeared at 8:30 a.m. The patients by themselves ceased the annoying practice and instead of flocking around the staff members each morning as they appeared, now paid them passing attention. We saw in this changed demeanor growing maturity and increased security.

Attendant (1)'s verbalizing awareness of the similarity of her problems with those of the patients can be viewed as a minor therapeutic triumph. This was a highly emotional and explosive woman, who at times of stress fleetingly lost almost complete control of herself. She vividly and intensively identified with the 13 patients who in the old plan were assigned as her responsibility. Misconduct of any one of them meant a personal failure for her. She had a good intellectual and emotional understanding of her charges, but her own emotional fragility and low self-esteem led her to become uncontrollably upset at the slightest indication of failure. This was further intensified by her inordinate sense of justice and her own brand of honesty characteristic of sensitive people.

Later in one of the sessions, she burst into tears and abruptly quit the seminar when a supervisory staff member distorted the facts (which were known to me) in order to whitewash herself as they related to the treatment of a patient. This attendant's sense of justice was too outraged to bear up under the stress and to prevent a scene, she fled the premises.

Her recognition of her feelings and reactions at this early session was only the first step in her self-therapy, but it did not alter her conduct or the intensity of her feelings for a considerable time. It took many months and many discussions at the seminar sessions in which she was the most active participant. Because of her long emotional dissertations, many began to view her as a disturbing monopolizer. On two separate occasions she was the subject of deliberation at the supervisory luncheon meetings, the only staff member so singled out.

A few days after her weeping outburst and quitting the seminar, Dr. Beckenstein, on meeting her and sensing her embarrassment, said in part, "All of us get upset at times and lose control of ourselves." She said nothing, probably restrained by her embarrassment, but later wrote to him, expressing her gratitude for his "understanding." She concluded by saying, "Thank you for all the things you are doing on the ward and thank you for Mr. Slavson. . . He goes deep, very deep." The latter part of her missive reflects her profound desire to help the patients and her deep involvement with them.

Gradually a noticeable change in this woman's facial expression and carriage was occurring. Her permanent mien of being driven, of anxiety admixed with suffering and unhappiness was visibly disappearing. In its place, calm seemed to be settling over her countenance. Her defensive semipermanent smile of embarrassment and placation was no longer in evidence. With this change, her ingratiating demeanor gave way to a growing self-assurance, and her dealings with patients became more objective and more restrained.

This very impressive transformation did not escape the attention of either her fellow workers or herself. As for the former, a few commented about the favorable change in this woman and her increased effectiveness in her work. She, on the other hand, revealed her awareness when on few later occasions she volunteered the statement, "I know I used to baby my patients. I don't do it any more." Such self-confrontation on the part of this formerly intensively defensive woman can be viewed as a triumph in automatic therapy that sometimes occurs through a fundamental change in one's life situation.

At the same sessions, the problem the staff encountered with a patient which had been discussed at a preceding session was again brought up. A portion of this discussion is reproduced here to indicate a change in the approach toward patients wrought by the seminars:

Mr. S.: Is there anything else that occurred during the week that you would like to talk about?

Att. (4) (from Ward A): Well, I tried to do what you said with J—, your honor system. You said trust the patients if they want the keys to go some place. And she wanted to go downstairs for a cup of coffee from the machine. She's usually quite pesty when she's on the first floor (where the coffee dispenser was). Instead of going for coffee she runs around and bothers everybody (where the offices are situated). So I said, "I'll give you the keys, but promise me you'll come right back; that you won't bother anybody." And she did. She went down and got her coffee and came right back up, handed me the key and said, "Thank you."

Mr. S.: Is this the first time she didn't "pester" people? Well, let's try to understand why this was so.

Att. (4): I think because she was trusted to go by herself. I figured that anyway she had to go in for change because she had only a dollar bill. She usually used to go into Dr. C—— because she always said she was in love with him.

Mr. S.: Did she bother other people as well?

Att. (4): This is what the attendants on the other wards said: She tried Dr. C——'s door, and when she came up she said, "Well, Dr. C——'s door was locked." So evidently she tried to get in. . . .

Social Worker: She came to me and asked me for change for a dollar. I said to her that I didn't have it. But as a rule when she comes down to my office I just can't get rid of her, but this time she said, "All right" and left.

345

SUPERVISORY NURSE: She told me the reason she had to come back so quickly was because she had somebody's key. "Otherwise I could have stayed longer," she said.

MR. S.: Was it because she had the responsibility for the key?

ATT. (4): Yes, she had to come back with the key. She had to rush.

MR. S.: Let's try to understand why she came back right away . . .

Initiated by the supervising psychiatrist, there followed an extensive review of this patient's psychosocial history and family problems that led to her break. Various staff members participated in this discussion. They became aware that as disturbed as our patients were, many could still be reached if we were genuinely convinced of this fact, and our approach assumed on a basis of equality and mutual respect and if we interacted with them.

Another situation that came up at the same session was one of the habitual negative approach of attendants toward patients. Their propensity for negative, tentative or evasive circumstantial responses to patients' requests, rather than definiteness that would give patients security, was one of the banes of our existence and proved one of the most rigid habits which we were never able to fully eradicate.

Our second or third most cooperative and empathic attendant complained about the "unreasonableness" of a patient in becoming upset because she was not immediately allowed to go down to the storehouse to fetch the daily household supplies, a chore usually, but not always, performed by a staff member. This was an entirely responsible patient who was trusted with keys and free movement through the hospital and off grounds during her periods of remission. In fact, she was transferred to an open ward, but found life there "too monotonous" and came back, making herself useful on Ward A in many ways.

After she had brought up the laundry on the morning of the seminar, she asked the attendant in charge (in the absence of the nurse) whether she could go down for the supplies. "No, I think Mrs. L—— (an attendant) will go down for them," said the attendant; "Thank you, K——." The patient became very agitated and in a hurt tone of voice, red face and tears gleaming in her eyes, exclaimed, throwing the keys at the attendant: "Well, am I not as capable as Mrs. L——? Why can't I bring them up? If that's the case, I'll not go down to get the laundry tomorrow, then!" Attendant: "All right, all right. You can bring them up." "We would have had a lot of trouble if I had not allowed her to do it," added the attendant.

Part of the discussion that ensued follows:

MR. S.: She obviously became upset by the fact that you had no confidence in her. You considered her inadequate. What would have happened if you had said to her: "Yes, you can go down."

ATT.: Well I did say that after.

MR. S.: After.

ATT.: Yes.

MR. S.: First you said Mrs. L——.

ATT.: Yes.

MR. S.: But supposing you said immediately, "Yes, dear, you can go down," what would she have done?

ATT.: Well, she would have cooperated right away.

MR. S.: Then why didn't you say this to her?

ATT.: Because that's the hospital rules against employees to go down and get the supplies.

SUPERVISING NURSE: They [supplies] have to be checked.

MR. S.: What would happen to hospital rules if the patients were allowed to go down?

CHIEF ADMINISTRATOR: One reason is because we must verify the amount of linen they get. Our linen supply, unfortunately, is very limited and many of our things have disappeared. So we do have to have a responsible person.

MR. S.: Now, how can this girl become responsible if we don't give her responsibilities?

CHIEF ADMINISTRATOR: There are other responsibilities we could give her.

MR. S.: But she wanted this one. I think we will have to change much in our philosophy if we aim to help patients. There are two ways of keeping these patients. One is custodial, just keep them, you know, keep them going, have a place for them to stay, and the other is to help them go out into the world and do something with their lives. Therefore, we will have to make some changes, even if it will cost a couple of rolls of paper, and maybe a hundred rolls. But we'll have to give these patients a feeling that they are important people. It was proven over and over again, that when we consider patients as responsible human beings, not just as patients, many of them live up to our expectations. But if we treat them as though they're helpless and unable to do anything, they

347

will remain the way they are for the rest of their lives. We have to make up our minds about what we're going to do; whether we will take a girl like this, who is striving to become independent and reliable and useful, and cut her off just because there's a rule in the hospital. By the way, what about the sheets? We were talking about sheets before. Was she allowed to go down to get sheets?

ATT.: Oh yes, she brings up sheets, pillowcases, blankets.

MR. S.: Without supervision?

ATT.: Without supervision.

MR. S.: She does that all right?

ATT.: Yes.

MR. S.: Has she ever gone down for supplies before?

ATT.: To my knowledge I have never sent her down for supplies.

MR. S.: Well, what is the evidence that she would create the kind of problem we're discussing—namely, that she'd spread around the ward what supplies you have. What evidence do you have that she would do that?

ATT.: Well, she can cause a lot of confusion. She has certain patients she likes, too. She'll tell those patients, "I brought up supplies and I brought up tobacco, I brought up paper." She's very talkative.

MR. S.: How do you know in advance that she will do that?

ATT.: Well, I know her ways. I know she will.

MR. S.: And do you think that if she got responsibilities she would not be able to control herself?

ATT.: I don't think she would be able to control this, keep this (to herself).

MR. S.: Would you want to experiment with this, or do you want to continue according to your own conviction of what she *will* do?

ATT.: Well, I don't know. I wouldn't suggest to send her down for supplies all the time.

MR. S.: What do supplies consist of, by the way?

ATT.: Napkins, soap, tobacco.

MR. S.: Therefore, what is the danger there? The tobacco, right?

ATT.: What's the danger?

MR. S.: It's the tobacco that's going to create a problem, not the soap and not the napkins?

ATT.: Well, but this is how we are trying to prevent confusion on the ward, because she'll tell the other patients that she brought up tobacco. Now all the patients will get upset and want tobacco.

MR. S.: How do you know that?

ATT.: Well, I *believe* she will. I know she cannot keep a secret.

MR. S.: Yes, but the point is that if we expect patients to act in a certain way, they will. If we expect them to act in another way, they will, too. But they still deserve the chance. They have a right to the opportunity to test and to find out—to test themselves—and you will then find out whether they can or cannot manage things. If we discover that they cannot, then we do something about it. But if they can manage, even if they slide back once in a while, and give us trouble, as it happens in every family, then we allow it. None of us is perfect. We all make mistakes; all families make mistakes and once in a while we, too, slide back. But patients have a right, as human beings, to be given a chance. When problems arise, we deal with them, or we'll try to find ways of dealing with them. Our job here is to find ways of dealing with such problems. At times it may be hard, but eventually we will overcome.[7] But you've got to have patience and patients must be given a chance to *try to live.* This is her life. She wanted to test you—will you trust her? And you failed her.

It will take a long time. It is not going to happen in one or two days. But the patients have to be given a chance to find their own way to life and we must not block that road. Let the patient do the job she chooses day after day and see what happens. If after a week you still have trouble about it, then you discuss it with the psychiatrist, Mr. G——, or myself; or, better still, at our meetings and we'll see what can be done. Or have a meeting of the whole ward, with the staff and the patients. Say to them, "Now we have trouble about this." [Mr. S. describes the solution of a similar problem in another institution by group action, not in a mental hospital, but where there were psychotics in the population.] There will be two or three of the patients who will give you ideas on how to control the situation. When it comes from them, the other patients will accept it. Because it came from them. . . .

We did not end the discussion with theoretic considerations. Rather, several solutions were suggested by the participants. One was that the patient be allowed to handle tobacco as she did all other supplies, and observe the subsequent results; another was that the tobacco supplies now used for "rolling their own" should be placed in the care of the ward nurses and used as part of occupational therapy. We had introduced mechanical devices so that patients could easily roll cigarettes in quantity for themselves and the ward population. At first, most of the patients continued to prefer the packaged cigarettes, but eventually they began to settle for what was available. One of the interesting phenomena was the absolute willingness with

[7] This phrase was used some years before it became the shibboleth of the civil rights movement.

which patients shared their supply of cigarettes with one another, and even in giving draughts on cigarettes they were smoking when asked. One wondered whether this kind of generosity with such a "precious" possession as are cigarettes for inmates stemmed from their fear of each other, from mutual identification, or as investments in expectation or reciprocity in the future. Refusal to share smokes seemed to be one of the more frequent causes for quarrels and fights.

Another attendant raised the question of the particular patient's inability to withstand frustration and the difficulties she creates when her needs are not met at once. This gave us another opportunity for sensitizing the attendants to the need for individualizing patients in meeting their needs.

Appendix II:
A Case of Differential Diagnosis with "Mental" Deficiency

Miss Joan Lawrence came to our attention when on a visit to Ward A, we heard loud screaming emanating from one of the small rooms, the door of which was locked. At first the screaming voice kept repeating the name of one of the attendants who, we knew, was one of the two most maternal and sympathetic on that ward. The screaming went on for some 10 minutes; then it changed to, "I want a cigarette! I want a cigarette!" in the same raucous voice for another 10 minutes or more, accompanied by kicking of the door. No one, neither patients nor staff, seemed to pay any attention. Apparently, being accustomed to such sounds, they seemed completely oblivious to the ear-splitting monotonous refrain.

Becoming annoyed both by the assault on our eardrums and by the callous indifference of the staff, we asked the attendant who was being summoned what all this was about. She informed us that this was a "lodger" who was sent up from a lower floor for temporary residence (which was the practice then) to be quieted down as she was giving the staff there "a lot of trouble" and was breaking windows. "Why don't we unlock the door and see what she wants?" we asked. Somewhat hesitatingly the attendant walked over to the door and unlocked it. I followed her.

351

Before us appeared a mountainous young woman of 18 years in appearance (though she was past 30 years as we later learned), nearly six feet in height, and weighing about 300 pounds. She wore a huge, plain white nightgown, grown gray with dirt, her arms immobilized by a camisole. Tears streamed down her unclean face, and mucous dripped from her nose. Her hair was disheveled, her round, fleshy, sallow face bore the marks of exhaustion, and her eyes were narrowed by the fear of confrontation and her suffering.

The patient was standing in the middle of the room in the narrow passageway between the two double-decker beds, with an expression of a beaten dog, and meekly responded to the very friendly attendant's query: "What do you want, honey?" The cautious and meek response came: "Please give me a cigarette." With considerable alacrity and obvious relief (since punitive treatment of patients was actually never to her liking) the attendant produced a cigarette and matches, asked the patient to sit down on the lower section of a double-decker bed nearby, put the cigarette in her mouth, struck a match and lit it. She then sat down next to the patient and "fed" her the cigarette. Since this occurred in the early phase of our ward program and because of shortage of personnel, I asked whether another patient might not be able to attend to this. One of the several patients, who had gathered nearby to watch the proceedings, gladly volunteered. The chore was thus turned over to her.

The attendant returned to her activities but I remained to observe what at the time appeared to me a bizarre scene: a perfectly healthy looking person rendered helpless by the camisole, and another alternately inserting and withdrawing, with an air of urgency, a cigarette from the mouth of her charge. This she did in such rapid succession as to prevent the recipient from enjoying the "taste," for even before the latter had fully exhaled the smoke, the cigarette was again thrust into her mouth. Thus the cigarette lasted for only a few minutes.

The patient's facial expression during this performance, however, seemed significant. As she was being "fed" the cigarette and received the "nursing" attention, she relaxed and a very faint smile of satisfaction appeared on her face. It struck me that this was either a person whose development was arrested by parental overgratification or a mental defective. The latter seemed more plausible by the speed with which she recovered from her disturbed state and the rapidity of her mood swing.

The patient was continued in a camisole for several weeks, but now she was no longer isolated. She could always be seen sitting in a row among the older "burnt out" patients presenting a picture characteristic of immobility and content. She was still clad in a dirty nightgown and bedroom slippers with her arms still tied down. Once as I was passing, I noted that her eyes were piercingly focussed on me. It struck me that *she wanted to be noticed.* In reflecting on these two phenomena—the infantile smile of gratification when nursed by the attendant and the urgency to be noticed—it occurred to me that this patient was psychologically an infant and that breaking of windows was a means of attracting attention to herself. It seemed that an exploration of the psychodynamics of this case by the seminar staff might make palpable the procedures we advocated for dealing with patients. We believed that such an exploration should make clear the inappropriateness of the punitive treatment this type of patient was receiving. We, therefore, arranged for a discussion of this case.

Miss Lawrence had been in treatment with a very gifted caseworker who, although she had recently left the hospital, was willing to come to our session to present the case, which she did in a masterful fashion.

The patient was the youngest of three children. An older sister and brother were school teachers and out of the home. At the time of the foregoing episode, she was 32 years old; her mother had been dead for about eight years and the patient lived alone with her 60-year-old father who was described as "dull, evasive and denying." The mother was described as being 4' 11" tall, very obese, always ill, and as having "died of high blood pressure." The patient, as a child, was "about average in school" but suffered from seizures "about six times a year, sometimes less," the first of which occurred at the age of eight.

These seizures took place only during periods when she was home for lunch (alone with her mother). The doctors had prescribed medication in the belief that these seizures "could be controlled." At about the age of 15 "she isolated herself from friends and confined herself exclusively to the family group." She became obese at about 12 years of age. The seizures had become more frequent during her high school years. She dropped out of school after three-and-one-half years at the age of 18. The seizures stopped at about that time.

During all these years, Miss L. was perpetually "babied." Her every whim was satisfied by all the members of the family, though her demands had become increasingly more bizarre. After quitting school, she shifted from job to job as a clerk, keeping to herself all her earnings, which she spent on clothes. At about 20 years of age, Miss L. grew extremely violent, screamed, and demanded that she be taken for rides in the family car. Various members of the family would accede to her screams and would drive her around for hours. Quite frequently her father would spend the entire night driving her in his car. On occasion she would fall asleep on these prolonged excursions.

At that time, the patient was described as being, "on good behavior" with strangers, although demanding and tyrannical, "noisy, nasty, and grouchy" with members of her family, using "bad language, obscenities and profanities of the vilest type." She was described as given to frequent mood swings. "She seems to ignore the social aspects of life," declared the informant. "She has never been to a party, does not dance; has never spoken to a boy and was never on dates; *has never done anything for herself*; never been known to read a book. Her reading was limited to movie magazines." The patient was described at the admission interview as "having an amazing memory for names and numbers. She amuses herself looking up numbers in the telephone book. . . . She is clumsy with her hands; is always agreeable with strangers, except with someone whom she knows well; then she treats them like the family. . . . She resorts to tears quickly when she does not get her way." The family treated her as mentally retarded and she retained a small-child facial expres-

354

sion and a girlish, "cute" manner to this day.

The patient was admitted four times to private sanitaria and four times to state mental hospitals between 1954 and 1960. The first diagnosis established was "psychosis due to convulsive disorder; Epilepsy." This diagnosis was continued in all the subsequent facilities, in some of which she had been placed on her insistence. Her stays in the hospitals were usually of several weeks to two months' duration. During the intervals in the community she had made "fair to moderate" adjustments for varying periods and had held clerical jobs for short spells. On one of these visits home, she became interested in an older man in her neighborhood and insisted on seeing him frequently, demanding that her family call him to come to see her. Later she fixated on a young teen-age boy, much younger than herself, whom she claimed she loved and whom she would constantly call on the phone. It was not unusual for her to appear at his door at 4 A.M. and ring the bell. The boy's family complained that she interrupted his studies and disturbed his peace of mind. However, she could not be made to desist.

At this time she was becoming increasingly agitated and unmanageable, despite the various medications she was receiving from various doctors. On her last admission to a private institution in 1959, she was found "tense, restless, confused . . . removed from contact with reality . . . completely unable to concentrate on any topic . . . insight was lacking. She had the idea that she was in the hospital only for a rest so that she would be able to see the boy she thinks she is in love with and that he would come to see her. . . . Patient was discharged in custody of her father (two months later) against the advice of the staff." However, her condition at home grew worse and permanent hospitalization became imperative.

On arrival at the Brooklyn State Hospital, the patient was in "a restraining sheet, her hair disheveled, with no make-up, agitated, unable to relax, high psychomotor activity, speech under pressure frequently incoherent, affect constricted and inappropriate ideation." There were also auditory hallucinations and thought disorder, e.g., her "boy-friend" communicating with her by beating pots and pans: "I wanted to answer and I knocked the T.V. over," she said. "Intelligence is low. Abstractions are marked by concretion."

When the patient calmed down, four months later, she became inordinately attached to the ward doctor and would bring him refreshments during ward meetings. "But when she felt she was losing the group's attention, she would resort to some attention-getting mechanism such as screaming or provoking another patient."

The caseworker who had summarized this patient's anamnesis thought that she had been greatly infantilized and that "her *potential for growth and maturation* [had] *atrophied*." During one of the weekly interviews, the patient revealed that she had witnessed the primal scene at the age of seven years. The father, who lived alone with his daughter, was described as "a very guilt-ridden man" and "completely unable to cope with her."

The caseworker had made a rather serious error with regard to the patient's insistent desire to spend the 1964 Thanksgiving holiday in her brother's home. The family had shied away from taking Miss Lawrence on home visits because of her unrestrained acting out. Her brother's family, as well, did not wish to receive her at their residence. In order to convince the patient that she had tried her best, the caseworker called the brother's home in the patient's presence. The sister-in-law answered the phone and the caseworker, obviously to convince her of this fact, arranged the telephone receiver so that Miss Lawrence could overhear the conversation. Hearing directly the sister-in-law's refusal, the patient broke into tears, sobbed loudly, then proceeded to break windows. She became so violent that she had to be put in restraint. The resulting disturbance on the ward was so great that she was shipped off to Ward A as a "lodger" to quiet her down.

On Ward A, Miss Lawrence went to bed where she lay in a foetal position for several days, refusing to rise, complaining that she was wet, demanding that she be powdered, and cream applied in the diaper area.

We brought this case up for discussion at the seminar January 14, 1965. The attendants displayed keen interest in this case, which illustrated a number of theoretic points covered in previous discussions and they actively participated in the deliberations. It became clear that we were dealing here with a person profoundly *fixated* at a childhood level and who, therefore, needed to be assisted in "growing up." For this a special attitude and approach would have to be evolved. We suggested that she must no longer be treated and catered to as though she were a baby; that she must be *helped* to take care of herself and take on some responsibilities. We warned the staff, however, that this change of role was to be implemented with gentle firmness, without criticism or rejection, or arousal of guilt or authoritarianism. The patient's need for attention, which we believed was an important factor in her behavior, had to be satisfied, as well, provided that it occurred on an adult, rather than infantile level. The staff would have to try to involve her in activities *with them* which would give her a feeling of acceptance and status.

The caseworker supported our treatment plan offering as evidence a number of strategies she had employed along the same lines. For some months she had held the interviews on the ward. Realizing that by this she had unwittingly played up to the patient's demand for maternal indulgence, she asked Miss L. to come to her office, which was situated in another building. At the appointed time, Miss Lawrence did not appear. The following week she was sent for and was told during the interview by the caseworker that she would no longer come to see her on the ward; that she would have to come to the office on her own. Miss L. never failed a session from that time on.

We also called attention to the obvious incest element that operated in this case. In previous seminar discussions the fact was established that in the psychotic syndrome there are present the factors of incest and homicide and that psychosis is most often a defense against these urges. This case unequivocally demonstrated the operation of these two dynamics. We noted that the outbreaks occurred at home where the patient was alone with her father and had subsided during the brief stays at hospitals only to be reactivated when faced again with the threatening condition upon return home. As a result of the struggle with the forbidden impulse, she would become uncontrollably disturbed. She would then have to be placed, and on several occasions she, herself, had asked to be returned to the hospitals, thereby evading her impulse.

This process—including both psychotic outbreaks and the desire to return to a hospital—was a good illustration of the attempt at self-cure, which was further evidenced also by her becoming attached to "an older man," as a replacement for her father, and demanding reunions with him, in which she was frustrated. Failing in this, she rediverted her libidinal strivings toward a teen-age boy, who was acceptable to her superego, for it extirpated the parental libidinal object (the father). When his family complained, and she, herself, recognized that he was unattainable as an escape from the pressure of her superego, she found escape in the full-blown psychosis, in a world of hallucination. We also noted that her attachment to the psychiatrist and her bringing him refreshments were acts of ingratiation with a father figure.

It was much later that the significance of the cessation of the convulsive episodes which occurred during her teen years (for she was never a victim of one during her entire stay at the hospitals, even during very intense agitation when one could have expected these to recur) became clear to us. We viewed the patient's demandingness, violence, and outbreaks as "epileptic equivalents," but further cogitation brought forth the significance of the temporal proximity of Miss Lawrence's witnessing the primal scene and the first "convulsive" attacks. One was placed at seven years of age, the other at eight. Though actual dates are not pinpointed, it is quite possible that they may have been spaced a few months or even a few weeks apart, but in different calendar years. Also, it is not impossible that in recalling incidents so many years back, approximations were offered, and the two events may have been separated only by one or two days. The locus of the first attack is also significant: the patient was alone with her mother during the school luncheon interval:

These circumstances would rather point to an hysterical reaction at being alone with her mother after the circumstances in which she had seen her in the act of coitus and she was overwhelmed by the memory and the accompanying feelings of fear, anger and humiliation that it aroused. This reaction now became a *modus vivendi* whenever an intense feeling overtook her. Further, being very infantile, the patient found secondary gains in the "fainting" mechanism (getting attention, being attended to, punitively creating distress for the parents).

As a result of the seminar discussion, the restraint was removed at once and she was treated in accordance with our suggestions by the staff.

On our next visit to the ward, Miss Lawrence confronted me full of smiles and friendly greetings. She was now clean, tastefully coiffured and trimly dressed. (Her family supplied her clothes.) She participated in the activities on the ward only sparingly. Though one of the younger members of the ward community, she did not seem to be able to find a lasting interest and could be seen most often sitting with the old inactive patients. On occasion she would read a magazine that was supplied by the hospital. She spoke to me whenever I came. Her conversation was lucid, carried on smilingly with the mien of a little girl. At every one of our encounters her conversation trailed off to the problem of "meeting a nice Jewish boy" and asking me to help her in doing so. Frequently she would end by asking, "Do you know some nice Jewish boy that I would like?"

Her fixation on the teen-age neighbor seems to have dissolved. In this her former caseworker had helped her. For months Miss Lawrence continued to indulge in her fantasy during the weekly interviews about this boy. Any effort by the caseworker to question the possibility of consummating the relation brought violent ire from the patient. However, the caseworker persisted cautiously to plant doubt in the girl's mind until one day when the therapist stated flatly that she did not think there was any substance in this futile relation, the patient, instead of being thrown into a rage, as was always the case before, asked meekly: "Do you think so?"

Unfortunately, the therapist was scheduled to leave the hospital at this point in the treatment.

Some notations in the patient's record by our (second) psychiatrist may be of interest:

Feb. 8, 1965: This patient is presently out of the camisole and this morning was downstairs attending music therapy.

Feb. 15: Patient is ambulatory on Ward A and is no longer in a camisole, apparently in response to the ward personnel's threat not to feed her or give her cigarettes as long as she stayed in the camisole. She is now up and about. . . She asks to be transferred to her old ward.

March 1: . . .patient has participated in some activities. Her condition seems improved.

July 7: She has been given the privilege of going (by herself) to another ward for activities. There has been improvement in her behavior. She seldom, if ever, screams or creates difficulties. She tries to participate in activities.

Aug. 24: Continues on Ward A where she is reasonably cooperative. When offered a transfer to her original ward (as she had requested), she changed her mind and stated she preferred to stay on Ward A. . . . This patient has not been assaultive or disturbed for quite a number of weeks. She still continues in her very childish attitude, but this seems her characteristic behavior even at its best.

The patient was transferred to the "better" ward on the insistence of her family members who considered her being on what used to be known as the "disturbed ward" as an affront to their dignity and a threat to the patient's security.

On the ward of more intact patients, the psychiatrist noted that, "The patient is ambulatory . . . She is friendly and cooperative with personnel and patients. She appears neat and clean. Participates in ward activities. There is no change in patient's delusions. She is presently on the following medication . . ."

The first time she confronted me on the lower floor of the building, the transformation in her personality was so marked that it took me a few moments to place her. She was dressed in an attractive, tailored suit, much slimmer, neat and clean and due to her good build and natural dignified carriage, impressed one as a lady of the upper class. She was effusively friendly, spoke distinctly in a quiet voice and carried on the conversation of several minutes appropriately and lucidly. However, toward the end she again inquired whether I knew a suitable boy for her, but at our subsequent encounters she did not broach the subject again. She received no individual therapy after her caseworker had left the hospital, which was the case with all the patients on the service, due to lack of budgetary provisions for such services.

We considered the monthly case presentations (usually of our most difficult patients) and the free group discussions of the anamneses as they related to the patients' personalities, their symptoms and behavior in the community and on the wards, the most effective means in our armamentarium for sensitizing the staff—psychiatrists, supervisors, nursing instructors, as well as attendants—not only to our patients, but all patients and to people generally. In our discussions, we repeatedly reiterated the natural law of cause and effect, that is, that "nothing occurs without a cause, even though we may not be able to recognize, or ever ascertain the cause." We have demonstrated this principle innumerable times during the seminars by helping the attendants through questioning to recall incidents that triggered disturbances in individual patients and in the ward population as a whole, on the one hand, and sanguine reactions on the other. These causative incidents may have stemmed from acts by a patient, by relatives, by afternoon or night staff, by administration, the ward staff themselves, by the physical condition of the patient or automatic psychic changes. "There is *always* a cause for everything that occurs, as obscure as it may be," we repeatedly told them. This served to reduce the onus of guilt against patients.

The discussion of individual cases gave us the best kind of opportunity to witness this law of nature in action. It was this awareness of the forces that operated in the causation of the psychotic syndrome (in which constitutional factors had always been included), that influenced the staff to view their charges with "compassion" and instilled the concept that "patients are people like other people and not only patients to take care of."

To be involved in the study of patients *in depth* on a par

with the professionally trained staff, including psychiatrists and the hospital director, gave the attendants a status of which they had never dreamt. The notebooks (and pencils) we supplied which had in fact been utilized in some cases gave the sessions an academic ambiance. This, coupled with being served coffee during the sessions, frequently by the supervisory staff, including the seminar leader, had helped to raise the attendants' self-images. Of even greater value was the fact that the information and insights derived from these discussions tended to improve judgment in some of the more intelligent and the more interested members. The total outcome of this was that a number of the more qualified attendants and other staff members became less dependent on directions from supervisors, took greater initiative, and demonstrated improved judgment in dealing with the various situations which presented themselves.

Another encouraging consequence of the experience on the wards and participation in the seminars was, according to Dr. Lippman, our psychiatric consultant, the fact that a number of attendants entered training in psychiatric nursing and a larger number took examinations for higher positions in the hospitals.

Index

Half-way house on hospital grounds, 271
Hannah
actions, 24, 25, 113, 115, 116, 135
attachment to Slavson, 24-25
attitudes, 254
diagnosis, 62
progress, 25-26, 181, 197, 288
Harrow, Miss, case history, 218-220
Health education class, 216
Helplessness. *See* Dependency of patients
Home visits, patient improvement and, 170-171
Honor cards
grounds for granting, 280n
patient use of, 279-280
privileges for holders, 172
resentment against, 280
Hopelessness
air of, 14-15
decline of patient, 203, 233
of staff, 14-15, 51
Hostility
acting out and discharging, 49-50
attendants on patient, 325-326
effects of repressed, 43-44
staff: toward each other, 248, 251-252; toward patients, 89
See also Aggression; Rages, patient; Violence

Identification
of attendants with patients, 343-344
of psychotics, 224
Identity. *See* Ego; Self-identity
Immaturity. *See* Regression of patients
Incestuous content of psychotic psyche, 41
Individual(s)
case discussion, importance of, 361 ff
democracy and egalitarianism in treatment of, 10
participation and self-choice, 178
regarding patients as, 15-16, 136-140; importance of, 117, 118; staff comprehension of, 183-187, 284-286, 288-291, 334; staff training in, 226, 233
work with, 217-224; psychiatrist and, 297
Industrial social workers, 309, 310
Initiative
patient, 17, 34; attendants on, 346-349;

development of, 15-16, 171 ff; eating situation and, 83; increase in, 261, 262, 290; previous activation, 17; responsibility assumption, 34; staff encouragement of, 259; staff understanding of, 185, 186, 187; stimulation of, 106-107, 107-112, 139-140, 178, 259, 293-294
staff, 73-74, 93-94, 234 ff
Insecurity
decline in patient, 263, 344-345
hospital as security representation, 185, 186
staff complaints as reflections of, 137-138
staff resistance and, 237-238
Interaction, therapy and, 2
Interest. *See* Initiative; Participation of patients
Interpatient visits, 104, 174
Interpersonal relationships
effectiveness in therapy, 12, 217-224
of patients, 20, 22, 23, 24, 25-26, 28-29, 32, 33-34, 37, 39, 45, 52-55; conditions encouraging formation of, 177, 178, 274-275; confidences, 52-53; deficiencies in, 210; improvements in, 258-259, 262-263; of mentally defective patients, 356; Miss K and, 219-223; need for, 18, 203; promotion of, 122, 126; with staff, 37, 54, 73, 219-224, 227-228
sources of, 177, 178, 274-275, 306
Interruption technique for agitation, 94-95, 180
Introspection, avoiding with psychotics, 216n
Involvement
attendants' sense of, 276-277
bases of, 295
See also Participation of patients
Isolation of mental hospital patients, 2, 10, 109
Ivy League, 71, 124, 125

Jeanne
actions, 21, 40-41
improvement, 41-42, 288
Job adjustment, social worker and, 309, 310
Justina
actions, 22-23, 160-161
appearance, 22
attachment to Slavson, 23

371

73714